DATE DUE		

RECENT PHILOSOPHERS

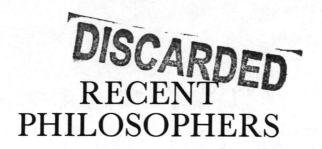

RECENT
PHILOSOPHERS

John Passmore

Emeritus Professor of Philosophy
Australian National University

OPEN COURT PUBLISHING COMPANY
LA SALLE, ILLINOIS 61301

Published by arrangement with Gerald Duckworth & Co. Ltd., London.

OC 872   10 9 8 7 6 5 4 3 2 1

ISBN: 0-87548-448-4

Printed and bound in the United Kingdom.

Contents

Preface

To the second edition of *A Hundred Years of Philosophy* (1966) I added a new chapter covering the years since the first edition (1957). That is what for a long time – the composition of this book has been greatly interrupted – I tried to do again. But I dismally failed. The chapter grew and grew and yet still left me dissatisfied with its brevity. In my introduction I have partly explained why. There is this to be added: contemporary philosophy is above all else meticulous; to describe it briefly is to fail to describe it. Often enough, too, it is composed over time, in a series of overlapping periodical articles, rather than boldly stated in a single work. It is often singularly compressed or written in a way which assumes that the reader knows what is being taken for granted; it needs, to be made intelligible, expansion rather than the contraction of summary. I can scarcely hope, even at the present length, to do more than give a taste of it. This is a descriptive, informal, necessarily summary account of some recent controversies, not a deep analysis or a final judgment about who 'really matters'. Someday, someone will do it very much better.

What counts as 'recent philosophy'? I must emphasise – for not everyone, I find, is conscious of the fact – that the second edition of my earlier book already contained studies of such active contemporaries as Quine, Strawson, Feyerabend. In general, then, 'recent' begins in 1966. But I have often enough gone back beyond that date, whether to provide background or to repair omissions. The terminating date is equally flexible. Even in the main text, there are references to books which were published in 1983. But the authors principally discussed were all of them familiar figures a decade ago; almost all the Anglo-American names, indeed, were already mentioned, if only in passing, in 1966. Except in the notes, the younger generation must still await its historian.

As for the notes, they are as up to date as, from my remote Australian eyrie, I could make them. They are, however, much less complete than were the notes to the original volume. Those notes left out very little that was relevant. That is nowadays not only impossible but unnecessary. In 1957, perhaps in imitation of the great classical philosophers but going even beyond their practice, bibliographical austerity was the order of the day. Now philosophers prefer to think of themselves as quasi-scientists, collaborating in a research programme. Their PhD training has multiplied their references. So although I seldom refer to periodical articles, let alone to reviews, bibliographies in the books I cite, many of them eye-pickings from periodicals, will repair these omissions.

One awkwardness arises from the decision to publish separately. I hope, before too long, to publish a revised edition of *A Hundred Years of Philosophy*, in the version published by Pelican Books. In the notes, I have often made cross-references to notes in that volume. There is, for the moment, a gap between the literature there mentioned and the literature here referred to; all going well, that gap will shortly be filled.

This book has been written by a retired Professor, without the exceptionally generous degree of assistance which was previously available. My wife has been called upon to help to an even greater extent than has been normal: I am very grateful for that help. At a time and in a country where the elderly are expected quietly to vanish I have also been exceptionally fortunate in that the Australian National University granted me first a University Fellowship and then a Visiting Fellowship in the History of Ideas department, under the congenial leadership of Professor Eugene Kamenka. Mrs Helen Hookey, in that Department, has been of great assistance in typing parts of the final version. Several of my colleagues, at home and abroad, have commented on sections of the book. It would be unkind to particularise them, as they have not seen the final version. But they have helped me to avoid a number of errors. I should be glad to have other mistakes drawn to my attention.

Canberra   J.P
February 1984

1

Introduction: Change and Continuity

Tumultuous, ill-defined, immensely variegated in aspiration and method – how can one hope to describe, briefly but comprehensively and comprehensibly, the contemporary Anglo-American philosophical enterprise?[1] Answer – impossible. So many philosophers writing, so many problems raised – completeness is no longer a rational ambition. A more modest title, let us say *Some Recent Philosophical Controversies Too Briefly Described*, would have been more accurate, if scarcely in the modern style. Given the need for drastic selectivity, I have begun with a broad survey of the contemporary scene before focussing on the relatively few themes, the relatively few philosophers, later examined in more detail. This is to dispel any suggestion that philosophy has no mansions other than those we shall be inhabiting, if by temporarily trespassing beyond the boundaries which were laid down in *A Hundred Years of Philosophy* and are otherwise rigorously adhered to in the present epilogue.

The title of that book, too, promised more than ensued. Not only was it largely confined to Anglo-American philosophy but, in the hope of constructing a coherent narrative, it did not move outside the closely intertwined fields of epistemology, philosophical logic, metaphysics, the philosophy of language, the philosophy of the physical sciences. That was already, in 1957, to exclude a great deal: moral and political philosophy in its entirety, to say nothing of aesthetics and the philosophy of the social sciences.

In the immediately post-war decades such a decision was, however, as much symptomatic as stipulative. To be sure, there were influential contributors to these excluded forms of philosophising, who tried to set them on new paths. In moral philosophy the name of R.M. Hare at once comes to mind, in the philosophy of law H.L. Hart, in the philosophy of history W.H. Dray. To a striking degree,

1

nevertheless, professional philosophers concentrated on precisely those areas of philosophising – calling them 'central' – to which *A Hundred Years of Philosophy* was confined.

When they embarked upon the less-fashionable topics, furthermore, this was usually in order to engage in a specialised version of 'philosophical logic'. That is most easy to illustrate in the case of moral philosophy: Hare set out to analyse the most general moral concepts, such concepts as 'ought', to delineate the structure of moral argument, to determine the logical status of moral assertions – whether they were genuinely statements, or rather disguised prescriptions, commands, recommendations, expressions of feeling. To give an account of the 'central' issues of philosophy was at the same time, then, to prepare the reader to enter its wider spheres.

That is no longer true. Moral, political, legal philosophers do not wholly confine themselves to conceptual studies, to examining 'the logic' of morals, or law, or political controversy. So *Justice* (1971) was one of the most widely-discussed books of the 1970s. There John Rawls, in a closely reasoned, certainly philosophical, argument, set out to consider not only how it is to be determined in what justice consists but, in detail, in what it *does* consist. A little later, in 1978, Sissela Bok wrote her *Lying*. Casuistry is no longer set aside as being unphilosophical; the Aristotelian emphasis on virtue and on the distinguishing characteristics of specific virtues is once more in fashion.

More remarkable still – at least from the standpoint of the earlier post-war decades – philosophers have begun to write about such socially controversial topics as feminism, abortion, environmental degeneration, nuclear warfare. The radical movements of the 1960s, for all that they so rapidly faded, have not been wholly inconsequential in their effects. To be sure, earlier philosophers, from Plato to Mill, had by no means thought of such topics as lying outside their province – or, indeed, of philosophy as having any fixed boundaries. Nearer to our own time, Bertrand Russell had addressed a wide public on education, marriage, peace and war. But Russell specifically told that public that in so doing he was stepping outside philosophy, writing as a father, a husband, a citizen, rather than as a philosopher. To that degree, he conformed to a convention which he had, indeed, helped to establish: that philosophy should be so defined as, even when it was moral and political philosophy, to preclude advice on practical issues. The 1970s, in contrast, witnessed the emergence of such periodicals as *Philosophy and Public Affairs* (1971) which sought to apply philosophy to political issues. In the 1980s societies and journals for 'applied philosophy', or such particular branches of it as 'the philosophy of medicine', have proliferated, to the surprise of an intellectual public conditioned to supposing that philosophy was a sophisticated intellectual game. With mingled feelings of embarrassment, incredulity, gratification and apprehension, philosophers have found themselves members of advisory committees on contemporary policy issues, or being called upon to lecture in medical or engineering schools. They were no longer prepared to grant that to participate in fundamental social controversies was to step outside philosophy.

That much of this work can properly be described as 'applied philosophy' rather than as lay sermonising is open to question. Hare, for one, has complained that its authors are too often content 'with appeals to their own and others' intuitions or prejudices' when what is expected from a philosopher is close reasoning. If in what follows it is ignored, this is not, however, as being unphilosophical but rather because – except in so far as some environmental philosophers raise metaphysical issues about man and nature – the most carefully reasoned 'applied philosophy' is in fact applied *ethics* and as such automatically excluded from the present narrative. But even this brief reference to it will serve to emphasise that the more technical issues to which this epilogue is confined by no means constitute the sole pabulum of contemporary philosophy.[2]

The case of Marxism is more complicated. The Great Boom of the 1960s succeeded in doing what the Great Depression of the 1930s had largely failed to do, to popularise Marxism among Anglo-American philosophers. Of course, their Marxism was rather different from the sort of Marxism most prevalent in the 1930s; it was no longer indissolubly linked, in the eyes of most of its adherents, with the desperate task of defending the Soviet Union. Indeed, many Marxists wholly averted their eyes from Eastern Europe. Marxism, we were told, 'had never been tried'. (That was particularly true in the Anglo-American world; France for long remained the principal home of the older Marxist attitudes.) There came to be as many versions of Marxism as there are of Christianity; a 'Marxism' could be chosen to fit one's particular temperament. They ranged from the humanistic Marxism of the *Economic and Philosophical Manuscripts* – written in 1844 but not published until 1932 and first translated into English in 1959 – to the austere dehumanised Marxism created in France by Louis Althusser. The humanist Marx was often amalgamated with a humanised Freud to give intellectual body to the inchoate ideals of the 1960s. Althusser's Marx was favoured by those whose ideals were of a more ascetic sort.[3]

If Marxism thus came to assume, in the 1970s, a prominence in Anglo-American philosophy departments which by no means characterised the preceding decades, it, too, will largely be ignored in what follows. That is for a number of reasons. Marxism is most effective, and most widely cultivated, in relation to political philosophy, the philosophy of art and the practice of social criticism, all of them lying outside my present concern. When Marxist-style philosophising does take the form of epistemology or metaphysics, it is most commonly a variety of scholarship, devoted to discovering what Marx 'really meant'. That is not at all surprising, seeing that Marx did not himself write in a systematic fashion on such topics. Indeed, he can most naturally be read as an anti-philosopher, as arguing that philosophy is a thing of the past, now to be replaced by science, to which it is related, he notoriously remarked in his *German Ideology* (1845-6, first fully published in 1932) 'as onanism is to sexual love'.

For a time a Marxist philosophy was nevertheless constructed, as it was in *A Hundred Years of Philosophy*, by turning to Engels and Lenin. Soviet Marxists still proceed in that way. But many other Marxists both in the Anglo-American world and on the European Continent – to which one has to go for the most influential restatements of Marxism – looked elsewhere for a Marxist philosophy, often back to Fichte, Hegel or Feuerbach. Their work, exegetical, apologetic, no more belongs to the present narrative than does comparable work on, let us say, Frege or Russell, even when it has epistemology or metaphysics as its theme.

It will already be sufficiently apparent why this epilogue, in its later chapters, will be much less representative of what now goes on in philosophy departments than was the volume to which it serves as epilogue. But there is still more to be said on this point. In 1957, when *A Hundred Years of Philosophy* was first published, the Anglo-American philosophical world was comparatively small, cosy, self-contained, reading very few philosophical periodicals, writing relatively little. A decade later the multiplication of books, the burgeoning of articles, had already reached a point at which, as I confessed on the appearance in 1966 of the second edition, the historian could no longer hope to 'cover the field' to the degree, quite considerable, that had previously been possible. If what had once been little more than a brook had by then been converted into a broad stream, in the 1980s the inevitable comparison, however banal, is with a flood.

To be sure, like any other flood, the flood of publications brings with it mud, débris, even corpses. These the historian can ignore with a clear conscience. And most of what is written, even when it is worthy, respectable, technically competent, is as irretrievably minor as is comparable work in science. A hive of activity is not necessarily a nest of geniuses. Nevertheless, many a philosopher must now be relegated to a footnote who would in earlier times have been thought worthy of extended treatment. Otherwise, this epilogue would swell to disproportionate dimensions.

The flood metaphor is, I granted, a banal one. But in the present instance it has a double force. A flood is remarkable not only for its volume but for the way in which it unites in a single flow what were once distinct streams, obscuring boundaries, breaking down fences. That is what has happened in philosophy. It is much more difficult than it once was to determine either the boundaries of philosophy as a whole or the boundaries of particular branches of philosophy. Under Marxist, or post-Marxist influence, one finds it questioned, for example, whether philosophy of science can be fruitfully distinguished from the sociology of knowledge. In the writings of the Frankfurt School, particularly Jürgen Habermas, epistemology and social theory flow into one another, not without reference to American pragmatism;[4] for Michel Foucault, French 'structuralist', what counts as knowledge is inextricably related to who possesses power; in Great Britain there is an active group of writers, encouraged by Paul Feyerabend's anarchism and the historical approach to the philosophy of science initiated by T.S. Kuhn, who seek to show that there can be no solution, except in sociology, for the leading problems in the philosophy of science.

To take a second case, nobody could have supposed that 'ordinary language' philosophy, even when Austin began to lecture on speech-acts, was a branch of linguistics, as then conceived by professional linguists. But later the interplay between philosophy and linguistics came to be so considerable, the boundaries so unclear, as to raise doubts whether we were not indeed witnessing, as Austin had anticipated, yet another breakaway of a new science from philosophy. Or if not quite a new science, at least a transformed linguistics which incorporated much that had been previously counted as philosophy. Where such a linguistics ends, where philosophy begins, is far from being obvious. Yet it is precisely in this disputed territory that much of the most influential contemporary philosophy now resides.

Similar uncertainties arise in the case of logic. Suggesting rather than reporting a usage, one might roughly distinguish three levels of logical activity: mathematical logic, philosophy of logic and philosophical logic. Mathematical logic constructs formal systems and tests them for such formal properties as completeness and consistency. Philosophy of logic looks at such systems and asks questions about the range of their application, whether, and in what sense, they are genuinely alternative logics, to what degree they are applicable to particular forms of reasoning. Philosophical logic considers, rather, the vocabulary of logic: what constitutes a statement, in what 'logical form' consists, or implication, or entailment, or disjunction, or modality ... A particular logician, of course, may move from one level to another, perhaps as he encounters problems at a particular level which he cannot solve at that level.[5]

There can be no doubt that philosophy of logic and philosophical logic both form part of philosophy – except in so far as philosophical logic fades into philosophy of language and that, as we saw, into linguistics. Indeed, many would still agree with Russell that philosophical logic *simply is* philosophy. It will bulk large in what follows. But to an ever-growing extent, mathematical logic has fallen into the hands of mathematicians. (One has to remember, of course, that Frege was a mathematician and so were many of the later logicians.) To be sure, analytical philosophers no longer, as many did in the palmy days of ordinary language philosophy, regard formal logic with scorn or dismiss it as wholly irrelevant. Indeed, a comparatively advanced acquaintance with the major logical systems has come to be taken for granted in contemporary Anglo-American philosophy; logical symbols proliferate. So far,

Carnap and Quine have vanquished Ryle. Nevertheless, few philosophers now read the *Journal of Symbolic Logic*, which has indeed set up for their purposes a *Journal of Philosophical Logic*. Although analytic philosophers use symbols derived from the logical systems of the past decades, their symbols are often decorative abbreviations rather than elements in philosophical derivations. They refer to mathematical logic but do not engage in it, any more than an engineer engages in mathematics; they are consumers rather than producers.

Setting out to describe the philosophical scene, then, one might well ignore developments in mathematical logic. The divorce, or amicable separation, between mathematical logic and philosophy does not however go undeplored and is sometimes refused recognition, especially by that minority group of dissenters who can summarily be described as 'deviant logicians'. They have two complaints: first that the divorce trivialises mathematical logic, leading to the construction of systems which are nothing more than mathematical games, with no right to call themselves 'logic', the second that it leads philosophers to rely on systems which they should in fact reject, whether as involving intolerable paradoxes or as being quite incapable of giving a satisfactory account of the difference between good and bad reasoning – at least outside mathematics and perhaps even within it.

Such earlier critics of mathematical logic as Schiller and Strawson had already argued that there are large classes of valid arguments which are not recognised as valid in formal systems and, in Strawson's case, that the mathematical logician's use of such logical constants as 'or', 'and', does not capture their role in everyday argument. They had not concluded, however, that a better formal system should be developed but rather that formal logic should be replaced, or supplemented, by an informal logic, which would capture the inferential force of specific concepts – what follows, for example, from 'being the brother of'. To this mathematical logicians have replied that such a logic could never be anything more than a miscellaneous hotch-potch and that their critics were confusing logic and rhetoric. No doubt, they have granted, we use all sorts of devices in the process of trying to persuade others that what we say is true. They have often granted, too, that we should not normally try to persuade people, for example, that q follows from p by telling them that *p* is false. But none of this matters, they would argue, if the outcome of accepting such material implications is the construction of a logical system which is clear, precise, adequate for deriving theorems from axioms and free of any confusing talk about 'meaning'.

In the 1970s, however, quite a few logicians, if still very much a minority, came to be dissatisfied with this defence. They were unhappy with the suggestion that a logic could be regarded as adequate which could give no account, in a large class of cases, of the difference between acceptable and unacceptable reasoning; they were not convinced that such paradoxes as the paradox of material implication – that a false proposition implies the truth of any proposition we care to mention – can either be set aside as of no consequence or defended as not being paradoxical at all.

The classical logician, so Richard Routley argues in his *Relevant Logic and its Rivals* (1982), behaves like an engineer who has invented a device to lift water from a stream. It is so badly designed that it spills most of its freight. Instead of trying to improve the device he devotes his energy to 'constructing ingenious arguments to prove that the device is admirable', this on such grounds as that 'there is nothing wrong with wasting water' or that the device has 'beautiful, clean, simple lines' which it would go 'totally against his engineering intuitions' to modify. Meanwhile, most of the community's water is obtained by 'the traditional tedious, limited hand-carrying methods' – this last a reference to the fact, to many shocking, that when philosophers want to bring out the fallacies in a philosophical argument, they often fall back on traditional, 'Aristotelian', logic, finding nothing in 'classical' Frege-Russell logic to help them. 'Relevant' logicians, unlike Strawson, are not ready to abandon formalisation: they want a formalisation which 'works', which really does distinguish valid from fallacious reasoning.

Of course, many formal logicians, G.H. von Wright for example, had already sought to supplement classical logic – ignoring the protests of that staunch defender of minimalist logic, Quine – by developing modal logics, or deontic logics, or logics of imperatives and questions. In so doing, they were working on the assumption that there were classes of argument, relating the necessary to the possible, or the obligatory to the permitted, or commands to their acceptance, or questions to their answers, which the classical logic did not suffice to formalise. Jaakko Hintikka had even sought to develop an 'epistemic logic' relating knowing to believing. But these supplementations left the central bastions of classical logic untouched, except when they drew upon C.I. Lewis's theory of 'strict implication'. That had certainly attacked classical logic at a central point – its theory of implication. But it introduced fresh paradoxes of its own, particularly the paradox that a sentence of the form 'A and not-A' strictly implies any sentence whatsoever.[6]

In search of a logic which would more closely relate to our ordinary inferential practices, W. Ackermann briefly sketched as early as 1956 a system which had as its centre the concept of 'strong implication' and rejected whatever axioms of classical logic did not satisfy that concept. His logic was developed over the suceeding years by A.R. Anderson and N.D. Belnap – with a number of collaborators – into a 'relevance logic', summed up in their *Entailment* (1975). One statement entails another, it is now said, only if, as we might informally put it, 'they have something to do with one another'. In more philosophical language, there has to be some connection between their content. (Relevance logic is unashamedly intensional, talking freely about meanings.) Such a connection can be more formally defined in terms of 'common variables'. Originally associated with Pittsburgh, this approach to implication – and more broadly to conditionality – has subsequently been developed in highly heterodox directions in Australia and South America, giving birth to 'paraconsistent' logics. The requirements it lays down for implication automatically rule out the paradoxes of both strict and material implication. To take the former case, it cannot be true that p and not-p together imply any proposition q chosen at random since they have no sentential variable in common. (Contrast 'p and q imply q'.) We shall not explore the intricacies of the resulting debate, asking whether the modifications required in classical logic bring the original project to ruin – especially if, to avoid Lewis's argument for the paradox of strict implication, the disjunctive syllogism 'p or q, not-p, therefore q' has to be rejected as invalid – or whether 'relevance' is a formal as distinct from a rhetorical notion.[7] What has already been said will serve to illustrate the case of those who deny that mathematical logic can safely be left to the mathematicians, like a colony which has won independence. In its more detailed reaches, however, it will subsequently be ignored.

There are many other points at which the boundaries between

philosophy and other forms of intellectual activity have become less easy to trace. It is at first astonishing to encounter a history of contemporary philosophy by an Austrian philosopher of science, Wolfgang Stegmüller, which includes, in its second volume, lengthy discussions of contemporary cosmology and contemporary theoretical biology, together making up almost half the volume. But Stegmüller hopes thus to illustrate what he calls 'the convergence between general philosophical theories and empirical investigations' in contemporary thought. He is by no means, one should emphasise, a 'nature-philosopher' of the kind so prevalent in nineteenth-century Germany, intent on arguing that for true science one must look to metaphysics – the sort of 'nature-philosopher' who stimulated the logical positivist onslaught on metaphysics. Far from it; he is one of the few German-speaking philosophers who resisted the blandishments of Heidegger and philosophised in the manner of a latter-day Carnap. Few Anglo-American philosophers would agree that a history of philosophy should go so deeply into science. Nevertheless, there is a widespread yearning after the speculative freedom of the Presocratics, for whom the distinction between philosophy and speculative science about the cosmos and the origins of life still did not exist. One finds it in such diverse thinkers as Heidegger, Popper, Feyerabend, not only in Stegmüller, and it is encouraged by the highly speculative character of contemporary cosmology.

At the very least, philosophers of science are much less willing than they were in the earlier decades of the century – especially between about 1925 and 1960 – to agree with Wittgenstein that 'the propositions of natural science have nothing to do with philosophy', that science is relevant to philosophy only in so far as philosophers of science can logically analyse the general structure of scientific theories. Quine has argued that there is no sharp distinction between philosophy and science, Putnam that philosophy of physics is 'continuous with physics'. For a time very few philosophers – with such notable exceptions as Reichenbach and Grünbaum – had ventured to write at length about space-time or quantum mechanics. These, it came to be felt, should be left to theoretical physics. In the 1970s, as we shall see later, that was far from being the prevailing attitude. The comfortable doctrine that philosophers could, and should, confine their attention to conceptual issues, leaving the empirical aside as irrelevant to their purposes, has been undermined on a variety of fronts, not only in respect to physics and biology. Cognitive psychology, information theory, computer theory – particularly in relation to 'machine intelligence' – have all offered challenges and opportunities to philosophers, especially to epistemologists. Books like the art historian E.H. Gombrich's *Art and Illusion* (1960) or the neurophysiologist Richard Gregory's *Eye and Brain* (1966) are by no means neglected by philosophers. The boundaries between philosophy and social science are once more fluid. If, as I said, few philosophers would expect me to follow the example of Stegmüller, there is much contemporary philosophy into which only someone trained in mathematics or physics or economics can hope to penetrate at all deeply.

Philosophy, then, is both expanding and contracting; at certain points it is losing ground to other forms of inquiry, whether to linguistics or mathematics, at other points advancing where it had earlier retreated. Geographical boundaries, too, are not so clear as they once were. The familiar contrast between 'Anglo-American' and 'Continental' philosophy was never, of course, geographically accurate. One had to include as 'Anglo-American' most Finnish philosophy, much Polish philosophy, and to remember that if 'Anglo-American' philosophy has roots in the British empirical tradition it owes a great deal to the German Frege, to such Austrian philosophers as the Vienna positivists, Karl Popper and, further back, Brentano. Nevertheless the contrast roughly worked. On the one side lay Franco-German-Italian philosophy, centring around Heidegger, Sartre, Jaspers, prophetic in style and, even when its outcome was atheistic, centrally concerned with the issues which have preoccupied theology. It allied itself with literature rather than science and claimed that to be deep, to say something genuinely new, one was forced to be obscure, calling upon the poet's right to twist language to one's special purposes. On the other side lay analytical Anglo-American philosophy, with clarity as its central virtue, the linguistic principles laid down by the Royal Society in the seventeenth century still its guide, sympathetic to science, devoting its attention to epistemology, mind and language, centring around Ryle, Ayer, Austin, Quine – brothers from a 'Continental' point of view, for all their differences.

These two kinds of philosophising still survive. Philosophy is not, as science is, a single intellectual community. It is not just, as is also true in science, that philosophers specialise. In a much more divisive way, they have different philosophical heroes, different ideas about what constitutes good and bad philosophising. At the 1983 World Conference of Philosophy in Montreal it was still true that considerable segments of the participants neither understood nor wished to understand what other segments of participants were doing, or why they were doing it, even when the topics under discussion were, to judge from their titles alone, of common interest. The difference is that the division between types of philosophising no longer corresponds to geographical boundaries even to the degree it once did.

True enough, France remains faithful to its insularity. Only a very occasional French philosopher takes an interest in analytical philosophising. One such exception, the philosopher of language Jacques Bouveresse, has described his philosophical position in an article with the revealing title 'Why I am so very unFrench'. 'Insularity', to be sure, is not quite the right word. Such German thinkers as Husserl and Heidegger have continued to be very influential in France, even although their influence in Germany has steeply declined. But Anglo-American philosophy continues to be almost completely unacceptable, whether in respect to its style, its methods or its conclusions. That is no longer true in Germany.

For many years, Wolfgang Stegmüller stood almost alone in Germany in philosophising in a Carnapian manner. But in the 1960s the German-speaking world at last discovered its own Frege, Wittgenstein, Popper, Brentano, Meinong, the Vienna positivists. More than that, it discovered Peirce, Quine, Austin and some at least of the later philosophers we shall be considering.[8]

It often criticised them, admittedly, from the standpoint of a more familiar German tradition. So at the hands of Ernst Tugendhat, one of Heidegger's last pupils, linguistic analysis is set against and linked with Husserlian phenomenology in its earlier form. Each is criticised in the light of the other, phenomenology for its failure to realise that the starting point of reflection is not the isolated essence but the sentence, linguistic philosophy as lacking 'the historical dimension and a comprehensive concept of understanding' – that concept of understanding as always dependent on membership of an 'intellectual tradition' which is central to the 'philosophical hermeneutics' particularly associated with the name of Gadamer, growing out of Heidegger's work.[9] Karl-Otto Apel, while making considerable use of Anglo-American philosophy of language, still has his heart set, in a quasi-Kantian manner, on the concept of an ideal use of language, illustrated in rational discourse and governed by rules which flow from the very nature of reason.[10] This is a far cry from Anglo-American semantics, and very much in the German tradition.

Yet the fact remains that no really thoroughgoing history of the Anglo-American tradition could properly ignore these developments. And it would be difficult not to follow them, as we have already suggested, into the social theories where Habermas has led them. On the other side, even if the influence of many 'Continental' philosophers has been much deeper in social theory and in a literary criticism perpetually in pursuit of a sustaining theory than in 'Anglo-American' philosophy, there are many geographically 'Anglo-American' departments – in English-speaking Canada perhaps the majority but elsewhere a sizable minority – where Hegel, Husserl, Heidegger count for more than Hume, Frege, Quine. It is no longer considered disreputable to write with approval of Hegel or even of Heidegger, to say nothing of their hermeneutic successors.[11] If Russell's admonition to concentrate on 'piecemeal, detailed, verifiable results' is still widely observed, many 'Anglo-American' philosophers have begun to write on a larger, bolder, scale.[12] So the boundaries between 'Anglo-American' and 'Continental' philosophy are being breached from both directions.

Obviously, then, great changes have come over the philosophical scene during the last decades. But the chapters which follow, while still, as an epilogue, confining themselves within the narrow bounds of the volume they supplement, will perhaps exaggerate the novelty of recent philosophy by largely confining themselves to 'new directions', especially in the philosophy of language. For philosophy is still in many ways the most striking example of that familiar aphorism, 'the more things change, the more they remain the same'. To be sure, there are novelties, questions raised which Plato would not have understood. Yet for all the greater sophistication of method, the use of technical tools deriving from logic and semantics, it is surprising how much philosophical effort is still devoted to trying to solve problems which Plato, or Descartes, or Hume, first saw as such.

A particular case will serve to illustrate two points, the familiarity of some of the issues and the novel manner in which discussion of them is now often carried on. One of the questions which greatly troubled Plato is how knowledge differs from belief. For a time it looked as if philosophers were happy to suppose that they had the answer, that knowledge is a kind of belief which has two peculiarities. First, it is true; secondly, the believer is fully justified in believing that it is true. In 1963 E.L. Gettier published a two-and-a-half page article in the journal *Analysis* which set out two counter-examples to this way of making the distinction. If, to take the first of them, we have good grounds for believing that Jones will be appointed to a particular position and that he has ten coins in his pocket, then we certainly have good grounds for believing that a person with ten coins in his pocket will be appointed to the position. This may turn out to be in fact the case but only because another person, also with ten coins in his pocket, is appointed. Then we did not *know* that a person answering to this description would be appointed even although we had good reasons for believing that such a person would be appointed and he was in fact appointed. Gettier's miniscule article generated some hundreds of replies, a clear sign that the old issues are by no means dead but also indicating just how many philosophers sit, with their typewriters ready, to comment on a new twist to an old controversy.[13]

There are some philosophers, too, who wholly devote themselves to classical philosophical questions, discussed in a classical manner. Descartes would contest their conclusions but would not be surprised by what they take to be centrally important. A case in point is the Australian philosopher David Armstrong.[14] Armstrong defends, in the classical manner, a world-hypothesis. The world, he says, 'contains nothing but particulars having properties and related to each other', it constitutes a single spatio-temporal system and – this more hesitantly – it is wholly describable 'in terms of a completed physics'. To any such world-hypothesis there are a number of familiar objections. The world as we actually apprehend it consists, so it is often said, not of particulars with properties but of isolated elements – ideas or sense-data or perceptions. It contains minds, others have argued, which are not spatio-temporal, and properties – secondary qualities – about which science is silent. That beliefs cannot be adequately analysed either in terms of properties or relations, that properties have no part to play in an accurate description of the world – these, too, are familiar contentions which Armstrong has to meet. Armstrong's reply to these objections is worked out in detail; we can do no more than summarise it.

To begin with perception, Armstrong first formulates his theory in *Perception and the Physical World* (1961), modifying it in detail but not in essence in his subsequent writing. Like his teacher, John Anderson, he argues that perception consists in acquiring knowledge or belief about particular states of affairs. This is certainly as a result of sensory stimulation. Nevertheless, what is perceived is not a copy of that stimulation, a sense-datum. Perceiving that there is a book on the table is, for Armstrong, believing one to be there. So the world as we perceive it, he concludes, already contains properties and relations; it does not consist of simple sensory elements.

As for minds, Armstrong takes as his starting point the Place-Smart doctrine of central state materialism, with its *locus classicus* Smart's essay on 'Sensations and Brain-Processes' (*PR*, 1959), as further developed by Smart, in the context of a broader discussion, in his *Philosophy and Scientific Realism* (1963). Armstrong's ambition in *A Materialist Theory of the Mind* (1968) is to present a central state theory not only of sensations but of mental states in general, many of which Smart had originally been content to describe – he later changed his mind – in terms of a Rylean behaviourism. For Ryle, such mental states as desires were dispositions, simply. For Armstrong, they are states which have a certain disposition, states 'apt for bringing about a certain kind of behaviour' – that is why one can think of them as 'intentional' – just as a brittle substance has a structure such that it is particularly liable to break. As for sensations, they, too, are states, but states 'apt for being brought about by a certain sort of stimulus'. As against a Feyerabend-style materialism, there are, then, mental states. But science, Armstrong says, has shown them to be also brain states and therefore spatio-temporal, not a counter-example to Armstrong's world-hypothesis.

Armstrong's account of secondary qualities runs along similar lines. Smart had argued that colour is an anthropomorphic concept, definable in terms of the human capacity to make certain kinds of discrimination, that in so far as it is the task of philosophers to see the world *sub specie aeternitatis* they 'must eschew the concepts of colour and other secondary qualities'. This, Armstrong suggests, is a relic of Smart's earlier operationalism; his own view is realistic. He identifies the secondary qualities with properties of physical objects, properties, however, of which we are aware in everyday perception only as structures, being aware that a rose and a geranium are both red, but not in what being red ontologically consists, as a disjunctive set of light waves.

What of beliefs? In his *Belief, Truth and Knowledge* (1973), Armstrong picks up Ramsey's suggestion that our system of beliefs is 'a map by which we steer', a belief differing from a thought we merely entertain in so far as it is always 'a potential cause or inhibitor of action'.[15] This, Armstrong thinks, is clear in the case of such beliefs as that the book is on the table; that is a state of mind, encoding information, and like other mental states disposing to action. But what about scientific laws with their unrestricted generality?

Armstrong's answer, again Ramseyan, is that to believe that a scientific law holds is to have a disposition to 'extend the map', or to 'introduce general relations of causal sustenance between portions of the map, according to general rules'. So if my belief that X's head is cut off generates and causally sustains the belief that X is dead, and a similar causal relation holds, whatever person is substituted for X, this constitutes my general belief that the decapitated are dead.

In this analysis, properties are taken for granted as against any form of nominalism. But does the world in fact contain properties, and if so how do we know *what* properties it contains? These questions Armstrong explored in his two-volume *Universals and Scientific Realism* (1978). He criticises in detail the classical theories, whether nominalist – in several varieties – Platonic, 'particularist', in the manner of G.F. Stout, or 'universalistic', as in Russell's suggestion that particulars are bundles of universals. His conclusion – Anderson's in outline – is that neither particular nor universal is dispensable, that the world consists of states of affairs, particulars having properties, particulars related to one another.

Scientific laws assert relations between universals. How do we know what universals there are? We cannot tell, Armstrong argues, by simply considering what predicates our language contains. Science discovers what universals there are, in the process of formulating general laws. Armstrong sharply distinguishes between 'the semantics of predicates' and 'the theory of universals'; questions about meaning are very largely set aside in his attempt to construct a 'first philosophy'. That there can be any first philosophy except a theory of meaning, any theory of universals except a semantics of predicates, is precisely what many of his contemporaries would most vehemently deny. But Armstrong remains quite unmoved by 'the linguistic turn'.

If Armstrong is unusual in having written on so many of the classical topics it would be difficult to mention any classical philosophical problem which has been left entirely unscrutinised over the last decades. Consider for example the detailed examination of identity by David Wiggins in his *Sameness and Identity* (1980).[16] This is in many ways an extreme example of a prevalent contemporary philosophical style. A meticulous, very difficult text is buttressed with a multitude of explanatory and defensive footnotes and supplemented by some thirty pages of 'longer notes'. Its formalistic approach, its manner, is 'post-Fregean', the most general description one could offer of Anglo-American analytic philosophy in the 1970s. Yet Wiggins's argument is rooted in Aristotle and Leibniz – the centrality of Aristotle for Oxford-trained philosophers persists, the interest in Leibniz is newer, but widespread.

Wiggins's first objective is to refute the view that identity is relative, that *a* can be identical with *b* when considered in a particular light and yet not identical with it when considered in a different light.[17] Take that famous London landmark, Cleopatra's Needle, and suppose the original stone is gradually replaced by concrete, as the stone weathers away. Then, on the relative identity view, it is or is not identical with the originally-erected Cleopatra's Needle, according as we think of it as a landmark or as a stone structure. Against any such doctrine, Wiggins argues that to be identical *a* and *b* must have all their properties in common, so that there can be no question of their being identical when considered in one respect but not in another respect. All apparent counter-examples, so he suggests, rest either on a confusion between 'is identical with' and 'is composed from or constituted out of' or on 'the deceptive designation of certain referring expressions'.

At the same time, Wiggins defends what has often been taken to be the same thing as the 'relative identity' thesis, namely that if *a* and *b* are identical, this must be in respect to some sort, or kind, which would answer the question what sort of thing they are.[18] This is in the strong Aristotelian sense in which to determine 'what they are' is to point to some general characteristic, a sortal property, which determines 'identity, persistence and existence conditions for the members of its extension'. The paradigm instance is a living organism. Describing something as a horse is in that process pointing to forms of activity, or functioning, or operations which, by way of natural science, can be used to determine whether something is a horse, when it began and ceased to be a horse, under what circumstances *a* and *b* are the same horse – even though, of course, I can recognize my favourite horse without knowing exactly what these forms are. Artefacts, Wiggins admits, are more difficult. There is in such cases nothing like the developmental laws which let us say that an acorn is the same *quercus* as the oak-tree into which it grows. A watch that has been extensively repaired no doubt fulfils the same function as the original watch, but so would any other watch. Wiggins grants that in such instances a degree of conventionality may attach to the notion of identity but not to such an extent, he thinks, as to destroy his general thesis.

What of personal identity? One traditional view is that the identity of a person consists in a person's ability to think of himself as being himself in different times and places and, in particular, in the continuity of memory. But consider, apart from other problems, someone who suffers total loss of memory. Is he a different person from the time of memory-loss onwards? We might feel inclined to answer: 'Yes, he is, although, of course, he is the same animal.' That answer, however, Wiggins has ruled out by rejecting relative identity. Yet he is not content, for Strawson-like reasons, with the alternative suggestion that a person *simply is* a living body. A person, in his view, is any animal, not necessarily human – although the human being, Wiggins insists, is our only clear paradigm of personhood – which belongs to a species whose *typical* members can *typically* reason and reflect, and can *typically* consider themselves as being still themselves at different times and places and ... The person who suffers from amnesia, for all that he cannot himself remember his own past, still belongs to a species which typically has such powers; he has not lost the animal human form. So he is still a person – more than that, he is the very same person who lost his memory.

This is by no means the sum total of Wiggins's argument. He considers carefully many of the questions we shall later be looking at, questions about necessity, about essences, about realism. But enough has been said to indicate that a discussion of the traditional issues can be sustained within the framework of a distinctly contemporary manner, as well as in the more classical style of Armstrong's work. One should note, too, for the benefit of those who suppose that problems about identity are of only technical concern, philosophers' games, meticulous trivialities, that Wiggins ends with conclusions, however briefly sketched, about the objectivity of ethical standards and ethical values, as supposedly derivative from his rejection of that alternative view of persons which regards them not as animals but as 'social constructs'.[19]. One should not conclude from the fact that a book looks forbiddingly technical – although most of Wiggins's formal symbols are nothing more than abbreviations – that its conclusions cannot be of deep human concern.

We have now arrived at a parting of the ways. We could devote our remaining space to those authors who continue working at the more familiar classical philosophical themes, not uncommonly by reconsidering Kantian views – for empiricism of the classical British sort is now at a low ebb.[20] But it will be more appropriate, I think, to concentrate on the theory of language and meaning. For it is here that the principal emphasis has lain, even when, as in Wiggins's case, the newer developments are invoked in the attempt to settle a problem in 'first philosophy' – or indeed, as in other cases, to deny that the classical problems of philosophy are worthy of serious consideration.

There is, it might be thought, no novelty in such an emphasis on language. Did not Oxford 'ordinary language' philosophy seek to solve the perennial problems of philosophy by appealing to linguistic usage? In the 1970s, however, ordinary language philosophy fell into disrepute; so much so that one of the 'new generation' of Oxford philosophers can write cuttingly of it as 'impoverished and fraudulent'.[21] Nevertheless, something still survives – Austin's theory of 'speech acts' is by no means dead, especially in the refined versions developed by John Searle and Paul Grice. Those refined versions will serve as a useful point of transition.

In his *Speech Acts* (1969), Searle begins by explaining that he is doing philosophy of language, not linguistic philosophy. Whereas linguistic philosophy tried to solve, or dissolve, classical philosophical problems by paying careful attention to the way in which certain words are used, philosophy of language sets out 'to give philosophically illuminating descriptions of certain general features of language such as reference, truth, meaning and necessity'. However much they might disagree with Searle's procedures and conclusions, most contemporary 'philosophers of language' would accept that characterisation of their task. What has fallen into disrepute is linguistic philosophy, not philosophy of language.

Searle himself, one should add, does not participate in the total denigration of linguistic philosophy – which he is still prepared to describe as 'a revolution in philosophy'. Yet he nevertheless criticises its principal exponents, on the ground that although they certainly had 'a nice ear' for linguistic distinctions, they also had 'little or no theoretical machinery' and often went seriously astray in consequence. His own object is to provide the 'theoretical machinery'. For that purpose, Searle begins from Austin's theory of speech-acts; his starting-point is not, as it is for most philosophy of language, the word or the sentence but rather the producing of such words or sentences 'in the performance of a speech act'. His systematic presentation and modification of that theory, his relating of it to contemporary debates, has had the effect that discussions of speech acts often take Searle rather than Austin as their point of departure.[22]

Searle is also ecumenical. Even though the theory of speech acts has often been thought of as a rival to those theories of language which look to the internal structure of sentences rather than to the intentions and the acts of the speaker, they should rather, he argues, be thought of as complementary. A complete theory of language must take account both of what a speaker *means to do* in speaking and what is *meant by* the sentences he uses. This particularly comes out in Searle's analysis of predication. Whereas in general we can distinguish, he says, between the 'content' and the 'function' of a speech act, as between the fact that I am promising and what I am promising, predication does not specify a particular function. The force of predicative acts comes entirely from the character of the specific illocutionary act in the course of which the predication occurs. This left it open for his critics to maintain that the crucial thing to get right is how to determine the meaning of this common predicative content. Illocutionary force is, on their view, an extra.

But that is not the route Searle wants to take. Indeed, in the preface to his *Expression and Meaning* (1979), he explains that the essays in that volume were originally designed as contributions to a book in which the theory of meaning would be shown to form part of the philosophy of mind, in which, in particular, speech acts would be linked with intentionality. As matters stand, he is content to suggest, as against Austin's view that there are a thousand or so different kinds of illocutionary acts, that there are but five general categories of such acts, without trying to deduce – as is, he thinks, ultimately demanded of him as a philosopher – from the philosophy of mind that there *must be* just five, no more and no less. (Strawson made fashionable the Kantian concept of such transcendental arguments, in which it is demonstrated what *must be* the case, in respect to categories.) For the rest, Searle takes up, not to the general satisfaction of his critics, the very difficult question what his theory is going to make of metaphor and fiction. In the process he looks critically at the concept of 'literal meaning' which is central to much contemporary philosophy of language. He explains, too, why he is discontented with the attempt of certain contemporary linguists to incorporate both his analysis of speech acts and Grice's analysis of 'conversational implications' into an elaborated theory, with its roots in general linguistics rather than in the philosophy of mind.[23]

To discuss Searle before Paul Grice is to throw chronology to the winds. Grice was already a well-known Oxford teacher when Searle went to that university as an American student. But Searle has been the systematiser, the book-writer. Grice's articles are sparse and complexly protected against counter-examples. In general terms, he, like Searle, stands by Austin's central emphasis on 'that notion', as he put it in 'Utterer's meaning, sentence-meaning and word-meaning' (1968) – 'which is involved in saying of someone that by (when) doing something, he meant that so-and-so', as distinct from that sense of meaning in which a word, or a sentence, in and of itself, 'means so-and-so'. A particular language, according to Grice, forms part of the repertoire of communicative devices which agents, in acting meaningfully, have at their disposal. Linguistics studies those devices, whereas philosophy of language concerns itself with the total speech act, in which an utterer intends by making an utterance that an auditor should recognise his intention for what it is and in virtue of that recognition respond – or at least intend to respond – to the utterer's intention. (As someone calling out 'Fire' intends his auditors to try to move as a result of recognising that this is what, by calling out 'Fire', he intended them to do.) Oxford philosophy of language was thus, in the 1960s, intimately linked with post-Wittgensteinian theories of action; intention lay at the centre of them both.

In his 'Logic and Conversation' (1975)[24] Grice particularly relates his theory of language to the practice of conversation, to talk exchanges, rather than to separate utterances or utterances linked only in formal logical relationships. Such conversations, he argues, are governed by rational principles – to be as informative as, but not more informative than, is required, not to say what one has no good grounds for believing, to be relevant and so on. In virtue of that fact a listener can draw conclusions which go beyond, and in such cases as irony can conflict with, the formal implications of what is said. So if I remark 'Either Grice or Searle said that', I 'conversationally implicate' that I am not sure who said it, even although I am formally entitled to make such a remark even when I know that Grice was the speaker. More generally, and slightly to simplify, if somebody says p and would not do so, assuming that he accepts the principles of rational conversation, unless he believes q, and if he is aware that I shall draw this conclusion and intends me to do so, then he has 'conversationally implicated' that q. So there is an informal logic of conversation somewhat as, so Grice's pupil Strawson thought, there is an informal logic of implication. Whether there is such a logic, or only a set of British conventions, has been much disputed.

2

Structure and Syntax

Calvinist Geneva, with its emphasis on a divine plan rather than on human intentions, is intellectually remote from Pelagian Oxford. It was in Geneva that Friedrich de Saussure delivered his *Course in General Linguistics*, posthumously published from outlines and lecture notes as early as 1915.[1] Like Grice, Saussure argued that the theory of language is but a part of a wider theory. This is not, however, a theory of actions but a general theory of signs, 'semiology', which itself forms parts of social psychology. Influential though this suggestion was to be, in Saussure it remains programmatic. His principal theme is *langue*, that general linguistic structure – defined as 'a sum of impressions deposited in the brain of each member of the speech community' – upon which each such member draws in every *parole*, speech-act. Thus envisaged, language is made up of signs, not sentences. Each sign, he argues, has a double aspect, as signifying a concept and as signified by an auditory image, a sound pattern – aspects as inseparable as the opposite sides of a piece of paper. Where there is no signifying, there is not a sign but only a noise; where there is no being signified, there is not a concept but only an amorphous intellectual blur.

The relationship between auditory image and concept is, for Saussure, arbitrary, just as it is arbitrary – Saussure, like Wittgenstein, is fond of analogies from chess – whether a chessman is made of wood or ivory. What is not arbitrary, and therefore the proper subject for linguistic theory, is the relationship between signs. Such relationships resemble what Saussure calls the 'grammar' of chess, which determines the 'value' of a piece in a rule-governed manner.

The 'value' of a piece varies with the state of the game. We can describe that state without knowing what has happened previously.

Similarly, Saussure argues against those who identify linguistic theory with philology, the linguist can develop a *synchronic* theory of language, analysing a language as it is at a particular time. He need pay no attention to the *diachronic* changes which have shaped it. There is, to be sure, one fundamental distinction between language and chess. The chess-player deliberately alters the state of the game whereas language, according to Saussure, 'in some way always eludes the individual or social will'. (In this, language contrasts with speech, sentence-forming, which is voluntary.)

How are signs related? The crucial relation for Saussure is their difference – which, indeed, constitutes them as individual signs. At the *signifying* level, he says, sounds are differentiated if they distinguish words from one another, as the letter 'r' distinguishes 'lip' from 'rip'; other distinctions we do not hear. (A Japanese does not hear any difference between 'l' and 'r' because that difference does not play a word-differentiating role in his language.) So, Saussure concludes, the auditory image is not simply 'given' as a 'sense-datum'; the nature of our language determines what we take to be a 'distinct sound'. The *significance* of a sign, he similarly argues, depends on the fact that it occurs where other signs might have occurred, as 'ran' in 'he ran up the hill' might have been 'walked' or 'climbed' or 'drove', and it signifies just in virtue of that fact. (Compare 'It is a long way ... go'. Only 'to' will fill this gap. Just for that reason 'to', in this context, does not signify.) Concepts, indeed, 'are purely differential and defined not by their positive content but negatively by their relation with other parts of the system'. A concept is not simply *there*, waiting to be named; if it were, he says, words in different languages would be precisely equivalent, as they are not. Languages differ by differentiating differently.

If Saussure's theory of language has created interest well beyond the ranks of linguists, that is because it permits of being generalised to other spheres. Saussure is arguing, in the first place, that even when phenomena are historical, subject to change, as languages clearly are, to analyse them theoretically we may nevertheless need to cut them away from their historical roots, to treat them as if they were unchanging – this in opposition to the nineteenth-century assumption that to understand is to see historically. Secondly, although languages are used by individuals in the pursuit of individual purposes, in the course of their meaning to do this or that,

Saussure's *langue* ignores all such purposes; it treats language as a formal system, which determines how individuals, whatever their purposes, divide up their world. It is so far Kantian in style, rather than empiricist, and raises the question whether there are other such world-organising codes. Thirdly, *langue* is self-enclosed. Whereas we ordinarily think of signs as existing in order to point to what is not a sign, to their reference, Saussure's signs point only to other signs. So the movement, as in so much later philosophising, is away from representation to internal coherence. Fourthly, each sign exists only in and through negating other signs. Some of these ideas had earlier exponents, in particular C.S. Peirce, but on the Continent it was through Saussure that they came into circulation.

Saussure was a linguist, not a philosopher. And it was fellow-linguists who immediately picked up and developed his ideas – especially the Moscow linguist, later to emigrate first to Prague and then to the United States, Roman Jakobson.[2] At his hands, they were linked with aesthetics, with the formalistic tendencies of the Moscow avant-garde in the 1920s. A painting, like a sentence, had ordinarily been supposed, by its very nature, to refer, whether to the world around the artist or, in some forms of Romantic theory, to states of the artist's mind. In formalist analysis it appears, rather, as a world of its own, or at the most as a member of an art-world, referring only to other paintings. Literature, too, had been thought of as a referential personal expression. Now, it came to be described, rather, as operating with a particular code – as exemplified in the pattern of a detective story – which the writer does not invent but takes over, and as referring only to other literary works. A Mallarmé, who sought to cut all connection between the language of poetry and reference, a Sterne, writing, so it is said, a novel about novel-writing, is taken to be exemplary. One other characteristic of post-Saussurean linguistic theories is notable: an obsession with 'binary opposites', the 'contraries' of traditional logic. These ideas were absorbed into the intellectual movement known as 'structuralism'.

Does structuralism fall within the province of our history, narrowly confined as that has been? There are good reasons for answering in the negative, abandoning the structuralists to the historian of ideas. None of the structuralists has written a metaphysical work comparable to Sartre's *Being and Nothingness*. (The comparison is inevitable; structuralism, in the 1960s and early 1970s, replaced existentialism as the Parisian intellectual fashion.) Several of them have specifically denied that they are philosophers, as distinct from intellectual historians, anthropologists, political scientists or psycho-analysts. They resent, as inappropriate, philosophical criticisms; they firmly maintain, appearances to the contrary notwithstanding, that they have no purely philosophical theses to maintain. Like the existentialists before them, furthermore, their influence on the more widely-discussed Anglo-American philosophers has been slight – even if, outside philosophy departments, they have often been what counts as 'contemporary philosophy'. Such Anglo-American philosophers as they have influenced, with very few exceptions, work in social and political philosophy and intellectual history, not in those areas on which we have concentrated our attention.

The structuralists, indeed, are often wilfully obscure, or wholly silent, precisely at the epistemological and ontological points where the Anglo-American philosopher seeks illumination. This is so whether the question at issue is the ontological status of language, its relationship to 'the world', or the manner in which it is related to individual speech-acts. Their philosophical framework, to the not inconsiderable degree to which they either rely upon, or react against, or allude to, philosophical doctrines, derives from Nietzsche, Husserl, Heidegger and, beyond that, Descartes. Such occasional references as they make to Anglo-American philosophy are usually, to put the point with excessive tolerance, more than a little misleading. Yet, even though to discuss the structuralists in any detail would be quite out of place, it would be a mistake wholly to ignore them; they represent in an extreme form certain tendencies which are also detectable in Anglo-American philosophy.

What, then, is structuralism? That is very hard to say, as hard as it was to define 'existentialism'. One is sometimes tempted to take over Engels' definition of Hegelianism: 'A compilation of words and turns of speech which have no other positive function than to be at hand at the right time when thought and positive knowledge are lacking.' It is easy enough to recognise the structuralist vocabulary – 'structure', 'signs', 'differences' – and its allusive, precious style, with its deliberately anti-Cartesian preference for the obscure and the indistinct. To set out the operating principles of structuralism, or even to decide who is to count as a structuralist, is much more difficult.

We might, no doubt, follow Piaget by describing as 'structuralists' only those who go in search of systems containing law-governed transformations which 'neither offer results external to the system nor employ elements external to it'.[3] But then we should find ourselves, as he does, at once taking our major examples from science and mathematics, well beyond what usually goes under the name of 'structuralism', and excluding many of those whom the world knows best under that name. Such a definition might roughly characterise the anthropologist Claude Lévi-Strauss, but only after considerable stretching the 'intellectual historian' Michel Foucault, the 'psycho-analyst' Jacques Lacan, the 'Marxist' Louis Althusser, the critic-novelist-'sociologist' Roland Barthes, the critic-'philosopher' Jacques Derrida. Not that this failure of application would worry them. Like the 'existentialists' before them, they often disclaim the label. To take only one case, in the preface to the English translation of his intellectual history *Les Mots et les choses* (1966) – in English, *The Order of Things* (1970)[4] – Foucault writes thus: 'In France, certain half-witted commentators persist in labelling me as a structuralist. I have been unable to get it into their tiny minds that I have used none of the methods, concepts or key terms that characterise structural analysis.' Yet this same Foucault, in one of those media-interviews which have come to be so characteristic of contemporary intellectual life, has described the attitudes of a 'we' who in the 1950s suddenly found 'ourselves' intellectually and morally dissociated from the existentialists. Whereas the existentialist passion was for life and politics, 'our' passion, he says, was for 'the concept and the system'. The existentialist 'I', he continues, has been destroyed, translated into a 'one'. 'It is not man who takes the place of God, but anonymous thinking, thinking without a subject.' Foucault's suitably anonymous 'we' can only refer to the structuralists – even if Foucault is not a semiologist.

What most repelled the existentialists, the domination of man by systems, is, from the structuralist point of view, not only inevitable but even desirable. Indeed, 'man' is dead as surely as, for Nietzsche, 'God' is dead. This is so whether 'man' is considered, in Husserl's style, as a subject who is the source of meaning and value, or in Sartre's style, as a capacity for freedom, or in Merleau-Ponty's style, as a being whose centre is 'lived experience' or, in the Oxford style, as a bearer of deliberate intentions. 'Man' is a concept invented, so Foucault tries to persuade us, in the nineteenth century. He is, so Althusser argues, an ideological creation, a 'subject' designed to be 'subjected'.

For the structuralist, two forms of intellectual activity are exemplary: a Saussurean philosophy of language and the mathematical theory of groups as expounded by the French mathematicians collectively described as 'Bourbaki'. Such a collective self-description is in itself attractive to the structuralists, with their emphasis on 'the collectivity'. But, as well, Bourbaki teaches that the nature of the individual group-members is of no importance, a group being defined by the laws which govern its transformations. Music, too, is a favourite example, especially in Lévi-Strauss.

Nearly as exemplary, oddly enough, are Marx and Freud. In the French intellectual atmosphere of the 1960s and 1970s a French intellectual could scarcely dare pronounce himself not to be a Marxist. Freud, like Hegel, came very late to France, and to be a Freudian was, from the 1960s on, no less essential. Yet there was a certain problem. Freud, on the face of it, was writing about instincts and their vicissitudes. Marx was committed to historicism, to diachronic rather than synchronic theorising, and in his earlier writings, what is even worse, to the 'humanism' which structuralists deride. So they had to be reinterpreted. In bitter opposition to the 'Socialist humanists', Althusser[5] in his *Reading Capital* (1965; trans. 1970) rejects Marx's earlier humanistic writings. Indeed, even *Capital* is suspect as compared with Marx's *Critique of the Gotha Programme* (1875) and the scarcely-known *Notes on Wagner*. This is on the ground that, even if Marx only very slowly shook himself free from Hegelian evolutionism, the 'real Marx' is nevertheless concerned only with formal relationships between 'processes without subjects', between modes of production and relations of production, not with historical sequences or individual intentions.

As for Freud, Jacques Lacan in the series of essays published as *Ecrits* (1966) interprets him as having discovered 'the language of the unconscious'.[6] Just as Althusser directs his fire against socialist humanism, so Lacan directs it against psycho-analytic humanism, as developed especially in the United States, for which psycho-analysis came to be primarily a method of helping a patient to 'adjust to reality'. The structure of the unconscious, he finally concludes, is the structure of language. Saussurean linguistics, not biology, provides psycho-analysis with a scientific model, just as for Lévi-Strauss it, rather than biology, provides a model for understanding kinship relationships.[7]

'Like phonemes,' Lévi-Strauss tells us, 'kinship terms are elements of meaning; like them they do not acquire this meaning except as a condition of their taking part in a system.' Again like phonemic systems, he goes on to maintain, they are 'spiritual elaborations at the level of unconscious thought'. And in their case, too, 'the visible phenomena are the product of the interplay of hidden general laws'. (One sees why he is fascinated by geology, which reveals the visible landscape as the product of such hidden laws.) As for the myth, that, like music, is a language which can 'transcend the level of articulate speech'. At the same time it 'obeys the same laws as symbolic logic'. Replacing the proper names and the elements of a myth by mathematical signs, we can reduce the myth to a formula. This, along with Lacan's psycho-analysis, is 'structuralism' in its purest form, from which Foucault naturally dissociates himself.

In that broader sense, however, in which Foucault and Althusser are 'structuralists' quite as much as Lacan and Lévi-Strauss, the philosophical significance of structuralism lies in the fact that it reduces to a minimum the role of human intentions, the human being as a free agent. It does not do this, as others have done, by arguing that human actions are determined by physical laws; rather, what determines them is a differentiating and differentiated system.

To be sure, the 'minimum' of agency thus left over is sometimes enlarged, sometimes diminished, in the writings of this or that structuralist. In *The Archaeology of Knowledge* (1969; trans. 1972) Foucault is finally prepared to say that the structures to which he has pointed are 'the set of conditions in accordance with which a practice is exercised' rather than 'a set of determinations imposed from the outside on the thought of individuals'. To understand the degree and vehemence of their hostility to 'man', one must always remember, too, what the structuralists were reacting against: the exaltation of the subject in Husserl and in Sartrean humanism.[8]

Jacques Derrida is sometimes described as 'post-structuralist' rather than as 'structuralist'.[9] In his *Writing and Difference* (1967; trans. 1979) and indeed elsewhere, he criticises Foucault,

Lévi-Strauss, Lacan; he rejects the concept of a total structural 'system'. There is a point, he argues, at which every system is forced to move outside itself, and in the process to abandon its claim to be total. Yet one can still think of him as, from a certain point of view, carrying structuralist themes to their extreme limits, some have said to absurdity.

One does not know whether to say of Derrida that he is a philosopher, or, like the later Heidegger and Nietzsche before him, an anti-philosopher, seeking in his case to replace philosophy by literary criticism. For all that Continental philosophy – Descartes, Rousseau, Husserl, Heidegger – is his starting-point, it angers him to be described as a 'Continental philosopher'. The defects to which he draws attention are common, he thinks, to Franco-German and to Anglo-American philosophy. Both try to discover something which is absolutely *present*, which acts as a 'source' for what is absent, and which is at the same time logically prior – as, for example, the 'simple' is taken to be prior to the complex. And one has certainly to grant to Derrida that the quest for an immediately present, logically prior, starting-point has characterised British empiricism quite as notably as Continental transcendentalism.

Were he to attempt to construct a metaphysical system, Derrida argues, he would inevitably fall into the same trap; it is implicit in the metaphysical enterprise. He cannot hope wholly to avoid doing so, he indeed confesses, even although he has largely confined himself to commentary – a commentary often both subtle and acute – rather than to system-making.[10] Only once does Derrida present a brief systematic account of his own views (1968, repr. in *Marges de la Philosophie*, 1972). Even then it takes the form of a commentary on himself, as if to illustrate one of his leading theses – that the unified self is a myth; he is not identical with the writer he is commenting on, even if he bears the same name. In Derrida's work, the manner exemplifies the content.

One general objective runs through that work – to 'shake up' our familiar conceptual systems, and, in particular, to free our thinking from its domination by such hierarchically ordered binary opposites as presence/absence, primary/derivative, necessary/possible, speech/writing, literal/metaphorical, serious/playful. Beginning from what is commonly taken to be the 'inferior' member of such pairs, he sets out to show that its defining characteristics apply just as much to its allegedly 'superior' opposite. Thus shaken up by 'deconstruction', the hierarchical pair is displaced by an over-arching 'concept' – the quotation-marks are meant to suggest that this new 'concept' has none of the fixity or determinateness usually ascribed to concepts – the range of which, however, is considerably broader than was at first suspected. So, for example, presence/absence is displaced by a neologistic, and distinctly elusive, 'différance', conjoining the French words for 'difference' and 'deferment'.

Consider the case of the sign. One cannot think of it as simply 'present' not only because, as Saussure had argued, it exists as a sign only through its relationship to other signs, signs which are *not* present, but also because its 'signification' is never wholly present to us, is perpetually 'deferred'. Derrida is not making the banal point that a sign can have more than one meaning and that it can change its meaning over time. Or so he assures us. It is much less plain precisely what he *is* saying. The sign is, for him, a 'seed' – he links, in a Heidegger-style etymology, 'semen' and 'semantics' – a seed which 'disseminates'. This key notion is developed in *Disseminations* (1972; trans. 1982) but in jungle-like obscurity; in one of the interviews which makes up *Positions* (1972), Derrida tells us, indeed, that dissemination 'ultimately has no meaning and cannot be channelled into a definition'. But in this, it would seem, it is not unique. For Derrida appears to be telling us that *every* sign is in this position. There is nothing that can be described, once and for all or even at any particular point in time, as 'its meaning'.

The case of signs illustrates a wider principle: identity/difference is everywhere displaced by 'différance', the identity of the self no less than the identity of the sign. To go in search of one's identity is to pursue a will o' the wisp. Our 'identity' lies in the manner in which we are differentiated from others within a particular differentiating system and there is no time at which it is fixed, determined; our 'nature' is always 'deferred'.

For the Anglo-American philosopher the most 'accessible' of Derrida's essays is his critique of J.L. Austin's *How to do Things with Words* and the subsequent controversy with Austin's defender John Searle.[11] Not that this is by any means a clear-cut discussion. (Derrida tells us that he hates discussion.) His manner of arguing, he himself says, is and has to be 'a strategy that is complex and tortuous, involuted and full of artifice'. Indeed, as he does not tell us, it is reminiscent of an electric eel. But at least what he is opposing is familiar.

Derrida welcomes Austin's recognition that not all speech consists in the communication of ideas and, above all, his rejection of the true/false and values/facts opposition. But he attacks Austin on three grounds: first, because Austin presumes that 'speech' is simpler, more straightforward, than writing – Derrida takes as his epigraph Austin's phrase 'still confining ourself for simplicity to spoken utterance'; secondly, because his thinking is dominated by such hierarchically paired opposites as serious/jesting, ordinary/parasitic, even if he rejects the fact/value opposition; thirdly, because he still describes speech-acts as communications, if not of ideas then of intentions.

Consider first the hierarchical opposition speech/writing. The preference for speech over writing, the assumption that writing is an inferior, derivative, form of communication, runs through the philosophical tradition from Plato's *Phaedrus* onward; it constitutes, Derrida argues, a fundamental intellectual error. (Lévi-Strauss had been very strongly on Plato's side.) 'Writing' comes to have a very special meaning for Derrida, so much so that he can calmly assert that writing precedes speech. Anything is 'writing', according to *Of Grammatology* (1967; trans. 1973), which *gives rise* to an inscription (my italics) – where 'inscription', too, has to be very widely interpreted. Sometimes he prefers the neologism 'archi-writing' for this new 'concept' which has displaced not only 'speech/writing' but even 'the world/writing'. (The French intellectual's dream, most openly expressed by Mallarmé, of a world which exists only in so far as it enters into a book, is here powerfully operative.)

It is commonly supposed, or so Derrida tells us, that in speech, as distinct from writing, the speaker is 'present with' his utterance, that he understands his own intentions by hearing himself and that the auditor in hearing him also understands that meaning, grasps that intention. (The French 'entendre', it is worth recalling, can signify 'to mean, to intend, to hear, to understand, to know all about'.) But this analysis presumes that the speaker *has* a determinate intention, is fully conscious of it, and can use language in such a way that, in and through hearing him, his auditor is bound to be aware of this intention. To take any such Gricean view is to overlook – Derrida would say 'repress' – the fact that language never 'holds fast', so as *necessarily* to carry a certain signification. The capacity of 'marks' to be repeated in different contexts – 'leaves us no choice but to mean (say) something that is (already, always, also) other than what we mean (say) ..., to understand something other than ... etc.' The very fact that I am using language makes it impossible for me simply to say what I mean; my complexity as a human being makes it impossible for me simply to mean what I say.

One final feature of Derrida's reply to Searle deserves attention. He makes great play – the 'play' of a cat and a mouse – with the fact that Searle's article has attached to it 'copyright © 1977 by John R. Searle'. One might suppose this 'play' to be merely an exercise in controversial viciousness. That is not so. For a leading doctrine of structuralism is that neither ideas nor language belong to anyone. And beyond that, indeed, that the very concept of 'ownership' is bound up with an untenable theory of the self. 'Structuralism,' Derrida remarked like Jakobson before him, 'is the end of private property.' But Derrida's remark has a broader application: structuralism, he could also have said, is the end of the private *person*.

On the face of it, Noam Chomsky is no structuralist.[12] Far from asserting that 'man is dead', he attacks behaviourist psychology, industrialised capitalism and State socialism precisely for their inhumanity. A political activist, his sympathies lie with the anarchist wing of Socialist Humanism, anathematised by the structuralists.[13] And the starting-point of this theory of language is not language as a collective phenomenon but the *creativity* of each and every language user, his capacity to utter and to understand sentences he has never before encountered. As against the structuralists, too, language is for Chomsky primarily a means of expressing thoughts rather than a system of social communication by the use of signs. He emphasises, where they play down, the differences between natural languages and other sign-systems.

Then, setting aside Derrida's semi-flirtation with Austin, why is it that the structuralists refer only to Chomsky, among contemporary Anglo-American thinkers, with any degree of respect? In the first place, he was trained in the tradition of structural linguistics; indeed, his teacher Zellig Harris wrote a book (1951) with that title. Chomsky's transformational linguistics is at many points in the sharpest possible opposition to American structural linguistics, rejecting as he does the view that linguistic theory sets out to characterise complex linguistic entities in terms of lower-order linguistic entities – sentences in terms of words, words in terms of phonemes. Nevertheless, his indebtedness to Harris and to such post-Saussurean linguists as Jakobson is still considerable.[14]

Secondly, even though the 'creativity' of the ordinary language-user is a leading motive in Chomsky's investigations, in his *Reflections on Language* (1976) he sets aside the creative use of language as a 'mystery', not, at least as matters now stand, a 'problem' for scientific investigation. (A disconcerting reminiscence of Gabriel Marcel's terminology.) His actual linguistic theories, as presented in his first published work *Syntactic Structures* (1957) and developed in his *Aspects of the Theory of Syntax* (1965), are sufficiently formalised, rule-centred, mathematised, indifferent to individual idiosyncrasies and intentions, to satisfy the most demanding of French structuralists.

The French structuralists were attracted, too, by Chomsky's distinction between 'deep structures' and 'surface structures'. That did for language, they supposed, what Freud had done for the mind and Marx for society. The 'deep structure', as Chomsky defined it in 'The current scene in Linguistics' (1966), is 'the abstract underlying form which determines the meaning of the sentence'.[15] In contrast, the surface structure is a representation of the 'physical signal' which we speak or hear, as when I hear some one say 'Come in!' The 'surface structure' is 'generated' from the 'deep structure' by such transformations as combination and deletion and a phonological input, determining its pronunciation. ('Generated' does not mean 'causally generated': grammar does not tell us why an individual says 'Enter' rather than 'Come in'. It is mathematical in kind, as when an algebraic equation 'generates' its various numerical solutions.) So the deep structure of 'Come in!' would contain such elements as 'you' and the verb 'to be' which are absent from the surface structure.

For all that it is so intimately associated with his name, by the time he came to write *Reflections on Language* Chomsky had nevertheless abandoned the terminology of 'deep structure' and 'surface structure', partly for technical reasons but also because – and this is more important for our purposes – he had been misunderstood, as the French structuralists had misunderstood him, by those who supposed that 'deep' structures were 'deep' in a metaphysical sense, that the properties of surface structures were, in contrast, 'superficial, unimportant, variable across languages and so on'. That was not his view; phonology, confining its attention to surface structures, could be quite as universal, he thinks, quite as 'revealing', quite as universable, as syntactical theory. Indeed, as he freely admits, phonology is the most fully worked-out branch of 'grammar'. (Chomsky uses the word 'grammar' very broadly, to include semantics and phonology as well as syntax.)

The French structuralist, so much is clear, will get little comfort from Chomsky's 'deep structures'. But there is another side to Chomsky's theory, which may still attract him. American structuralism, as formulated in Leonard Bloomfield's very influential *Language* (1933), had rejected what was fundamental to Saussure, the view that the sign signifies a concept. (Bloomfield's earlier writings had defended a version of this view, re-stated in terms of Wundt's psychology, and it has since had something of a revival.) Under the influence of behaviouristic positivism Bloomfield defined language use as the substitution of a sign for a non-verbal response to stimuli; the sign 'means', in his view, what it substitutes for. In a notorious example, Jill asks Jack to climb a tree and get an apple for her; her making that request, as a response to the stimulus of hunger, is a substitute for her climbing the tree, exactly as he would were he himself hungry. Whereas the structuralists are reacting against the characteristically French emphasis on the centrality of the individual consciousness, for Chomsky Bloomfield-style behaviourism is the enemy, as his review (1959) of the arch-behaviourist B.F. Skinner's *Verbal Behaviour* made abundantly plain.[16] But they both set against their enemy the concept of underlying modes of apprehension which affect individual decisions without the individual being conscious of that fact, and in a manner which does not wholly derive from his own experience, the 'stimuli' to which he has been subject.

Chomsky is reacting, too, against a classical American empiricist conception of the task of linguistics which naturally flourished in the special circumstances of that continent: to record as accurately as possible the languages spoken by the vanishing North American Indian tribes and then, by the use of 'discovery' methods, to generalise from such recordings to the grammar of their languages – in the broad Chomskian sense of 'grammar'. Chomsky rejects the view that there is any such 'discovery method'. A grammar, as he sees it, is a *theory* of a language, which tries to explain why, in that language, only some sentences, some transformations, some sequences of sound, some verbal combinations are grammatically permissible.

For a 'discovery procedure', he substitutes an 'evaluation' procedure. The linguistic data at the linguist's disposal, like the data at a scientist's disposal, always permit of more than one explanation. An 'evaluation procedure' selects between different possible grammars by the use of such criteria as 'simplicity in relation to the theory being employed'. (He denies that 'simplicity' has an absolute sense.)

Merely to record a language, Chomsky also argues, is to include sentences which are 'acceptable' but not grammatical and to exclude sentences which may never be uttered but which are nevertheless perfectly grammatical. A sentence may, he says, in a particular context be 'acceptable' in the sense that no one doubts the speaker's meaning, even though it incorporates a 'slip of the tongue' or a grammatical error. On the other hand, a sentence may be grammatical but so complicated that a listener would be unable to 'accept' it; he would find it incomprehensible. The linguistic theorist is interested only in grammatical sentences and in every such sentence. Grammar, then, is not a theory of 'performance', of, in Saussurean terms, 'parole'. Its concern, rather, is with what Chomsky calls 'competence'.[17]

Ryle had drawn a distinction between 'knowing how' and 'knowing that' and had associated competence with 'knowing how'. Indeed, we usually suppose that 'competence' is a characterisation of a person's capacity to perform. In the case of language-competence, Chomsky however suggests, 'knowing-how', as in 'He knows how to talk English', must rest upon a rather special sort of 'knowing that', rather special because it is not explicit. The grammarian tries to uncover this 'tacit knowledge' of the language user, a tacit knowledge which explains how he can distinguish what is grammatical from what is not grammatical.

Why suppose that a language-user has such a tacit knowledge? A person can 'pick up' music, can not only sing but compose songs, without being able to say what a key is, or a half-tone, or a note. We normally suppose that a child picks up his first language in a similar manner. Certainly, he cannot tell us what the rules of his language are; if, as Aristotle argues, it is a sign of the man who knows that he can teach what he knows, the child does not know the rules. (It scarcely helps to substitute the word 'cognize', as Chomsky at one point suggests, for 'know'.)

While not denying such sufficiently obvious facts, Chomsky wholly rejects the received, 'empiricist', account of language learning. In his *Cartesian Linguistics* (1966) he associates himself, although not in detail, with an older rationalistic theory of the human mind, according to which experience stimulates the mind to make use of a knowledge which already forms part of its own structure, is 'innate'. Unless we suppose, he argues in *Reflections on Language*, that human beings are 'specifically designed' to learn language, we cannot possibly understand how 'on relatively slight experience and with no training', a child can learn 'to make use of an intricate set of specific rules and guiding principles to convey his thoughts and feelings to others'. The mechanisms to which the empiricist appeals – such mechanisms as generalisation, analogy, conditioning – are, in Chomsky's view, simply not *strong* enough to explain how anyone learns his first language. (Learns, as distinct from being taught, since teaching is in this instance of minimal importance.) That is why we have to suppose that the child already has in some sense, a *knowledge* of language.

His 'competence', then, does not consist simply in his being able to perform competently; it incorporates the fact that he has certain principles at his disposal. An 'innate faculty' in the mind – 'represented', for Chomsky is no dualist, 'in some still unknown way in the brain' – creates an abstract cognitive structure which then enters into 'the system of capacities to act and interpret'. To study 'competence' is to study this entire set of mental structures and mental processes. Like Lévi-Strauss, Chomsky is happy to admit what Lévi-Strauss calls 'spiritual elaborations at the level of unconscious thought'. Linguistic theory uncovers them. Language, as Leibniz had suggested, is a 'mirror of the mind'; linguistic theory is a theory of the human mind, a branch of *cognitive* psychology – not, as for Saussure, of *social* psychology.[18]

Are we to suppose that an English child is specifically 'designed' to learn English, a French child French? Obviously not; an English child brought up in France will speak perfect French and no English.

The 'competence' of the child is, for Chomsky, universal; he is born able to talk English or French or Chinese, if he is brought up in the appropriate society. Yet if we suppose him to be born possessed of a 'universal grammar', any such grammar, to be a grammar, must be restrictive, ruling out certain grammars as humanly impossible.[19] 'The child cannot know at birth,' Chomsky therefore writes in *Language and Mind*, 'what language he has to learn, but he must know that its grammar must be of a determinate form that excludes many imaginable languages.' Endowed with that 'tacit knowledge', he selects a 'permissible' hypothesis about the grammar of the language he is using. Correcting his hypothesis in the light of experience, he finally comes to 'know his language' in such a way as to reject some of his linguistic experience as 'defective and deviant', i.e. as ungrammatical performances. This analysis, Chomsky grants, is most strongly supported in the case of phonology. Even though other sounds are physically possible, all languages, it would seem, make use of a sub-set of a limited set of sounds. Could there not be a language which contains different sounds? If there were, according to Chomsky, we could not learn it as readily as we now learn our own language. And in the same way, he believes, we are designed to learn any of a set of syntactical and semantic rules but only the members of that set.

Chomsky's linguistic theories have suffered many a change since they were put forward, to create a 'revolution in linguistics'. Sometimes they are said to be now 'in complete disarray'. This does not disturb him; an 'immature science', he argues, is bound to experience such a rapid rate of change, even in respect to its very general principles. But he continues to stand by its fundamental principles: that a grammar is not simply a descriptive but an explanatory theory, that to study it is to study 'competence' rather than 'performance', that an empiricist-style psychology is incapable of explaining how a child learns his first language, that linguistic theory is a central clue to the understanding of mind. It is in virtue of his attack upon empiricism, his resuscitation of Kantian-like concepts of inborn mental structures which limit what form our actions can take, their intellectual shape, that Chomsky has exerted his philosophical influence. So far, he and the structuralists can properly be run together.

3

From Syntax to Semantics

Chomsky has been described as a 'syntactical animal'; that description, with its imputation that he wholly neglects semantics, he rejects. But he would agree that his central emphasis has been on syntax – and to a lesser degree phonology. For all the human interest of semantics, deriving from the centrality within it of such notions as 'truth' and 'meaning', Chomsky thought himself entitled to concentrate on those fields where theoretical progress might readily be made. Towards the project of discovering a universal grammar and a universal phonetics he could, he thought, immediately contribute; universal semantics remained obscure. And syntax, he continued to argue, could be investigated quite independently of semantics.[1]

Some of his pupils sought to extend Chomsky's method to semantics.[2] In 'The Structure of a Semantic Theory' (1963) J.J. Katz and J.A. Fodor set out to describe 'the abstract form' of a semantic theory of natural languages. A semantic theory, as they understand it, explains certain kinds of speaker's competence: how he can pick out certain sentences as anomalous even though they are grammatically correct, how he can tell that one sentence is a paraphrase of another even when they are syntactically quite distinct, how he can go to a dictionary, look up a word, and determine which of the meanings there set out is the one appropriate to a given sentence. So an English speaker finds 'colourless ideas sleep furiously' anomalous, although it is syntactically and phonologically unexceptionable, recognises that 'The boy hit the ball', means the same as 'The ball was hit by the boy', and knows that 'ball' is not here being used to mean 'a social assemblage of persons for dancing'.

To explain such phenomena Fodor and Katz set up 'trees' consisting of 'semantic markers' and 'distinguishers'. The semantic markers are general concepts arrangeable in ordered paths, where the order is constituted by a progression from a broader to a narrower concept. Concepts which are mutually exclusive head, in their view, different paths. The 'distinguishers' reflect 'what is idiosyncratic to the meaning of a [lexical] item'. Suppose we take the case of 'bachelor'. A description of one of its various meanings will make use of such semantic markers – or, as they are sometimes called, 'components' – as 'human', 'male' along with the distinguisher 'has never married'. It can be set out thus: bachelor →︎ noun →︎ (Human) →︎ (Male) – [who has never married]. The semantic markers, 'human' and 'male', are, they tell us, as fundamental to our understanding of a language as the syntactical marker 'noun'; we can have no grasp of the meaning of a language until we have control over them. A particular distinguisher, in contrast, a speaker may never encounter. So semantic theory, as they understand it, is about relationships between semantic markers; such relationships determine whether a sentence is semantically anomalous. ('Semantic anomalies' turn out to be very like Ryle's 'category mistakes'.)

One question naturally arises out of this analysis. On the face of it, 'male', 'human' and the like are English words. It cannot be the case that we must have a tacit knowledge of these words before we start learning English. In the Katz-Fodor theory, however, 'human' is not to be thought of as an English word – it is sometimes written H U M A N to make this point – but rather as that construct in semantic theory which is represented in English by the word 'human'. As a 'semantic marker' it forms part of the 'language of thought' – David Lewis has called it 'Markerese' – which precedes the *expression* of thoughts in a natural language. (An animal, so it is argued, can think in such a language even although it never learns to express its thoughts in a natural language.)

Since its first appearance, this theory has been widely criticised and extensively modified. Sometimes the debate has been about issues which are of linguistic rather than philosophical concern – whether, for example, 'kill' forms part of the universal semantics or whether such a semantics will contain only 'cause' and 'to die', into which 'kill' can be 'decomposed'. Sometimes it has turned around the question at what level semantic analysis occurs – whether, as Katz and Fodor originally thought, it occurs at the level of 'deep structure' so that one first discovers the deep structure and then semantically analyses its constituent elements or whether, as Chomsky himself came to think, some features of the surface structure – stress, for example – have to be taken into account in semantic analysis. In the ensuing discussions the deep sometimes became deeper still, the surface often deepened, or the deep became more superficial. That is another reason why Chomsky finally abandoned this Protean terminology. At other times, the criticisms have been of a more obviously philosophical sort, attacking the conception of a 'language of thought', an implicit knowledge of which precedes the learning of any natural language, perhaps by arguing that a semantics of this kind merely transfers the problem of meaning from ordinary languages to the language of thought.[3] To this last criticism, we shall later return.

In a more fundamental way, the Katz-Fodor semantics has been criticised as, in its concern for linguistic competence, ignoring the central issues of semantics. This is not in the least surprising; there have always been marked disagreements about the nature and objectives of semantic theory. From the 1960s onwards, in opposition both to the Austinians and the Chomsky school, interest has re-awakened in the sort of truth-conditional semantics which derives from Frege, whether by way of understanding or misunderstanding, was developed by Wittgenstein in his *Tractatus* and, after him, was variously reshaped by Tarski, Carnap and Alonzo Church. Carnap, one might say, has won a posthumous victory over those ordinary language philosophers who thrust his semantics aside as, in Ryle's words, 'an astonishing blend of technical sophistication with philosophical naivete'.[4] (Why Ryle found such a blend 'astonishing', I do not know.)

Let us begin from the least accessible of the new semanticists, Richard Montague.[5] That may seem to be a foolish choice. Montague's work is exceptionally difficult to summarise. He died, murdered, without having put his ideas together in book form. His more philosophical articles – he also contributed extensively to mathematical journals and journals of symbolic logic – were posthumously brought together under the title, *Formal Philosophy* (1974). The title is appropriate: Montague assumes a knowledge of such branches of mathematics as set theory; his articles are as exceptionally devoid of explanation and illustration as they are rich in formal symbolism, often freshly coined, and succinct formal proofs. He changes his mind from article to article, often on such fundamental points as whether it is possible to construct a satisfactory semantics without appealing to Frege's distinction between sense and denotation. Had Montague survived to write the longer, less compressed works which he promised his readers – it is a large assumption that they would ever have got written – one doubts whether he would have been any more considerate. He once devoted five seminars, or so the story runs, to the exposition of a bare two pages in one of his essays. 'That,' he then said, 'is the rate at which I ought to be read.' Even if that is true, to write about him on the same scale would be grossly to exaggerate his centrality in contemporary philosophy. His influence, if by no means negligible, has been by the nature of the case distinctly confined. Some of his pupils, whether linguists or logicians, have carried on his work. But to most philosophers he has been, quite literally, a closed book.

The most one can hope intelligibly to do in a brief compass is to describe his ambitions and the means by which he sought to put them into effect. His importance in our story, which justifies using him as a point of departure, lies not in the details but in the fact that he illustrates in an unusually striking form the sort of link which now exists between linguists, logicians and philosophers of language. This is a link which such of his colleagues as Barbara Partee have sought to forge more firmly by suggesting that – although Montague usually writes with something close to contempt of Chomsky and his followers as lacking 'adequacy, mathematical precision and elegance' – his work can fruitfully be conjoined with transformational grammars. (Subsequent attempts to demonstrate formal equivalences between Montague's analyses and the analyses of linguists have brought relief to many who feared that they might be compelled to read Montague.)

'Formal philosophy' was, I said, an appropriate title for Montague's collected essays: 'formalised philosophy' might have been even better. In the conflicts between ordinary language philosophy and artificial language philosophy which marked the post-war decades, Montague had no doubt where he stood – alongside Tarski, with whom he at one time collaborated, and Carnap, whom he constantly quotes with admiration. He never changed his mind on that particular point.

One can neither do philosophy, he continued to think, nor give a satisfactory account of the semantics of ordinary language except in a formalised artificial language. He tells us in his 'On the Nature of Certain Philosophical Entities' (1970) – the article in which his linguistic analyses are most closely brought to bear on traditional philosophical issues about, for example, sense-data – that he wants to defend two positions which are often supposed to be incompatible: that 'there is philosophical interest in trying to analyse ordinary English' and that 'ordinary English is an inadequate vehicle for philosophy'.

Only on the first of these two points did he deviate from his post-Fregean predecessors. Most earlier post-Fregeans had despaired of everyday languages, as presenting insuperable obstacles to formalisation. So Tarski had argued that anyone who tried to describe the 'semantics of colloquial language' by using 'exact methods' would first have to undertake 'the thankless task of reforming this language' and that this reformed language would then lose its 'naturalness', being transformed, in the process of reform, into an artificial language.

One can easily understand this attitude. The expressions of an artificial language can be rigidly categorised. If 'V_0' serves as the name of a variable in an artificial language, then there are only certain places in the sentences of such a language which it can grammatically occupy – as in elementary algebra we can write '6x' but not 'x6'. 'Yellow', in contrast, is sometimes a noun, sometimes an adjective, and sometimes a verb. How then can its syntactical role be formally characterised? Many everyday words, too, are fuzzy or ambiguous or both at once. How high must a man be in order to be 'tall'? And why cannot we equally ask how high a 'tall story' must be? More important still, given the assumption that semantics has to do with truth-conditions and entailments, the form of a colloquial language often suggests that two expressions are precisely parallel to one another in their entailments which are in fact not so parallel. To take a familiar example, 'Jones is a skilful philosopher' entails, or so we would commonly suppose, that 'Jones is a philosopher', but 'Jones is an alleged philosopher' certainly does not.

In the light of such facts one is at first puzzled how, in his 'English as a Formal Language' (1970), Montague could so uncompromisingly deny, in total opposition to his earlier Carnapian view, that 'any important theoretical distinction exists between formal and natural languages'. Twenty years earlier, in his 'The Need for Abstract Entities in Semantic Analysis' (1951), Alonzo Church, after briefly exploring the syntax and semantics of formalised languages, had no doubt gone on to add that there was no difference *in principle* between such languages and natural languages; he had even drawn up a few rules for English in this spirit.[6] But he could do this, he freely granted, only by setting to one side logically irregular constructions and equivocal words. To lay down rules for a natural language, he had added in Tarski's manner, 'is as much a matter of legislation as of reporting'. Montague, on the contrary, even though his articles confessedly formalise only 'a fragment of English', hoped to extend the same principles to English as a whole, and in a way which *did* report rather than legislate.

Chomsky and his followers had also set out to develop a formal theory of natural languages. But Montague rejects their view that syntactical theory is, in the last resort, a branch of psychology; in his eyes, it is a branch of metamathematics, a formal analysis of a formal system. More than that, he condemns their failure to recognise that 'the basic goal of serious semantics and syntax is the construction of a theory of truth' – or more narrowly, of 'truth under an arbitrary interpretation'. (For in Montague, as we shall see, truth applies to sentences only when they are interpreted in a particular way.) This emphasis on truth unites the post-Fregean semanticists. They are not interested in linguistic distinctions for their own sake but only in so far as they bear upon the capacity of sentences to assert and entail truths. Particular classes of sentences – sometimes such improbable sentences as 'John wishes to find a unicorn in order to eat it' – preoccupy them just because problems arise about what such a sentence entails, whether it can be true, in that instance, if there are no unicorns.

Abjuring psychology, then, Montague hopes to construct a semantics for English which will be metamathematical in character. That carries with it two consequences, if his plan is to be carried through in a Carnapian spirit; English has to be mathematicised and a suitable formal language has to be constructed for talking about it. Montague attempts both these tasks. From Aristotle to Quine, logicians had 'regimented' ordinary English sentences to determine their entailments. Arguments incorporating everyday sentences as premises were for this purpose 'expressed in logical form', a logical form which made use of a very small number of logical constants – 'every', 'at least one', 'or', 'and', 'if ... then ...' The entailments of sentences were taken to flow from the presence of these constants, whatever the nature of the other expressions they contained; other entailments, as we saw, were set aside as merely rhetorical.

In the post-Russellian period, as we also saw, logicians added to the restricted vocabulary of Russellian formal logic, especially by employing additional logical operators – modal, imperative, deontic, tense and epistemic.[7] Quine, as a leading proponent of regimentation, dissented, arguing that modal logic, for example, could not permit such elementary, and essential, logical processes as quantification and substitution. (One cannot validly argue, he had pointed out, from '9 is necessarily greater than 7' to 'the number of the planets is necessarily greater than 7' even although 9 is the number of the planets.)[8] Most logicians, however, came to be convinced that such objections could be circumvented, especially when Saul Kripke (along with others) developed a Leibniz-style semantics for modal logic which overcame, or so it was supposed, traditional problems in interpreting such modal sentences as 'x is necessarily y'.[9] ('x is necessarily y' is taken to mean 'x is y in every possible world.')

Montague had at first agreed with Quine; he wanted a logic of a purely extensional sort, which made no reference to anything except individuals and sets of individuals. But like so many logicians of his time he came to feel that such a logic would not suffice if he was going to find a way of transposing natural language sentences into a form which made their entailments plain. (Although, as we shall see, in a certain sense the theory of sets continues to be primary.)

There were two stages in this procedure. First of all, the expressions of ordinary language had to be categorised; that was the syntactical task. Here Montague drew upon and modified the categorial logic of Kazimierz Ajdukiewicz ('Syntactic Connection', 1935) itself applying to syntax the semantic analyses of Lesniewski.[10] This syntactical analysis is for Montague of little interest in itself. 'I fail to see any great interest in syntax,' he writes in his 'Universal Grammar' (1970), 'except as a preliminary to semantics.' The syntactical features of a language could be categorised in all sorts of ways; the essential thing is so to characterise them as to provide a suitable basis for semantics. Similarly, he thinks, syntactical rules –

used to determine how categories of expressions can grammatically be concatenated into wider categories and finally into grammatical sentences – ought to be constructed in a fashion that runs parallel to the formulation of semantic rules. Another of Montague's objections to Chomsky is that he failed to take into account the need for such constant checking of syntactical analysis against semantical requirements.

The effect of this semantically-oriented approach is that Montague's categorisations of 'a fragment of English' look very odd indeed to anyone brought up on the normal categorisations of grammarians. Yet at the same time they are by no means identical with the restricted categories of 'classical' logic, with its variables, constants, brackets and quantifiers. Consider the list given for the fragment of English discussed by Montague in his 'Quantification in Ordinary English' (1973). It includes such familiar grammatical friends as common noun phrases and transitive verb phrases but also such grammatically unfamiliar categories as 'sentence-taking verb phrases', exemplified by 'believe that' and 'assert that', and 'sentence modifying adverbs', exemplified by 'necessarily'. An earlier list in 'English as a Formal Language', had been rather different; there 'believes that' belonged to the same category – or, more accurately, 'had the same index' – as 'necessarily'. (Each category in Montague's system is assigned an index.)

The change is one of relative detail but it will serve to illustrate Montague's procedures. Fresh 'difficult cases' had been drawn to his attention; to cope with them he had to make distinctions at a different point. If one were to ask how Montague would justify his categorisations the answer he would give is not at all a grammarian's answer. They make possible, he would say, a syntactical analysis of a sentence which will allow it to be semantically interpreted in a way that will avoid unacceptable entailments. He always has particular cruxes in his mind, whether they be the classical problems raised by Frege about the identity of the Morning Star and the Evening Star – how this can be both strict and empirically learnt – or a problem raised by Partee about why 'Ninety rises' does not follow from 'the temperature rises' and 'The temperature is ninety'. Much recent semantics, indeed, is preoccupied with such 'monster-barring'.

How is one to make the transition from syntax to semantics? By way, Montague replies, of a 'mapping' of the categories syntactical analysis reveals in English on to types within an intensional logic, a logic which allows references to concepts, propositions and modality, so that English expressions of a certain category can be rigorously translated into expressions of a certain type in intensional logic. (Although the relation is not one-one; English expressions are sometimes semantically ambiguous, so that we may have to say that the translation is either ... or ...) Of course, classical regimentations of, let us say, 'All men are mortal' into 'For all *x*, if *x* is a man, *x* is mortal', had also translated English expressions into logical form. But in the first place, so Montague argues, the translation was informal, not conducted in accordance with strict rules, and secondly the logical form into which English expressions were regimented in classical logic was too exiguous to serve the purpose of properly distinguishing between semantically different expressions – between, to revert to an earlier example, 'alleged philosopher' and 'skilful philosopher'.

Montague had been impressed not only by the 'possible worlds' semantics of Kripke and David Lewis – which we shall later be exploring in more detail – but by the tense logic of Arthur Prior and the special version of pragmatic logic suggested by Y.Bar-Hillel. Classical logicians had not only sought to translate all statements into statements about individuals and sets of individuals but had made use of no tenses except a timeless present – such as 'Socrates is mortal' where the 'is' has no special reference to the present moment. Prior, in contrast, interested himself in entailments which depend on tense distinctions, as in 'It's raining, so we'll need an umbrella' where the fact that the rain is occurring *now* is essential to the inference. One important feature of such expressions as 'It's raining' – if one refuses to regiment it in Quine's manner, into something like 'Rain is falling at 11.20 a.m. on December 13, 1984' – is that it can be true on one occasion of use and not on another. The same can obviously be said of such expressions as 'He's incompetent'. That can be true when it is said of Jones yet not true when it is said of Smith.

In Charles Morris's original distinction between 'syntactics', 'semantics' and 'pragmatics', pragmatics had to do with the special ways in which individuals use signs. By such later philosophers as Carnap, it was consigned, like so much else, to 'psychology'. Montague picks up Bar-Hillel's suggestion that it could be developed in a formal systematic fashion if it confined itself to what Peirce had called 'indexical expressions' and Russell 'egocentric particulars', such as 'he', 'and', 'it'.[11] And in his 'Pragmatics and Intensional Logic' (1970) an extended pragmatics is presented as being 'in a sense' a part of an intensional logic. Only 'in a sense' of course. In intensional logic, which includes such modal operators as 'necessarily', truth has to be thought of as truth in some possible world – counting our actual world as one possible world – or some set of such worlds; in a pragmatic logic truth is truth on a particular occasion of use. (In each case, however, it is truth on a certain interpretation of the sentence in question.) What is common to the two cases is that truth has to be 'indexed': it is truth on a certain interpretation, in a particular world – or truth at a particular time at a particular place.

Thus it is that Montague arrives at a language into which, once their grammaticality has been established by syntactical analysis, the sentences of everyday English can be translated in a way that will make plain their truth-conditions, allow permissible entailments and forbid impossible entailments. (Although what he counts as such does not always coincide with our intuitions.) If one asks where this intensional logic comes from, Montague tells us in his 'On the Nature of Certain Philosophical Entities' – the paper in which he first announced his conversion, after 'fifteen years dogmatism', to intensional logic – that within set-theory one can 'justify' a language or theory that 'transcends' set-theory and 'then proceed to transact a new branch of philosophy within that theory'. In his 'Universal Grammar' (1970), first delivered in 1969, two years after 'Philosophical Entities', both intensional logic and a fragment of English are 'justified' within this broader context. That is the respect in which set-theory is 'primary'.

As Montague's work proceeded, he was led into more and more novelties – novelties, that is, from the standpoint of 'classical logic' although they often have had predecessors in the history of thought. So whereas both in 'traditional' and 'classical' logic a sharp distinction is drawn between such quantifiers as 'all' or 'some' and ordinary adjectives, Montague argues that they are both, along with 'the', to be regarded as constituents in common-noun phrases. This means that he stands closer to traditional grammatical analyses, for which 'all men' is taken to be a noun phrase, the subject of such predicates as 'are mortal', than he does to the analyses customary in logic. At a more epistemological level, what we normally think of as individual names, and along with them quantified common nouns, come out, when translated, as expressions which denote sets of properties of individual concepts. These innovations, Montague believes, are essential if we are to give a straightforward account, without circumlocution and paraphrase, of the kind of puzzling cases which such linguists as Partee are adept at thinking up, to say nothing of more familiar semantic cruxes. Some will feel the price paid is too high, but no one can question Montague's Socratic willingness to 'follow the argument where it leads'.

If Montague makes considerable use, in his semantic analyses, of 'possible worlds', it is anything but plain – even his pupils are unsure – whether he takes them to be merely a technical device or rather to involve him in an ontological commitment. He uses them to explain such phenomena as this: we say that Scott and the author of Waverley are identical and yet we know that this is something which had to be learnt. If the identity in question is strict identity this is hard to understand. For it would follow that they have all their properties in common. Since there is then nothing to distinguish Scott from the author of Waverley, how, one naturally asks, could anyone have wondered whether he was or denied that he was? Yet they certainly did. Montague's answer is that although in our *actual* world Scott and the author of Waverley are *actually* identical, one can easily construct a possible world in which they were not, in which, let us say, Maria Edgeworth wrote Waverley and Scott only pretended to have done so. Strict identity, in contrast, is identity in all possible worlds; there is no possible world, to take the least controversial case, in which Scott is not Scott. One can wonder therefore if (in some world) Scott is the author of Waverley as one cannot wonder if Scott is Scott. Whether, in offering such an analysis, Montague was automatically committed to believing that in some sense there 'really are' possible worlds, even if he disliked this conclusion, or whether he was still free to maintain that they are 'just a manner of speaking' – like an atheist's 'God help us' – has come to be a highly controversial question.

David Lewis admired Montague, to whose memory he dedicated his most controversial book *Counterfactuals* (1973). The admiration was reciprocated. Lewis exerted a not inconsiderable influence on Montague as did, as we have already seen, Saul Kripke. The interplay between philosophers – with, in this instance, the considerably older Montague being shaken out of his dogmatic slumber by younger men – is a characteristic feature of contemporary philosophy. But in Lewis's case the metaphysical situation is plain. He is the most stalwart defender of the view that talk about 'possible worlds' cannot be reduced to a mere manner of speech, employed in order to facilitate the use of a technical semantic device.

It would be wrong, however, to treat Lewis simply as the proponent of what his critics see as metaphysical monstrosities. He has written on a wide variety of philosophical topics. In particular, he has made his own contribution to the running discussion about the proper approach to semantics. And in the process of doing so he has developed a theory of 'conventions' which has attracted wide attention both inside and outside philosophy.

It will be best to approach him through an essay he contributed to a volume on Chomsky, an essay entitled 'Languages, Language and Grammar' (1974). True enough, many of the views he there developed had already, and more fully, been expounded in his *Convention* (1969) and his 'General Semantics' (*Synthese*, 1970). But in the later essay they are not only modified but brought together in a way which will help us to sum up much of our earlier discussion of semantics. For his essay is in many respects a 'higher synthesis' – indeed, he presents it in that form.

There are two ways, as Saussure noticed, of looking at language. The first, in the manner of Lewis's 'General Semantics', considers language as assigning meanings to a sequence of marks and sounds and asks what constitutes such an assignment. This, Lewis argues, must be something which, when combined with information about an actual or possible world, lets us judge a sentence to be true or false. (As, given information about our actual world, we can judge 'Platypuses lay eggs' to be true and, given information about a possible world, we can judge false 'Had he taken his pills, he would have got better'.) A meaningful sentence, then, means in virtue of the fact that it makes assertions about a world – by various devices, Lewis assimilates questions and imperatives to assertions – which permit us to judge it to be, in its language, true or false, whether true or false in some particular world, or true in all possible worlds (analytically true), or false in all possible worlds.

But we can also, Lewis freely grants, look at particular languages in a Grice-like manner, as used by members of a particular population in order to change the beliefs and habits of fellow-members of that population. This is the context in which Lewis defends the view that to use a particular language is to defer to conventions. To this Quine had objected that in order to establish any such convention one would need already to have a language. Language on his view consists of regularities. That is all.

Now, of course, Lewis does not want to deny that to speak a language is regularly to behave in certain ways, regularly to use a certain grammar, a certain vocabulary, and so on. Nor does he want to argue that a decision to do this was made *at* a convention where, without having a language, it was generally decided that it would be a good idea to have one, with that grammar, these words. A group of enthusiasts for an international language might do just this, but could do so only because they already had languages in which they could communicate with one another. Conventions are not generally established at a convention.

If a convention is a regularity, it is, Lewis argues, a regularity of a very special sort. 'Conventions,' he tells us, 'are regularities in action, or in action and belief, which are arbitrary but perpetuate themselves because they serve some common interest.' What makes them a convention rather than a deliberate rational device is that they develop out of pre-existing regularities and are conformed to because of this fact; had the regularity been of a different sort it would have been equally sensible to conform to that.

Like many other recent semanticists, Lewis has recourse, in defending his view, to the 'theory of games'. Using a language is assimilated to playing one of those games in which the players come off best by coordinating their efforts. (The novelist 'Ouida' once described an eights race in which 'all rowed fast but none so fast as stroke'. She did not understand that victory in such a race can come only as a result of what Wittgenstein called 'silent adjustments'.) A population may be said to have accepted the convention of keeping to the left when, grossly to simplify Lewis, almost everybody keeps to the left, knowing this to be the convention, and expects everybody else to know and observe this same procedure but – and this is what makes keeping to the left 'merely a convention' – would prefer to keep to the right if they found that almost everybody else did so. (Unlike going to church, let us say, which some people would prefer to do, even if it 'wasn't done'.)

We know why people accept a traffic convention – which might, to be sure, have originated out of a specific agreement but is still a convention, not just a regularity, even when it has developed as a result of a habit which 'caught on'. It is in order to avoid collisions. Equally, we accept the conventions of a language because the alternative is a world in which we could no longer 'take advantage of, and preserve, our ability to control other people's beliefs and actions to some extent by means of marks and sounds'. But the ability to use a particular language in this way, Lewis also argues, depends on there being, among users of that language, a convention 'of truthfulness and trust'. We expect our fellow language-users to speak the truth, for the most part, and to trust in our doing so. Only in virtue of that convention does our language coordinate our efforts. If people were regularly to lie – not so regularly, of course, that the contradictory of what they said was always true – and expected us to do so, language would be pointless.[12]

For Lewis, then, a complete theory of language will answer both the questions a Montague asks and the questions a Grice asks – or at least a corrected version of these questions. What of Chomsky's questions? Many of Chomsky's concerns and preoccupations Lewis does not share. But he sketches a 'universal grammar' which will incorporate as special cases both the rules set up by logicians in relation to the artificial languages they study and the transformational grammars of Chomsky and Katz, in the form they took in 1965-6. Characteristically, however, he is dissatisfied – when the question is in what interpretations consist – with what, as we have already seen, he calls Katz's 'Markerese'. It leads to a theory, he objects, which 'leaves out such central semantic notions as truth and reference'. To overcome this defect, he calls upon Montague – correctly tracing the origins of this approach, however, to that increasingly influential thinker Carnap – in order to develop a theory of interpretation which not only 'specifies truth values for a sentence', in the conventional post-Fregean manner, but does so 'in all possible worlds, not just in whichever world happens to be actual'. (In the case of modal operators the specification is to 'sets of sets of possible worlds'.) As we discover from his other writings, we are now to take these 'possible worlds' very literally.

The dialectic interplay between philosophers is, as I earlier said, now considerable. So in relation to possible-world semantics and especially the area in which it is most at home – the conditional proposition – I shall try to give an account of a controversy with Lewis, Nelson Goodman and Robert Stalnaker as three of its most notable participants, all three of them, like so many of the philosophers discussed in this chapter, Americans. This will culminate in another American, Kripke's, own presentation of the metaphysical implications of the 'possible world' semantics he did so much to revive. In consequence the continuous presentation of Lewis's views will be seriously interrupted. But I hope that – as on later occasions when I shall be using the same method – the controversial points at issue will be more clearly delineated.

Why all this talk, we must first ask, about possible worlds? Why not develop a theory which refers only to our actual, everyday, world? The fact is that, so the exponents of 'possible worlds' argue, we constantly refer to possible worlds, whether we realise this or not, in the course of our daily activities. We do not confine ourselves to saying things like 'The book is on the table'. We regret, speculate, estimate chances, in such assertions as 'Had I taken his advice, I should now be happier', 'If I were to follow that advice, I should be bored', 'Following that advice, the chances are that I should be defeated'. Scientists, too, try to establish laws, which justify conclusions about what *would* happen *were* such and such to be done; they make use of 'dispositional predicates' which unpack into 'would ... if ...', where that follows the 'if ...' may never happen. (Gold is soluble in *aqua regia*, but very little gold suffers that fate.) They talk about probabilities, now often defined by philosophers either in terms of 'propensities' or estimates of what someone *would be* prepared to bet. Meaningful assertions abound, then, which, on the face of it, refer to possibilities, not to actualities, and which we nevertheless take to be true.

There have not been wanting those, nevertheless, who are prepared to argue that statements about possibilities can be reformulated as statements about actualities. Nelson Goodman finds 'unacceptable without explanation' all 'powers or dispositions, counterfactuals, entities, or experiences that are possible but not actual'. And the 'explanation' he demands is a reference to the actual: 'All possible worlds lie within the actual one.'[13] His struggles to establish this position in *Fact, Fiction and Forecast* (1954) were complex and honestly described. In the end, after critically examining many alternatives, he fell back on a concept of 'projection'. We can put his point thus: let us call a non-dispositional property like 'flexing' a 'manifest property' and think of 'flexible' as a 'projection' of that property to cases where something is not actually 'flexing' but would do so under appropriate circumstances; then that projection is justifiable when 'flexing' is related by laws to other 'manifest properties' which are also properties of those things we describe as 'flexible' – for example, a law to the effect that things flex only when they have an x-type structure. Similarly, a counterfactual conditional is a 'projection' from our knowledge of lawlike connections. So, to take the most plausible sort of case, 'If I put that gold ring into *aqua regia* it would dissolve' is a 'projection' of my knowledge that when gold is put into *aqua regia* it *does* dissolve.

This analysis – and Goodman grants that there are counterfactuals to which it does not seem to apply – raises an only too familiar problem. Clearly, not every generalisation supports a counterfactual. 'From every war, civilisation has eventually recovered' does not sustain the counterfactual 'If there were to be a nuclear war, civilisation would eventually recover'. What makes the difference? Goodman cannot reply – as Kneale had replied – that the lawlike proposition is distinguished from other generalisations by the fact that it justifies counterfactuals. What he wants to know is precisely why some statements sustain counterfactuals and others do not. So he is led into the notorious 'problem of induction'.

Confronting that problem, Goodman introduced an example which has given rise to even more discussion than Gettier's example. Suppose all emeralds examined before time t are green. That is usually taken to confirm the hypothesis that *all* emeralds are green – a projection to unobserved cases. But consider the more complex predicate 'grue'. This applies to all things examined before t when they are green but otherwise to anything that is blue. So at time t we have for each statement asserting that an emerald is green, a parallel statement that it is grue, each confirming the hypothesis that all emeralds are grue. But after time t an emerald could only be grue if it were, as it would not be, blue. Why can we, on the basis of the same evidence, project green but not grue?

Goodman believed that he could answer that question. In general terms, 'green' is better 'entrenched' than 'grue', in the sense that in the past it has often been successfully 'projected'. But we shall not follow him into his careful defence of this position against the more obvious objections to it – that, for example, it is unduly conservative. For the total effect of Goodman's capacity for pointing to problems was to discourage others from taking his route.

There were, of course, other ways of defending his view that counterfactuals, dispositional terms and the like do not commit us to 'possible worlds'. The Australian philosopher John Mackie, to take a case, argued that conditionals are not, strictly speaking, true or false. They assert the consequent only 'within the scope of' a particular 'supposition', a development of his earlier view that a conditional is a compressed argument rather than a statement.[14] Lewis is totally unconvinced by any such attempt to interpret all conditionals as being about the actual. It seems obvious to him that a particular class of hypotheticals, those where the 'if' clause, as in 'if I were a millionaire' interpreted as being about John Passmore, is 'contrary to fact' can only be about happenings in possible worlds. (What we normally call the actual world is for Lewis just that world in which we ourselves live and which we therefore, in Hume's phrase, 'choose to dignify with the name of reality'.) To understand his approach we shall move away from Lewis again to Robert Stalnaker's 'A Theory of Conditionals' (1968).

Stalnaker begins from a suggestion of Ramsey's about the circumstances under which we are entitled to believe a hypothetical proposition. But in a manner very characteristic of contemporary Anglo-American philosophy he immediately passes on from questions about belief to consider what are the truth-conditions of hypothetical statements. Whereas Ramsey had suggested that in order to determine whether to accept a conditional we should add the antecedent of the conditional to our existing set of beliefs and consider whether the consequent is then true, Stalnaker converts Ramsey's 'existing set of beliefs' into 'the actual world' and the 'existing set of beliefs' *together with the antecedent* into a 'possible world', a world in which the antecedent is true 'and which otherwise differs minimally from the actual world'. (Characteristically again, he adopts this procedure because he can then convert to his purposes Kripke's semantics for modal statements.) So 'If I had taken his advice, my life would have been happier' is true if and only if my life

would have been happier in a world in which I did take his advice but
which otherwise differs minimally from the actual world.

It obviously will not do to say that this statement should be
accounted true even when, taking his advice, I should have been
happy but only if all sorts of other conditions were also fulfilled.
(Provided, too, that the War had not broken out, I had not lost my
job, had not met William and so on.) Yet, on the other hand, one
cannot say that the proposition is true only in a world which differs in
no other respect from the present world except that in that world I
took his advice and was happy. For to differ in these respects the
world would have to differ in other respects. My being happy is not
without consequences; to take someone's advice means not doing
what I in fact did, and so on. So one has to say – whatever the
difficulties in filling this out – that the possible world differs
'minimally' from the actual world. To cope with a similar problem
Ramsey had admitted that I might have to 'adjust' my existing set of
beliefs in order to incorporate the antecedent I am adding to them.
For otherwise they might be rendered inconsistent.

Unlike Stalnaker, Lewis does not present a general theory of
conditionals. He entitles his book *Counterfactuals*; he begins by
arguing that although counterfactuals are like strict conditionals,
they cannot be assimilated to them. Nevertheless, the general outline
of his theory is very like Stalnaker's, even if he presents it in
geometrical terms, possible worlds being represented as nested
spheres. But he has two complaints about Stalnaker. First, Stalnaker
assumes that there is something describable as *the* closest world, the
world at the shortest possible distance from an alternative world, let
us say the actual world. This Lewis denies. There is no closest
possible world to a world containing a line an inch long. Secondly,
according to Lewis, Stalnaker does not give a satisfactory account of
that large class of counterfactual conditionals where the consequent
contains 'might' rather than 'would' – 'I might have been happier if'.

We shall ignore the subsequent dispute, arising out of Stalnaker's
attempt to reply to these objections.[15] Let us revert to Lewis's
'realist' interpretation of 'possible worlds'. It had generally been
presumed that when Stalnaker moved from Ramsey's talk about sets
of beliefs to his own talk about possible worlds there is no
metaphysical shift; they are both talking, in the long run, about sets
of statements. So it caused quite a stir when Lewis wrote: 'I

emphatically do not identify possible worlds in any way with respectable linguistic entities: I take them to be respectable entities in their own right. When I profess realism about possible worlds, I mean to be taken literally.'

One naturally objects. Suppose I say that if Jones were rich, he would drink champagne for breakfast. This, on the face of it, is about Jones here in this actual world. How can Jones also be in a possible world? This is the problem of 'cross-world identification' which Quine particularly emphasised. Lewis's answer is that although Jones can exist in only one world, he has 'counterparts' in minimally different possible worlds, none of whom, if the conditional is true, are both rich and not breakfast champagne drinkers. They resemble Jones 'closely enough' in 'important respects of intrinsic quality and extrinsic relations' and resemble him 'no less closely than do other things existing there'. This is a device Lewis had already used for analysing *de re* modalities, distinguishing the properties a thing *must* have in order to be what it is from those it has only accidentally. The properties Jones must have, on his view, are the properties which all his counterparts will have as distinct from the properties which only one, or some, of his counterparts will have. (As he might be rich, but couldn't be handsome, without ceasing to be Jones.)[16]

Saul Kripke will have none of this.[17] No doubt, he had invoked 'possible worlds' in the semantics with which he had made his name. Nevertheless, in the preface to *Meaning and Necessity* (1980) – first published in 1972 as a long article – he wholly rejects Lewis's 'realistic' interpretation of 'possible worlds'. Not only that – he sets aside as a pseudo-problem the Quinean problem of trans-world identity which had provoked Lewis's 'solution'. (He allows, as we shall see, 'trans-world identity' in a different sense.) Yet he is not content, either, with the view that 'possible worlds' are simply a technical device.

Consider, he says, two dice of the normal kind. Suppose, when we throw the dice on a particular occasion, one side turns up six, one five. We can describe this actual outcome as one of the 'possible outcomes' of throwing the dice. Each of the possible final states of the dice, Kripke tells us, can be thought of as a miniature 'possible world'. But had the outcome been different, it would still have involved these very same dice, not their 'counterparts'; there is no problem, then, about the 'trans-world identity' of the dice.

This, Kripke grants, is an unusually simple example. Normally, in asserting counterfactuals, we are theoretically considering not just two dice but ways the entire world might have been – even if in practice we confine ourselves more narrowly, to factors we assume to be relevant. But the complexity of such cases must never cause us to lose sight of the fact, made plain in the dice case, that 'possible worlds' are abstract states of the actual world. Indeed, everyday language – 'it is possible that' – will often make it plainer what is meant by talk about 'possible worlds'. (Quine's ironic comment: possible worlds were introduced to explain modality; if we now ask what they are, we find ourselves referred for explanation to modal statements.)

Kripke sets out to do four closely related things. The first is to distinguish between the *a priori* and the necessary; the second, to develop a theory of proper names; the third, to argue in favour of *de re* necessity, i.e. to maintain, as against the Carnapian view that necessity attaches only to statements, that *things* necessarily have certain of their properties; the fourth, to reject the notion of contingent identity. Given Kripke's formal powers we expect these questions to be discussed with a battery of logical apparatus. They are not: *Meaning and Necessity* is a set of informal lectures. (Had he tried to develop a worked-out theory, he at one stage tells us, he would certainly have gone wrong, like all his predecessors.) The problems in understanding him often derive from that very informality, from Kripke's refusal to be tied down.

Why such informality? At the end of a later, very technical, essay, Kripke preaches a lay sermon, directed against those philosophers who fail, for all their technical ingenuity, to 'keep basic conceptual distinctions in mind', who propose technical criteria simply to exclude philosophical approaches they dislike – sometimes 'as if it were thought that any technical criterion, however loosely defended, is superior to a mere (!) philosophical argument'. He urges philosophers to 'maintain a proper scepticism of attempts easily to settle linguistic or other empirical questions by quick *a priori* formal considerations' and to acquire 'a better sense of both the power and the limitations of formal and mathematical techniques'. Untechnical presentation, he obviously believes, is sometimes the right approach – even if the most rigorous formal reasoning is clearly called for when the question at issue is strictly a problem in logic.[18]

To turn now to the issues themselves. A person, Kripke says, knows something *a priori* when he knows it in a manner which is independent of experience. 'Necessity', in contrast, is a logical notion: to say that a proposition is necessarily true is to answer 'No' to the question: 'Might this proposition have been false?' 'This number is prime' is a necessary truth whether we work out its truth *a priori* or believe it because someone, or a computer, told us so. The mere fact that we have learnt something from experience does not of itself show, Kripke concludes, that what we have learnt is not necessarily true. This distinction between the epistemologically *a priori* and the logically necessary is, for Kripke, fundamental.

Now consider the second question, about proper names.[19] Kripke distinguishes three 'historical' views – his ascriptions are often questioned. He himself defends 'Mill's' view, that a proper name refers to something but does not carry with it any description of that thing. (We can know that someone is called Jones, without, on this view, knowing anything else about him.) The second, 'Frege-Russell', view is that a proper name is an abbreviation for a description – Aristotle, let us say, for 'the teacher of Alexander'. This raises the obvious difficulty that if some scholar were to discover that Xenocrates, rather than Aristotle, was Alexander's teacher, we should not normally conclude that Aristotle did not exist, that the name had no reference. The third, 'Wittgenstein-Searle', view tries to avoid this difficulty; for it, 'the referent of a name is determined not by a single description but by some cluster or family'. Our belief that William Tell did not exist depends on the fact that not enough of those descriptions hold good which would suffice to establish that this name had a referent.

Kripke's objection to the last two views takes substantially the same form. Suppose we say, 'Aristotle was fond of dogs.' To understand this statement, Kripke argues, is to understand both the conditions under which it is in fact true and the 'conditions under which a counterfactual course of history, resembling the actual course in some respects but not in others' would be correctly if partially described by it. (The conditions under which, even if Aristotle had not philosophised, he would still have loved dogs.) But suppose 'Aristotle' is regarded as an abbreviation for 'the last great philosopher of antiquity' (or of this along with other such descriptions as 'the teacher of Alexander'). Then in a counterfactual world in which someone else – let us say a certain 'Lysias' – was the last great philosopher of antiquity (and taught Alexander and ...) the question whether *that* person, Lysias, loved dogs would be the relevant issue for the correctness of 'Aristotle loved dogs'. And Kripke presumes this to be clearly not so. Taking over a technical expression from his logic, Kripke describes names as 'rigid designators': they have the same reference in every possible world. (That in our language, different persons can have the same name is confusing at this point but not, on Kripke's view, fatal. There are different readings of 'Aristotle loved dogs', depending on which Aristotle we are talking about. But so long as 'Aristotle' is being used as a proper name, each such reading uses it as a rigid designator.)

The reference of a name, he admits, can be first given by means of a description. Someone could say that he means by 'Alpha Centauri' the star with such and such coordinates. But that, on Kripke's view, is not the typical case of name-using. Even if name-using has to begin with a 'baptism', whether by pointing or description, thereafter the name is handed down from link to link; someone uses it correctly when, of intention, he uses it 'with the same reference as the man from whom he heard it'. In any case, Kripke argues, it is one thing to say that a description is used to fix the reference – to make it plain what is being referred to – quite another thing to say that the description is the *meaning* of the reference.

Necessity enters into this picture in so far as 'Aristotle' has the same reference in all possible worlds. Aristotle, then, is necessarily the person named Aristotle. (Kripke disputes at length the doctrine that this is a mere tautology.) But necessity ranges far beyond this point. Kripke suggests that we *necessarily* have the parents we actually have – since we could not otherwise be the person we are. Similarly a particular table is *necessarily* made of a particular block of wood – it could not otherwise be *this* table. (A very similar, sensorily indistinguishable table, serving the same function, could, of course, be made from a different block.) He goes on to argue that 'natural kinds' – including under this head not only 'species names' like 'tiger', 'cow' but 'mass terms' like 'gold', 'water' which do not have a determinate form – are, in crucial logical respects, like proper names.[20] (The old grammatical term 'common name' is, he says, so far justified. Montague, too, had used that term very broadly.) A nugget of gold, that is, would continue to be gold, a tiger to be a tiger, even if it were to turn out that 'gold' and 'tigers' had been systematically misdescribed.

But what then is the status of such scientific propositions as 'Gold has the atomic number 79'? If this is true, Kripke suggests, it is necessarily true. For it is a proposition about the stuff of gold, what makes it gold. Such a doctrine, as Kripke grants, is likely to puzzle us. 'Necessary' denies 'might have been otherwise'. And Kripke has told us that gold 'might have turned out not to be an element at all', let alone an element with a particular atomic number. How, then, can it be a necessary truth that gold is an element with the atomic number 79?

At this point, Kripke has recourse to a doctrine of counterparts. He had already re-introduced the concept of 'trans-world identity' in a somewhat similar context, as referring to the identity across worlds of a table and a particular set of molecules, a nation and a particular set of individuals. Now he tells us that the 'loose and inaccurate' statement that gold might have turned out to be a compound 'should be replaced (roughly) by the statement that it is logically possible that there should have been a compound with all the properties originally known to hold of gold'. Such a compound would not *be* gold for, necessarily, gold is an element but, as in the case of the table, it would be a counterpart of gold, sensorily indistinguishable from it. Once we express ourselves carefully – as, Kripke confesses, he has not always done – and remember too that to call a truth necessary is not to say that it could only have been discovered *a priori*, the apparent inconsistencies, so Kripke tells us, will disappear.

With this apparatus he turns to his final theme, the untenability of identity theories of the mind-body relationship. All identity, he holds, is necessary identity. (This is also Wiggins's view; there is a symbiotic relation between these two thinkers.) Identical objects, that is, are necessarily identical, and true identity statements between rigid designators are necessarily true. Admittedly, *descriptions* 'can be used to make *contingent* identity statements', e.g. that the man who invented bifocals was the first Postmaster-General of the United States. (Franklin could have invented bifocals without being Postmaster-General.) But there is no such possibility where the identity is asserted to hold between named objects – in the classical example 'Hesperus' and 'Phosporus'. And Kripke, as we saw, has extended his theory of proper names to include common names.

So much established, Kripke's argument against the identity theory can now assume the following general form: the things being identified, a brain state and a mind state, can be rigidly identified; the only identity which could link them is therefore necessary identity; it is, however, logically possible for the brain state to exist without the mind state existing; therefore they cannot be identical. Against the second premise, of course, the 'contingent identity' theorist points to such identities, which he takes to be contingent, as that of heat with molecular motion. But 'heat' and 'molecular motion', Kripke has argued, are both rigid designators; their identity is therefore not contingent but necessary. And the same would be true of the supposed identity of pain with stimulation of C-fibres. So, again, if there is to be an identity it must, in this case, be a necessary identity.

Could an identity-theorist accept this conclusion, asserting that the connection is indeed a necessary one which only seems to be, is not, merely contingent? (That would mean rejecting Kripke's third premise.) So, it would then be argued, pain is related to the stimulation of C-fibres just as heat is related to molecular motion; in each case science reveals to be necessary an identity which 'might nevertheless not have existed' in the sense that the pain or the heat could have had some other source. The analogy, Kripke replies, will not stand up. In the heat case, what is being said by 'Heat might not have consisted of molecular motion' is that someone 'could have sensed a phenomenon in the way in which we sense heat' – by way, that is, of a particular sensation – even although that phenomenon was not molecular motion. That possibility does not obtain in the case of pain. For, according to Kripke, pain, unlike heat, exists only as a sensation of pain. So brain and mind states cannot be *contingently* identified, since they do not satisfy the requirements for contingent identity, and they cannot be *necessarily* identified either.[21]

4

Davidson and Dummett

Of the many other contemporary philosophers who have studied the relationship between truth, language and reality, two particularly demand attention in virtue both of their originality and their influence, the American Donald Davidson, the Englishman Michael Dummett. In both cases one could otherwise wish, if for very different reasons, to be excused. Over a period of more than twenty years Davidson has written nothing but articles, exceptionally scattered in their place of publication and for the most part very short, carrying the virtue of compactness to the point at which it becomes a vice. These articles are interwoven one with another and with a network of philosophical controversy. They may give the impression of being repetitious, and certainly there are particular points which Davidson is constantly hammering home. But the apparent repetitions are often subtle reformulations, sometimes incorporating quite consequential revisions. It is part of Davidson's general theory that in order to understand a particular belief, we have to look at the general system of ideas and attitudes of which it forms part. This is certainly true in Davidson's own case. While he is not, in the ordinary sense, an obscure writer – 'elusive' is a better description – one is not surprised to find that expositions and criticisms of his views are so often prefixed by 'if I understand him aright'.

The difficulty with Dummett is at once similar and dissimilar. For a time he wrote little; his Oxford friends began to fear that he would never write the substantial books they expected from him. When he did, it was in the form of a lengthy book on Frege, followed by an even lengthier book on the interpretation of Frege – in all over a thousand pages – into which are interwoven his own doctrines, criticisms of his contemporaries and replies to their criticism of him.

63

The total effect is intimidating in the extreme. And then there is a large volume of essays to be taken into account, a book on mathematical intuitionism and several subsequent, very lengthy, essays.

But neither, as I said, can be ignored. Their work, Davidson's particularly, is, among other things, the point of departure for a flourishing group of young Oxford philosophers, the successor in a historico-geographical sense of 'ordinary language' philosophy but reacting violently, as we have already mentioned, against that philosophy, both in their interests and their style. (They write in a manner which is often ferociously technical and always formidably abstract, devoid of concrete examples.) One should by no means think of the new 'Oxford Group' as being uncritical Davidsonians. A member of the group, J.A. Foster, was indeed prepared to write in 1976 that 'Davidson's design is in ruins'. But Davidson was their initial inspiration.[1]

Davidson's thinking is a seamless web. We can nevertheless draw a rough and ready distinction between the set of articles, with their central interest psychological,[2] which he brought together in *Essays on Actions and Events* (1980) and his essays on semantic theory, published as *Inquiries into Truth and Interpretation* (1984). Let us begin with the somewhat more amenable psychological essays.

After some abortive work in the experimental psychology of decision-making, which had an important negative effect on his thinking, Davidson's interests were aroused by post-Wittgensteinian philosophical psychology, especially by Anscombe's *Intention*. We shall look at two lines of thought which developed within his psychological writings, which are linked with his semantics and which burgeoned into an ontology. The first of these arises out of his refusal to regard intentional action as 'rising above' the causal level. 'The ordinary notion of cause', so he sums up in his prefatory remarks, 'is essential to the understanding of what it is to act with a reason, to have a certain intention in acting, to act counter to one's own best judgment, or to act freely' – the very points at which it has so often been cast aside as useless.

This leaves Davidson with a problem, most plainly set out in his 'Mental Events' (1970): how to reconcile what, on his view, are two apparently irreconcilable facts. The first such fact is that human actions are clearly part of the order of nature, 'causing and being caused by events outside themselves'; the second fact is that there are, or so he thinks, 'good arguments against the view that thought, desire and voluntary action can be brought under deterministic laws, as physical phenomena can'.

The title of this essay is significant. 'Mental *events*', not 'mental states' or 'mental processes'. The second interwoven theme that runs through Davidson's thinking is that properly to discuss either causality, or intentional action, or the mind-body problem one has to evoke an ontology of events. Davidson had been particularly impressed by Anscombe's doctrine that the same act can be intentional under a certain description and unintentional under a different description – as I might intentionally write a Polish name but unintentionally spell it wrongly, without performing two distinct acts. What is it, at the ontological level, which carries these two different descriptions? To this Davidson answers: an event. Admittedly, when we say that someone has performed an action, we do not ordinarily mention an event. We say, for example, 'Brutus stabbed Caesar' as if nothing were involved except Brutus, Caesar and an act of stabbing. But such an analysis, Davidson argues in 'The Logical Form of Action Sentences' (1967), is a mistake. The logical form of such a statement is something like: 'There exists an event that is a stabbing-by-Brutus-of-Caesar event.' (The formal presentation is somewhat tidier.)

Why take this view? Here Davidson calls upon his semantics. If we put action-statements in an 'event' form, we can see, he says, why certain implications hold which would not hold on more conventional renderings, why, for example, 'Brutus stabbed Caesar in the back' entails 'Brutus stabbed Caesar'. Set out in a standard fashion, we have two distinct predicates ascribed to Brutus – 'being a Caesar-in-the-back stabber' and 'being a Caesar-stabber' – with no standard way of moving from the first to the second. But if we offer as the logical form of 'Brutus stabbed Caesar in the back' something like 'There exists an event that is a stabbing of Caesar by Brutus event and it is an into-the-back-of-Caesar event' this clearly entails its first part. (It is his regular test of such renderings that they permit all permissible implications.)

A difficulty then arises. Davidson has been very greatly influenced by Quine; he quotes Quine's quip, 'No entity without identity.' If Davidson is going to incorporate events into his ontology, he has, on this view, to offer some criterion for saying of an event described in one way that it is identical with an event described in a different way. One important criterion, he suggests, is that if events have the same causes and the same effects they must be the same event.

This may provoke the objection that events are not the sort of thing that *can be* causes and effects. For some philosophers – Mackie for one – had argued that causes, properly described, connect facts, expressible only in sentences. That position, Davidson had replied in 'Causal Relations' (1967), leads to difficulties as soon as we try to spell out the sort of logical relation which holds between the sentences in question – it seems at once that it cannot be, and that it must be, a material implication. Events, for Davidson, are precisely what causal relations *do* hold between. There is no problem, then, in asserting that two events can be identified as being the same event on the ground that they have the same causes and the same effects.

Davidson does not wish to deny what underlies Mackie's view, namely that to assert that one event causes another is to assert that the two events are linked in a law-like way. But he adds two comments. The first is that we can know that A causes B without knowing what law connects them, the second is that the law which connects them may not, and usually does not, connect them under the descriptions which we employ in asserting the causal connection. We can know, for example, that Jack broke his leg by falling downstairs and agree that there is some law-like connection between the event we have described as 'Jack's falling downstairs' and the event we describe as 'Jack's breaking his leg'. And yet, there is no strict law to the effect that if someone falls down the stairs he breaks his leg. If we were to try to construct such a law by adding more and more detail ('a man of such-and-such an age falling from such-and-such a height at such-and-such an angle on such-and-such a kind of floor') we should have on our hands a 'law' which is just a detailed account of what happened in this case. The event has to be redescribed in terms of physics, so Davidson concludes, before there is any prospect of discovering a strict law from which, given the attendant circumstances, the leg-breaking is deducible.

All this has to be kept in mind in order to understand Davidson's highly unusual defence of identity materialism, his manner of reconciling the fact that the mental forms part of nature, subject to normal causal influences, and the fact that relations between mental events are not law-like. In a typical psychological explanation, so he has argued in his earlier essays, we say that someone acted in a particular way because he had certain desires and certain beliefs. This, he had also maintained, is a causal explanation. Nevertheless, he adds, there are no strict laws of the form 'Whenever anybody has such-and-such beliefs and desires, and such-and-such other conditions are fulfilled, he will act in such-and-such ways'. How anyone acts will depend not on his having a particular belief, a particular desire, but on his structure of beliefs, desires, fears, hopes, expectations and the like. We may pick out one of these, as when we say that Tom married Mary 'because she is rich', as explaining an action. But this, Davidson suggests, is a simplifying device.

Psychologists have for long recognised as much. That is why they have sought alternative methods of explaining human action, whether in terms of conditioning or, in Ramsey's manner, in terms of willingness to bet on certain alternatives. But we can make no sense, Davidson argues, of these alternative forms of explanation without considering them against 'a background of coherent attitudes', the very thing they are supposed to render unnecessary.

We might expect these arguments to culminate in some form of dualism, not in what Davidson calls 'anomalous monism'. And it does lead Davidson to conclude that there are no strict laws relating the mental to the physical. (By 'the mental' he does not mean, as other identity theorists have meant, sensations and the like but any event which, in Brentano's style, essentially involves a propositional attitude – believing, hoping, expecting, fearing ... that ...) For if there is a law to the effect that whenever the physical event p occurs in my brain the belief m must occur in my mind, a belief would have to be something which we could ascribe to a person in the same sense in which we might ascribe some physical property to him. And on Davidson's view beliefs are not like that: in order to ascribe a belief to a person we have to take into account considerations of coherence, rationality and the like, in a way that has no application to physical properties.

Nevertheless, mental events are part of nature and, as such, both cause and are caused in a manner which is in principle governed by strict laws. This is only possible, in the light of what has so far been argued, if they are also physical events; the laws relating them to other events will then be strict physical laws, not psychophysical laws. But, so long as we confine ourselves to 'the psychological idiom', we can relate psychological events one to another by loose psychological generalisations without paying any attention to the fact that what we are relating are also physical events and in that capacity subject to strict physical laws.[3]

The analyses Davidson offers us of action statements and causal statements can be thought of either as contributions to philosophical psychology or as exemplifications of semantic analyses, based on a semantic theory which, Davidson tells us, he has been expounding since 1953. Discussion of the theory in its initial form does not usually go back, however, beyond 'Truth and Meaning' (1967) or the somewhat more systematic, if still programmatic, 'Semantics for Natural Languages' (1970). In 'Radical Interpretation' (1973) and 'In Defense of Convention T' (1973) his theory takes a somewhat different turn, although by no means a radical turnabout.[4]

What, Davidson begins by asking, does a semantic theory try to do? 'It aims,' he replies, 'to give us the meaning of every meaningful expression.' This sounds strange; we usually suppose that words are 'meaningful expressions' and it is hard to see how a semantic theory could do what a dictionary does. But a little later 'meaningful expressions' is rephrased as '*independently* meaningful expressions' and these in turn are quietly identified with sentences. Indeed, words come into the picture only in so far as sentences contain words; their meaning, like that of such phrases as 'is the father of', consists in the systematic contribution they make to the sentences of which they form part. (The contrast with Saussure will be obvious.)

So semantics, as Davidson understands it, does not tell us, for example, what 'good' means. (That had also been Montague's view.) It does, however, analyse such sentences as 'She is a good actress' to distinguish it from 'She is an English-speaking actress' in such a way as to make it plain, by setting out their logical form, why the second sentence entails 'She is English-speaking' but the first sentence does not entail 'She is good'. To generalise what he says about action-sentences, he sets out to 'give an account of the logical or grammatical role of the parts or words' of particular types of sentence which will be consistent with 'the entailment relations between such sentences' and with what is known of the role of those same parts or words in other types of sentence. He takes this to be 'the same as showing how the meanings' of such sentences 'depend on their structure'. The task of 'uncovering the logical form', he therefore says, is 'the central task of semantics'. His interest is in that fragment of a language – he relates it to Chomsky's 'deep structures' – which offers us a way of interpreting entire classes of sentences;[5] it does not worry him if the sentences which give the logical form scarcely sound English. Since every language has a finite number of letters, words and types of phrases, he hopes, by making use of concatenations of these repeatable elements, both in axioms and theorems, to 'give the meaning' of the infinitely many sentences a language contains.

When, in everyday life, we are puzzled about the meaning of a sentence in a language we imperfectly understand, we normally turn for help to a dictionary, with perhaps the aid of a grammar book. Fodor-Katz substantially tell us that this is what we ought to do, even if their theory incorporates rather special views about the nature of a good dictionary and a good grammar book. Such a procedure would not resolve Davidson's semantic qualms. He shares the common twentieth-century assumption that truth and meaning are linked, that we cannot claim fully to understand a sentence unless we know what its truth-conditions are. And neither grammar book nor dictionary tells us, or enables us to deduce, what the truth-conditions are of causal sentences, or action sentences. In fact, they will probably deceive us as, so Davidson argues, their analysis of 'Brutus killed Caesar' deceives us. So he looks elsewhere for his semantics.

In his *From a Logical Point of View* (1953), Quine had distinguished between 'the theory of reference', turning around such extensional notions as 'designates', 'satisfies', 'is true', and 'the theory of meaning', containing such intensional notions as 'is synonymous with', 'analytic', 'means'. And the theory of reference, he had argued, is in a considerably better intellectual condition than the theory of meaning. Davidson at first set out to develop a theory which would do what we demand of a theory of meaning – which would enable us to interpret sentences – but which 'falls comfortably within a theory of reference'. (Later, in his 'Reality without Reference', 1970, he denied that there can be anything properly describable as a *theory* of reference; we need, he says, the concept of reference as a 'posit' within semantic theory but the testable theory begins at the level of true sentences and the functioning of words in sentences – just as, he says, the tests of micro-physical theories are at the level of physical objects. Nevertheless, meaning theory makes use of 'reference' as it does not make use of 'meanings'.)[6]

Propositional logic, he thought, had shown how the truth value 'p or q' derived from the truth value of 'p' and of 'q'; Tarski had shown how the truth-value of 'open' sentences, containing free variables, such as x, derived from their satisfying ordered sequences – as, to take the simplest case, 'open' sentences of the form 'x is the father of y' are satisfied by such an ordered sequence as ⟨Duke of Edinburgh, Prince Charles⟩ – and by so doing had been able to give an account of the truth of quantified sentences; he himself had shown how the truth of action statements derived from the truth of statements about events. That was only a start but, he thought, a good start, whatever problems remained.

Davidson's semantics was to be an ontologically austere theory. 'I think theories of meaning prosper', he writes in his reply to Foster, 'when they avoid uncritical evocation of the concepts of convention, linguistic role, linguistic practice or language games'. Montague, Lewis, Kripke all offer us, on his view, too rich a diet; they in reply challenge Davidson to cope with what he admits to being problems – counterfactuals, for example – on what they regard as a diet which lacks adequate nourishment.

Tarski had shared Davidson's fondness for the extensional. The axioms of his 'truth-definition' – or what Davidson calls his 'truth theory' – contain only such expressions as 'class', 'sequence', 'sentence', 'structural description'.[7] To develop a similarly austere theory of *meaning* we need first, Davidson tells us, to discover some property 'T' which characterises those sentences which 'mean that p' (in a particular language L) and then to find some non-intensional relationship between sentences with such a property and p itself. We can do this, he says, by substituting 'if and only if' for 'means' and 'true' for 'T'. So we now end up with Tarski's truth-sentences – 'Snow is white' is true (in English) if and only if snow is white. And we are in a position to draw upon the formal resources of Tarski's theory, his methods of proving T-sentences. Given that theory and recognising it for what it is, a truth-theory, Davidson writes in his 'Reply to Foster': 'We could produce a translation of every sentence in the language and know that it is a translation.' Not only that – 'We should know in detail how the truth value of sentences in the language were owed to their structures and why some sentences entailed others, and how words performed their function by dint of relations to objects in the world.' Infinite riches indeed from a formal theory!

For various reasons, however, Tarski had argued that his definition of truth could not be applied to natural languages – not only because to do so would lead to semantic paradoxes, but because natural languages contain irreducibly indexical expressions, which do not indicate what would satisfy them. There was room in his theory for 'A book is stolen' or 'All books are stolen' but not for '*That* book was stolen'. For on the face of it, we have no way of judging this to be true or false unless we happen to be present when it is uttered and hence know which book is in question and what time the 'was' refers to. Davidson replied to Tarski by setting out a T-sentence thus: 'That book was stolen' is true in English as (potentially) spoken by p at t if and only if the book demonstrated by p at t is stolen prior to t.

This sentence is characteristic of Davidson's analyses. On the left hand side, as in Tarski, there is a sentence in the language which is being semantically studied and on the right hand side a sentence in the language of the theory. (In this case, both languages are English, but that need not be so.) The theory language contains no quotation marks and no reference to 'meanings' or any cognate intensional expressions. But it gives the 'logical form' of the original sentence and thereby contributes to our understanding of its meaning.

The method is Tarski's, but there are changes from Tarski in so far as the original sentence, in Davidson's analysis, is understood as being a speech-act, and the theory language still contains indexical expressions – 'the book demonstrated by p' (see on this 'In Defense of Convention T', 1973). And it becomes plain that the classical T-sentence – 'Snow is white' is true if and only if snow is white – would not really satisfy Davidson. For it conceals a semantic problem. 'Snow' is a mass term; Davidson would want an analysis which brought out the difference between this sentence and 'Punctuality is desirable' or 'The tiger is an animal' – perhaps, as a first analysis, 'Every particle of snow above a certain size is white'.

Such sentences, of course, we can understand only if we understand the meaning of their constituent parts. But parts of sentences, Davidson has said, have a meaning only in virtue of their 'making a systematic contribution to the meaning of the sentence in which they occur'. This sounds like a vicious circle: to understand a sentence we must know the meaning of its parts, to understand the parts we must understand the sentence. That consideration leads Davidson to defend a variety of holism: 'We can give the meaning of any sentence (or word) only by giving the meaning of every sentence (and word) in that language'. No single T-sentence, it would then seem, gives us the meaning of the sentence it is about. Rather it, along with its proof, which proceeds by way of a logical categorisation of the constituents of the sentence, tells us something we have to know in order to understand the part that sort of sentence plays in our language.

These are scarcely uncontroversial doctrines. (Neither, I should add, is my interpretation of Davidson uncontroversial.) Three questions have troubled his critics. The first is why an ordinary speaker of a language seems to get along quite well in his understanding of what is said although he is far from having – what Davidson himself would not claim to have – a total theory of his language or even a theory of some fragment of the language, to which Davidson *would* lay claim. The second question is how we are to tell whether a particular T-sentence is itself true. And the third question is how we know, even if we know it to be true, that it gives, or contributes to giving, the *meaning* of the expression it is about. It is a requirement of a good semantic theory, so Davidson tells us, that it be empirically testable. But just how are these last two claims testable?

Davidson's 'Radical Interpretation', supplemented by 'In Defense of Convention T', sets out to answer these questions. On the first point, he makes it plain that he is not putting forward a theory about how we ordinarily learn or interpret our own, or other people's, language. His theory is totally devoid of any reference to psychology, here unlike Chomsky, or even to epistemology. He is asking, rather, what theory we *could* know which would let us know that when Kurt 'under the right conditions' utters the words 'Es regnet' he has said that it is raining, and how we *could* come to know this theory. (He does not add at this point, what I have taken to be his view, that once we know this we should be able to interpret Kurt's statement in a sense in which Kurt cannot interpret it, which would bring out features of what this sentence means of which Kurt is not aware. Or at least that this would be true if Kurt had said 'Ich glaube dass es regnet', with the familiar semantic problems such belief-sentences raise.)

The second question – how we know the T-sentence is true – arises out of the fact that when a theory of truth is to be used as a theory of meaning we can no longer do what Tarski did, simply *stipulate* that the theory-language sentence is to be 'an adequate translation' of the original sentence. For if we take 'is an adequate translation of' to be equivalent to 'has the same meaning as', that sameness of meaning is precisely what we are trying to use the truth theory to give an account of.

All this becomes a little clearer if we think of ourselves as trying to establish, in English, a truth theory of French. Suppose the original sentence is 'La neige est blanche' and the theory-language sentence is 'Snow is white' so that we now have: 'La neige est blanche' is true in French if and only if snow is white. What ground have we for taking this to be so? In Davidson's earlier writing, his standpoint was that of someone building up a meaning-theory for a language he already knows rather than that of somebody building up a meaning-theory for a foreign language. Hence it did not worry him unduly how, considering sentences in a foreign tongue, we are to know that the truth sentences which test the theory are themselves true and are known to be truth sentences.

That is one of the problems with which Davidson attempts to cope in 'Radical Interpretation', in a manner greatly influenced by Quine but without relying on Quine's epistemology.[8] Putting the method crudely, we ask ourselves under what conditions Kurt says 'Es regnet'. If we find that he says this when it is raining then we have a piece of evidence of the form: 'Kurt belongs to the German speech community. and Kurt holds true that "Es regnet" on Saturday at noon and it is raining near Kurt at noon.' This is evidence for the T-sentence: 'Es regnet' is true in German when spoken by x at time t if and only if it is raining near x at t. Davidson is employing, then, the traditional 'descriptive' approach to language that Chomsky objected to, if only to gather evidence for a 'deep' truth-theory. But even if we are not dissatisfied with it on these grounds, we may still object that not only Kurt but any other member of the community from whose utterances we seek supporting evidence of the form 'Gretchen is a member ... and says ...' may be mistaken, or lying. At this point,

Davidson invokes a principle which in various forms and under various names has been very prominent in recent semantic discussions, in relation to the question of evidence. This is that unless we can interpret the utterances and behaviour of a creature 'as revealing a set of beliefs largely consistent and true by our own standards, we have no reason to count that creature as rational, as having beliefs, or as saying anything' – as having, that is, a language as distinct from a capacity to make noises.

The third question remains. Is a T-sentence automatically a meaning sentence? From the beginning, Davidson recognised that 'if truth-value were all that mattered the T-sentence for "Snow is white" could as well say that it is true only if grass is green or $2+2=4$ as say that it is true if and only if snow is white. For according to the extensional logic he is working with, any true sentence can be substituted for any other true sentence without this affecting the truth-value of any sentence of which it forms part. This did not worry Tarski because he postulated that the sentence must offer a translation. Davidson's case is different; as we saw, he cannot simply postulate this. We may hope, he says, that a satisfactory truth-theory will not generate such anomalous sentences. But this 'hope' does not allow us to *identify* T-sentences with sentences which 'give the meaning'. Nor can we relativise T-sentences to the theory that proves them, as some of his earlier formulations might suggest. 'If the theory does what it is designed to do, T-sentences alone must provide all we need for interpretation.' But this is exactly where the investigation of the habits of native speakers is to come into the picture. We shall not find that Kurt says 'Es regnet' if and only if $2+2=4$, which would be always. There will be some degree of indeterminancy but not enough, he thinks, to destroy our capacity to distinguish between good and bad truth-theories for particular sentences and thus to use them in meaning-theories.

Davidson is not in the end, then, despondent. And his particular analyses – along with those of such critical co-workers as Gilbert Harman and John Wallace – often have an interest which is independent of his general theory. Take, for example, his analysis of propositional attitudes. He begins from the suggestion – with some philological warrant – that the 'that' in 'Galileo said that the earth moves' is a demonstrative, the sentence as a whole being equivalent to 'The earth moves. Galileo said that', where we have two extensional sentences. This is worth discussing in its own right as a solution to the problem how the original sentence can be analysed in truth-functional terms even although it is certainly not the case that it retains its truth whatever true proposition we substitute for 'the earth moves'.[9] (He had already, as we saw, given an account of demonstratives.) But he does finally accept Foster's criticisms this far: 'Nothing strictly constitutes a theory of meaning.' 'A theory of truth,' he continues, 'however well selected is not a theory of meaning', and there are 'irreducible indexical elements'. He still thinks it possible, however, to call upon such a theory 'to say what it is that an interpreter knows' and so 'to give a satisfactory answer to one of the central problems of the philosophy of language'. Whether this leaves him subject to Putnam's gibe that Davidson's semantics is just 'Quinean scepticism under the guise of a positive contribution to the theory of meaning' remains a question. In general, Davidson is widely rebuked in the United States as an advertiser of programmes which make large promises but never come to fruition; his most devoted admirers have been in England, which is perhaps less demanding in this respect. But even there, as we saw, doubts have been expressed.

To turn now to Dummett.[10] Much of his intellectual life has been devoted to the interpretation and, with very considerable qualifications, the defence of Frege. The two immense books which flowed out of this project – *Frege* (1973) and *The Interpretation of Frege's Philosophy* (1981) – include, to be sure, very considerable independent discussions of most of the major issues in the philosophy of language. But in such a manner that to discuss, let us say, Dummett's theory of proper names, one would have to take into account what Frege himself says, what Dummett says about Frege, what Kripke says about both Frege and Dummett, together with Dummett's replies to, and his independent criticism of, Kripke. And this is clearly impossible in any reasonable compass.

Then there is a further difficulty. Uncompromising though Dummett is when he is defending his interpretation of Frege or castigating his opponents, his exposition of his own views is tentative, exploratory. No sooner is one on the point of ascribing to him a definite doctrine than there is a sudden twist in the argument; unexpected difficulties arise, new alternatives present themselves. Critics and defenders alike *harden* Dummett's views in order to begin discussing them. We shall have to confine our attention to two closely-connected aspects of his thought: his views about the centrality of the philosophy of language and his anti-realism.

Philosophy of language, as we have already seen, has attracted over the last decade a striking proportion of the ablest philosophers. Indeed, 'language' has been a key-concept in post-war culture generally, much as 'atoms' were in the eighteenth century and 'development' was in the nineteenth century. Even the major scientific discoveries of the period, in molecular biology, have recourse to such concepts as 'code' and 'transcription'; there are books on 'the language of architecture'. So powerful has been this tide that most philosophers of language do not even bother to justify their conviction that language is the proper starting point for philosophy, much as their empiricist predecessors quietly assumed that perception was the place to begin.

Dummett, in contrast, explicitly defends the 'linguistic turn'. 'Until we have achieved an understanding of our language,' he writes in the 'Justification of Deduction' (1973), 'in terms of which we apprehend the world, and without which therefore, there is for us no world, so long will our understanding of everything else be imperfect.' His predecessors would have written 'perception' or 'thought' where he writes 'language'. Why the change?

For two reasons, made plain in his 'Can Analytic Philosophy be Systematic and Ought it to Be?' (1975). First, Dummett is depressed, like many a philosopher before him, by the failure of philosophy to make progress in the sense in which the natural sciences make progress, to establish itself as a systematic investigation, proceeding 'according to generally agreed methods of inquiry', achieving results 'which are generally accepted or rejected according to commonly agreed criteria', issuing in an articulated theory. The epistemological approach had not succeeded in achieving that end. Frege, Dummett thinks, showed us the path to follow, by envisaging philosophy as a theory of meaning.

Not everybody accepts this interpretation of Frege, and the more sceptical may wonder whether Montague, Chomsky, Lewis, Davidson, Kripke, Dummett differ less than did Bradley, Russell, Dewey. But certainly the feeling that philosophy is at long last a cooperative enterprise, demanding a rigorous technical preparation, to which any individual, much in the manner of what Kuhn calls 'normal' science, can hope to contribute his moiety, has won the support of many Anglo-American philosophers – even if, as Dummett wryly admits, such hopes are by no means new and have so far always been disappointed.

Dummett is not saying that philosophers should entirely confine themselves to the theory of meaning. In the end, he nevertheless thinks, their speculations will have to be tested before the tribunal of meaning theory. And certainly, he is confident, 'it is only by the analysis of language that we can analyse thought'. The attempt to do so directly, in the empiricist manner, to 'strip thought of its linguistic clothing and penetrate to its naked essence' ends up by 'confusing the thought itself with the subjective inner accompaniments of thought', such accompaniments as images. If these final remarks are Wittgensteinian in spirit, Dummett has all the same rejected two of Wittgenstein's central theses: first, that philosophy cannot be a systematic inquiry parallel to the natural sciences; secondly, that philosophy of language is not a general theory of meaning but an investigation of how language is used in particular language games.

On this latter point, he bases his critique of Wittgenstein on Frege's distinction between 'force' and 'sense'. No doubt, he freely admits, in different language games the same linguistic expression can occur with different forces, as in a command as distinct from an assertion. Nevertheless, 'Close the window' used as an imperative has the same *sense* as it has in 'I forgot to close the window', whether this be an apology, an excuse, a reminder, or whatever else. Otherwise, Dummett argues, we could never learn a language. Wittgenstein, so Dummett tells us, was right in emphasising, as against Frege, that language is a social, a communicative, phenomenon, not just an expression of a thought. He was right, that is, in linking meaning with use; his mistake lay in his supposing that every difference in the occasion of use brings with it a total difference in meaning.

What form would a systematic theory of meaning take? In the first of a sequence of two articles entitled 'What is a Theory of Meaning?' (1975, 1976) Dummett sets out the general conditions such a theory must fulfil, while being anything but dogmatic about the details. It must issue in principles, he argues, which will make explicit the implicit knowledge we have of the language we use, the knowledge we display in our practice, in such a way as to show that these principles do adequately reflect that practice. (They must not, for example, ascribe to us a knowledge we could not possibly have.) Like Chomsky and many another, Dummett assumes that when we display a competence, that competence must rest on an implicit knowledge of the principles which investigation brings to light – that we have an implicit knowledge, for example, of the physical principles which are manifested in our capacity to ride a bike. He denies, however, that what is brought to light is something psychological. If a robot could talk a language, on Dummett's view, it would demonstrate an implicit knowledge of linguistic principles, but without possessing our psychological states.

A good theory of meaning, then, will be a theory of what it is to understand, of what one knows when one knows a language, so that, for example, 'Meaning is use' could serve as a thesis in such a theory only if to *know* the meaning is to *know* the use – implicitly or explicitly. At its 'core', it will have a theory of reference; its 'shell' will be a theory of sense. These will be supplemented by a theory of force. Finally – this, at various points, against Davidson, Kripke, and to a lesser degree Quine – it will be full-blooded, atomic, or at least molecular, and rich. A 'modest' theory, in contrast with a 'full-blooded' theory, begins from the assumption that we already understand certain basic concepts, on which the meaning of other concepts rests. It is liable, so Dummett argues, to the objection which notoriously attaches to translation theories – according to which the meaning of a sentence consists in its translatability into some other sentence – namely, that we can know that one sentence translates another without knowing what either sentence means. (Suppose we ask a scientist what a sentence means. He may tell us, and from the nodding of heads by other scientists we might know, that this is a correct translation. Yet we may still not understand.) So similarly, to know that the meaning of a sentence is a function of the meaning of certain basic linguistic expressions tells us what that sentence means only if we already understand these basic expressions. A theory of language, to be 'full-blooded', must give an account of what it is to understand *any* expression, basic or derived.

On holism, Dummett says that it is at first puzzling that Davidson's theory should be holistic, since on the face of it the meaning of each separate sentence is, on his view, deducible from a set of axioms relating to the words and constructions which comprise that sentence. But in fact Davidson does not tell us in what the meaning of the axioms consists, or the meaning of 'is true' in the truth sentences. So 'there can be no answer to the question what constitutes a speaker's understanding of any one word or sentence'. We understand, Davidson is forced to conclude, nothing short of the language as a whole. As for the view that we can break out of the threatened circle by considering what the members of a language community 'hold true', this approach, Dummett argues, cannot give any proper account of the difference between making a mistake and misunderstanding the meaning of a sentence. Any systematic theory of meaning has to be able to do this.

Dummett is quite willing to admit that our understanding of any one sentence 'will usually depend on an understanding not merely of the words which compose that sentence, and of other sentences that can be constructed out of them, but of a certain sector of the language, often a very considerable one'. He rejects, nevertheless, the view that we must understand the *whole* language in order fully to understand any sentence. A systematic theory of language must, he thinks, to that extent be either atomic, then concerning itself with the understanding of individual words, or molecular, with the understanding of sentences as its objective, not holistic. (Characteristically, he does not come to a final conclusion about what it must be.)

As for 'richness', a rich theory will attribute to any speaker who knows what a proper name means some knowledge of the conditions which must be satisfied by any object which bears that name or, at the very least, a capacity to recognise the bearer of the name when it is encountered. So to understand 'London' we must either be able to describe that city or to recognise it when we are there. This is in contrast with an austere theory, like Kripke's, which demands only that our naming of it should be continuous with previous namings.

That much established to his satisfaction, Dummett looks in detail, in the second of his two articles, at the relation between meaning and truth. To understand the development of his thinking at this point, we have to recall that he was for many years Reader in the Philosophy of Mathematics at Oxford, before he succeeded Ayer as Professor of Logic, and in that capacity lectured at length on intuitionist theories of mathematics. The first book he wrote, although he did not publish it, was on the principle of excluded middle; he did finally publish *Elements of Intuitionism* (1977), an introduction to mathematical intuitionism, based on his Oxford lectures. What particularly interested him in intuitionism was, first, its rejection of bivalence, of the principle that every mathematical proposition must be either true or false even when we do not know, are in no position to know, which it is and, secondly, its willingness to introduce considerable changes into both classical mathematics and classical logic in the interests of preserving mathematics as a consistent systematic inquiry.

The intuitonists did not generally seek to extend their conclusions to natural languages. Dummett makes that (modified) extension. Only by gradual stages, however. He begins from the prevailing assumption that to understand a sentence is to be able to state its truth condition. To this he raises two objections. First, to understand a sentence we need to know how its meaning derives from the meaning of its words. Merely being able to state its truth condition does not tell us this. Secondly, we often understand a sentence without being able to state its truth condition. Indeed, this must be so. For, Dummett points out, stating truth conditions is uttering sentences. Unless we already understand some sentences, stating the truth conditions of sentences is a process which could never get under way.

Then should we say that we must *either* be able to state the truth condition *or* have an 'implicit knowledge' of it? Dummett grants this much: provided only that there is some way of recognising that a person holds a sentence to be true – and Dummett has no real qualms on this point – we can *sometimes* determine, by way of that recognition, that he has an implicit knowledge of the truth condition of a sentence. But only under special circumstances. The truth condition in question must be one that a person is capable of recognising when it in fact obtains, and he must, whenever it does obtain, accept the sentence as true. (So someone can be recognised as having an implicit knowledge of the truth condition of 'That is red' if he accepts that something is red if and only if some demonstrated object is in fact red.) In some cases, of course, he may have to adopt special procedures to discover whether the truth condition holds, going into the garden to look when someone says 'the grevillea is blooming'. This, and more complex cases, present no problem for such an analysis. If a person has a practical procedure for putting himself in a position to discover whether the condition obtains, and can show that he has it, that demonstrates, so Dummett suggests, his implicit knowledge.

The problem remains that, as the intuitionists argued in respect to mathematics, there are a great many sentences such that we have no effective procedure for determining whether they are true – as when sentences are used to assert that *everything*, future, present or past, which is of a certain kind must possess a particular property, or are used to assert counter-factual conditionals, or are used to assert something about a spatiotemporal region which is in principle inaccessible to us. Such cases are more numerous, Dummett suggests, than we normally suppose. Two examples, on which he places much weight, are 'A city will never be built on this spot' and '*X* is good at learning languages', when said of somebody who has never in fact come into contact with a foreign tongue. (Compare Gray's 'mute inglorious Milton'.) Admittedly, in special cases there may be a possibility of directly recognising that the truth condition of a sentence of this class obtains, as when a person lives to see what he had regarded as a counterfactual conditional – let us say 'if someone were to step on the moon ...' – converted into a factual conditional. In general terms, Dummett nevertheless insists, the conditions for showing implicit knowledge cannot be satisfied in respect to these classes of sentences.

Developing this point, Dummett sets up his 'principle *C*', that if a statement is true 'there must be something in virtue of which it is true'. 'Observation statements' can be 'barely true', true simply in virtue of what we immediately perceive to be the case. But the class of sentences enumerated above are not observation sentences. Sometimes an attempt is made to turn them into quasi-observation sentences by imagining a being for whom the past and future are as observable as the present. Even if we can make sense of this, Dummett argues, we certainly cannot make sense of the concept of a being who has 'a direct insight into counter-factual reality'.

The only way out, Dummett concludes, is to abandon the view that a sentence *must be* either true or false quite independently of what we can know or not know, even if we have no possible way of deciding which it is, just as mathematical intuitionism dropped the assumption that a mathematical proposition *must be* either true or false even when we have no way of proving either its truth or the falsity of its negation. For intuitionism, correctly asserting a mathematical proposition consists in truly claiming that a proof of it either exists or can be created and understanding such a proposition consists in 'being able to recognise a proof of it when one is presented'. That a person has the capacity to do these things, he can readily show.

Extending this theory outside mathematics, in the manner Dummett attempts, involves substituting the broader notion of verification for the narrower notion of proof. 'We are entitled to say', as he puts it in 'Truth' (1959), 'that a statement P must be either true or false, that there must be something in virtue of which either it is true or it is false, only when P is a statement of such a kind that we could in a finite time bring ourselves into a position in which we were justified in asserting or denying P; that is, when P is an effectively decidable statement.' We 'correctly assert' a statement – the notion of 'correct assertion' comes to play a more central role than the 'truth' of sentences, since Dummett takes correctness 'to the primary notion' – when this 'something' obtains. We incorrectly assert it when it does not. And we know the meaning of a sentence only when we *know* what this 'something' is, what would count as conclusively establishing the correctness of our assertion. Inevitably, this doctrine reminds us of logical positivism in its first state and Dummett has sometimes been dismissed as a resurrectionist. But following Quine – once more, a major influence – Dummett, unlike the positivists, rejects the view that verification will normally take the form of pointing to a 'mere sequence of sense-experiences'. It can range anywhere from this to a mathematical proof, by way of a variety of inferential relationships.

Dummett, however, is still not satisfied. Further reflection leads him to wonder whether falsifiability rather than verifiability is not the primary notion. Here again the crucial question is how a person's implicit knowledge can be shown. We can more readily determine, he argues, that a speaker is ruling out a particular state of affairs than whether something has been shown to be 'true' or 'false'. Consider: 'If the President of Australia does not come, Mary will be disappointed.' We know, he says, that such a speaker is ruling out the possibility that there is no President of Australia. But we do not know whether, if the speaker suddenly discovers that there is in fact no President of Australia, he will take this to show that his original utterance is false – as distinct from, say, meaningless. And the same uncertainty attaches, more generally, to the circumstances in which a person will feel entitled to call a conditional 'false'; he may have different ideas from us on this point. So Dummett moves towards something like Jaakko Hintikka's game-theoretical semantics: 'An assertion is a kind of gamble that the speaker will not be proved wrong.'[11] In the end, and characteristically, his final conclusion is no more than that a falsificationist theory is a 'better bet' than the alternatives. For we still cannot use such a theory, he grants, to show how 'every feature of the use of a sentence can be given in terms of a recursive application to it of that central notion'. And so long as that is the case 'we remain unprovided with a firm foundation for a claim to know what meaning essentially is'.

Let us look, finally, at Dummett's anti-realism.[12] 'Anti-realism' is by no means a perspicuous concept; it is sometimes identified with phenomenalism, sometimes with instrumentalism, sometimes with nominalism. But in his 'Realism' (1963), Dummett specifically rejects the view that phenomenalism is anti-realist and in his 'Science and Commonsense' (1979) largely criticises instrumentalism, arguing that science is continuous with our everyday beliefs, except possibly in its highest reaches. Indeed, many a realist would read him with approval. Then in what sense is he anti-realist?

In the preface to *Truth and Other Enigmas* (1978), he writes thus: 'The whole point of my approach to these problems has been to show that the theory of meaning underlies metaphysics. If I have made any worthwhile contribution to philosophy, I think it must lie in having raised the issue in these terms.' What he does – and in some respects this is reminiscent of Carnap – is to state the case against realism in a way which closely relates it to his semantic theory. The controversy, he says, is about a class of statements, not about a class of entities – statements about the physical world or about mental events, mathematical statements, statements in the past or the future tense, and so on. And the question at issue is whether such statements 'possess an objective truth-value, independently of our means of knowing it'. (One could argue, of course, that certain of them do, but others do not. One might be, say, an anti-realist in mathematics but not in respect to statements about material objects.) The realist says that they do; the anti-realist that 'statements of the disputed class are to be understood only by reference to the sort of thing we count as evidence for a statement of that class'. The realist accepts the principle of bivalence, the anti-realist does not. (Later Dummett was to express himself more hesitantly on this contrast.) This ought by now to sound familiar. Indeed, expounding Dummett's semantics has been expounding his anti-realism. Of course, he takes up particular epistemological issues, especially in his 'Science and Commonsense', but we cannot follow him into these more detailed debates, except to emphasise that Dummett is by no means the totally convinced anti-realist that he is sometimes made out to be.

The realist, he thinks, has had victories which are too easy, because the real points at issue have not been clearly apprehended. Even when they are, however, the matters in dispute – such as whether 'we *could* not derive, from our training in the use of the past tense, that conception of truth as applied to statements about the past which the realist professes to understand' – are by no means easy to settle. Dummett is fully convinced, only, that he at least knows in what terms such debates have to be conducted, as being about the grounds on which statements are described as true or false.

Why, then, is it so regularly supposed that realism is about the existence of entities? Dummett looks at this question in relation to the philosophy of mathematics. The 'Platonist' is usually taken to assert that there is an objective mathematical reality, consisting of abstract objects related in abstract structures, the intuitionist that mathematical reality is something we create. Dummett does not deny that both work with this sort of picture in their mind, that the Platonist thinks of the mathematician as being like an astronomer or a geographer, the intuitionist as being like an imaginative writer. But these pictures, these metaphors, derive, so Dummett tells us, from views about whether mathematical statements must be determinately true or false; they are not the ontological foundation of the Platonist or the intuitionist argument. Similar observations apply to all realisms and anti-realisms.

Indeed, anti-realism is a global position, it offers us a way of approach to a wide range of controversies which turn out to have far more in common than we should at first suppose. It has one consequence that some will find unpalatable; in so far as it rejects the principle of bivalence, the effect is that some familiar forms of inference are no longer valid – inferences from 'that is not true' to 'that is false'. But that, Dummett argues, is not a *reductio ad absurdum*.

If the revision were too extensive then it would be, since the theory sets out, in general, 'to explain existing practice rather than to criticize it'. But, as in the mathematical case, some departures from classical logic and ordinary linguistic practice may be inevitable if we are to construct a systematic theory of meaning. 'Ordinary language' is by no means the final court of appeal. (Dummett makes it plain that although he thought of Austin as 'unquestionably a clever man', he also thought 'that the effect of his work on others was largely harmful'.)

Almost twenty years elapsed between the publication of Dummett's first article on realism and the appearance of his second article under the same title (*Synthese*, 1982). Dummett still stood fast on his principal theses: that the debate between realism and anti-realism turns around the interpretation of a class of statements and that it has something to do with whether we accept, in relation to that class of statements, the truth condition theory of meaning and the principle of bivalence. In the later article, however, he loosens the tightness of this relation. He admits, for example, that there is a 'comparatively mild' form of anti-realism, of which phenomenalism is an example, even if he still regards it as 'highly dubious whether a classical phenomenalist can properly be described as having held an anti-realist view at all.'

Classical phenomenalists, as a result 'of a lingering attachment to material-object statements', still accept bivalence for the subjunctive conditionals into which they translate certain material object statements: conditionals like 'If anyone were to have touched that object, he would have experienced a sensation of heat'. Yet at the same time they cannot, as a realist would, say that this is true because the body was hot. So they are in the position of maintaining that such a conditional must be either true or false while in many instances not being able 'to give any non-trivial answer to the question in virtue of what such a statement is true'. (Dummett regards a Tarski truth sentence of the translational sort as, in this context, trivial.) So Dummett concludes that, in consistency, phenomenalists *should* be anti-realists in his stronger definition of the term; that is why, he thinks, we commonly regard them as such.

He no longer wishes to say that anyone who accepts bivalence is automatically a realist. But he is still convinced that the issues turn around problems in the theory of meaning. He is still intent, too, on arguing that many of those whom we might be tempted to characterise as anti-realists, just because they hold that statements about certain classes of entities rest upon statements about some other class of entities, do not deserve to be thus 'honoured'.

5

Realism and Relativism

The debate between realism and anti-realism is not peculiar to Dummett; it has once again moved to the centre of the philosophical stage. 'The movement', Nelson Goodman tells us in his *Ways of Worldmaking* (1978), 'is from unique truths and a world fixed and found towards a diversity of right and even conflicting versions or worlds in the making' – a movement which, he says, Kant initiated, C.I. Lewis carried further and realists of various persuasions unsuccessfully sought to resist. Goodman's own position he describes as 'a radical relativism under rigorous restraints, that eventuates in something akin to irrealism'. There are 'rigorous restraints', then – fancy is not to be allowed unlimited liberty – but they are not the restraints which realism imposes, restraints imposed by facts. He is yet another philosopher who expresses his admiration for the boldness of those pre-Socratic philosophers who 'made almost all the important advances and mistakes in the history of philosophy', as they constructed systems on the basis of chosen starting-points.[1]

Unusually for an Englishman, Dummett had made a close study of Goodman's *The Structure of Appearance* (1951), a work of great complexity, modelled on Carnap's *Logical Construction of the World* (1928) if in a spirit influenced by Carnap's later 'principle of tolerance'. Like Carnap, Goodman set out from a set of primitive ideas, linked by elementary relations, and conjoined with definitions. On this basis, however, he tried to construct not *the* world but *a* world. He described his starting point as 'realist' in so far as he took as atoms such 'sense-qualia' as colours, sounds, degrees of warmth, temporal moments and physical locations rather than, in Carnap's manner, cross-sections of experience. (He differed from Carnap, too, in constructing his system with a 'nominalist' logic which permits no entities except individuals rather than a 'Platonist' logic which allows reference to classes.) But he was certainly, even in 1951, not a realist in the ordinary sense. He did not allow the question: 'But is the world *really* made up of sense-qualia, of segments of experience or of physical objects?'

Like Dummett, although very differently in his conception of what this would entail, Goodman thought it was more than time that philosophy became scientific. He did not take this to mean, however, that it should try to demonstrate, from an initial set of indubitable givens, what the general structure of the world must be. Science, on his view, is not like that. His sense-qualia are not pure objects of perception which offer us an immediate, indubitable apprehension of the world. Rather, they are his *chosen* starting point. He was not prepared to accept either Ayer's later view that phenomenalism is the only proper starting point or the position Ayer had once taken that the system erected on the basis of one starting point will just be in a different language from, translatable into, a system erected on the basis of a different starting point. Various starting points, on his view, are equally proper – even if a specific starting point may be preferable in terms of the fact that a more comprehensive system can be constructed by taking it as basic – and the systems erected on them can quite properly contain irreconcilable sentences.

In 1968 Goodman wrote a book called *The Languages of Art*. That fact is significant for two reasons. First, the title emphasises his predominant interest in systems of *symbols* as compared with Kant's emphasis on the structure of the mind and C.I. Lewis's emphasis on concepts. Secondly, it made plain the fact that Goodman, unlike most of his otherwise sympathetic contemporaries, takes the arts very seriously 'as modes of discovery, creation, and enlargement of knowledge in the broad sense of the advancement of the understanding'. That profoundly affects the range of 'worlds' or 'versions' he is prepared to take into account. Quine, for example, agrees with Goodman that it is possible to construct alternative scientific theories, which are not inter-translatable, and which would be 'equally sound'. But Goodman's attempt to treat with equal respect the world of commonsense – let alone the 'world' of Rembrandt or, even, the 'world' of abstract painters – 'founders', on Quine's view, 'in absurdity'.

In the light of these preliminary remarks, let us look at Goodman's case for 'radical relativism'. In a way, it is reminiscent of Berkeley's arguments against Locke's theory of substance. Everyone would admit that there are different, sometimes conflicting, sometimes reconcilable, 'versions' of the world. So, for example, visitors to China may offer us different versions of what life is like in that country. This may be simply because they have different interests or different concerns. In that case we can reconcile their different versions by saying things like: 'as an artist, he ...' or 'as a socialist, he ...' Or we may draw attention to the fact that they visited different regions of China or went there at different times. But sometimes these methods of reconciling fail us. The different versions are, as we say, 'flatly contradictory'. Then we normally conclude that one or the other is simply mistaken, and that which is wrong, or whether both are, depends on what actually happens in China. If philosophers disagree, at a much higher level of generality, about what the general structure of the world is like, we should normally take the same view, that their 'versions' of how the world is structured are correct or incorrect just in virtue of the way in which the world is *in fact* structured. Goodman is rejecting the assumptions implicit in this procedure, the assumption that a version is right if the world is of such-and-such a character.

We should rather say, so Goodman tells us, that the character of 'the world' depends upon the rightness of our description. For 'we cannot test a version by comparing it with a world undescribed, undepicted, unperceived'. 'All that we can learn about the world', he tells us, 'is contained in right versions of it'. There is no way of getting outside a particular 'version' in order to decide what the world is 'really like', any more than, so Berkeley argued, it is possible to get beyond our particular perceptions to discover what the 'underlying substance' is really like.

Goodman describes himself, then, as a pluralist. He is not, he explains, anti-scientific; he has no patience with the mystical, or humanistic, obscurantism so typical of the 1970s. Nor has he come to accept those Lewis-style 'possible worlds' which, he tartly remarks, 'so many of my contemporaries, especially those near Disneyland, are busy making and manipulating'. (Montague was at Los Angeles.) His multiple worlds are all of them, except when they fail to satisfy certain constraints, able to be regarded as *actual*, just as he took them to be in his earlier writings. What he is rejecting is physicalism, the view that physics is pre-eminent and all-inclusive, so that every other 'version must either be reducible to it or meaningless'; one cannot, he says, reduce Constable's or Joyce's world-view to physics.

How do we, whether artists or scientists or philosophers, construct a world? We do not make worlds out of nothing; what we do is to remake rather than to make, to remake that world to which we have become habituated. We remake, Goodman tells us, by decomposing, deleting, supplementing, reweighting, reordering. But under what constraints? And when are we to say that our world remaking is successful? The test, we would ordinarily reply, is truth. But this can no longer be regarded as 'correspondence with reality'. Rather, 'a version is taken to be true when it offends no unyielding beliefs and none of its own precepts'. 'Unyielding beliefs' may at a given time be 'long-lived reflections of laws of logic, short-lived reflections of recent observations, and other convictions and prejudices ingrained with varying degrees of firmness'. Precepts may be 'choices among alternative lines of reference, weightings and derivational bases'. The line between beliefs and precepts is 'neither sharp nor stable'.

So a statement about points – to take Goodman's own favourite example – can be true in a system in which points are defined in a particular way and which accepts nominalist precepts and yet false in a system which works from a different definition or accepts 'Platonist' precepts. Truth, he goes on to emphasise, is too easy to discover, provided only that we confine our attention to trivialities. Scientists go in search of scope and simplicity, rather than truths. And since, he also argues, we ought to count as a 'version' an unverbalised painting as well as a verbalised theory, it will be best to speak of 'rightness' rather than 'truth'. (It was for some decades said that Tarski had rehabilitated the concept of truth and with it the concept of 'correspondence with the facts'. But both in Dummett and in Goodman – to cite what are only examples – 'correspondence' goes and truth occupies a back-seat, whether as auxiliary to, or substituted by, 'correctness', 'rightness' or 'rational assertability'.)

The question still remains: 'What constitutes rightness?' What, exactly, are the 'rigorous restraints' to which Goodman's 'radical relativism' is subject? It is not at all easy to make out Goodman's answer to this question. He seems to be much happier when he is promulgating his relativism or discussing the ways in which even music and abstract art can count as 'versions' than he is in explaining why we should be prepared to accept constraints, as distinct from simply letting our fantasies run wild. 'Rightness of fit' comes to be Goodman's central notion. The 'fit' in question is not, of course, with an independently existing world. If we want to know whether 'a picture is rightly designed or a statement correctly describes' we 'try its fit', he says, but always in a system – for 'a design that is right in Raphael's world may be wrong in Seurat's'. When it comes to a choice between systems there are multiple criteria. These include coherence – which is having a notable revival, now that the fact that what is true in one coherent system may be false in another is no longer seen as a disadvantage – deductive rightness, inductive rightness, 'projectibility', simplicity, scope, initial credibility. Whether, with the aid of these criteria, radical relativism can be prevented from collapsing into scepticism is a crucial point at issue.

One should not suppose, of course, that in the 1970s realism had no defenders. In his *Objective Knowledge* (1972) Karl Popper carried realism of a certain kind – in the spirit of Plato, Hegel's 'objective mind', Bolzano and Frege – to an extreme point.[2] He distinguished three worlds, without wanting to insist either on the word 'world' or the precise number. World One contains physical objects and states; World Two mental objects and states; World Three 'objective contents of thought, especially of scientific and poetic thought and of works of art'.

About all three, Popper is a realist. His main concern, however, is to defend the autonomy of World Three, especially as against the view that whatever constituents he takes it to contain – problem situations, critical arguments, the contents of journals and books and, by analogy with physical and mental states, 'the state of a discussion' – either belong to or are expressions of World Two. He thinks of World Three as a natural product, like a spider's web. It has its origins in the efforts of human beings, just as it feeds back both on minds and on physical objects. Nevertheless, it develops autonomously, by processes rather like natural selection.

He takes as a case the sequence of natural numbers. We create, he grants, that sequence. But once created it sets problems. This in turn generates efforts on our part (World Two) to solve them. Our solutions add new objects to World Three – new entities, new conjectures, setting new, unintended, problems. 'Even though the third world is a human product', Popper writes, 'there are many theories in themselves and arguments in themselves and problem situations in themselves which have never been produced or understood and may never be produced and understood by men'.

Subjectivism is Popper's great enemy. It has infected, so he maintains, even science itself; he tries to drive it out of probability theory, out of quantum mechanics, with the help of his epistemology without a subject, for which what counts is *what* is before the mind, not *that* it is before the mind. It cannot be claimed, however, that his quasi-Platonic version of objectivism has succeeded in stemming the tide. Philosophers only rarely admire their children, almost never their younger children. What has been influential in Popper has been his critique of induction, his view that the choice of basic 'observation' sentences is conventional, that all observations are theory-guided. Quite against Popper's intentions, these doctrines, converging with other philosophical streams, have helped to form anti-realist rather than realist philosophies, to give heart to, rather than to subjugate, subjectivism. In other cases, what were once stalwart defenders of realism have undergone conversion. The intellectual history of Hilary Putnam is particularly striking in this regard, even if there are those who would say that to write about 'Putnam's philosophy' is like trying to capture the wind with a fishing-net.

Putnam's reputation as a vigorous contributor to contemporary philosophical controversies considerably antedates the first two volumes of his *Collected Papers* (1975). But it then became more obvious that his articles of the previous fifteen years were not just lively forays but a coherent volume of work with two main themes – realism and revisability – and a leading method: the destruction or weakening of antitheses. Let us look first at this pre-conversion Putnam.

Consider the philosophy of mathematics. In 'What is mathematical Truth?' Putnam joins Pólya and Lakatos in arguing that mathematical reasoning is much more like the reasoning of empirical scientists than the philosophical tradition has generally allowed, that quasi-empirical arguments can be, in mathematics, perfectly acceptable. He is not saying, quite, that mathematics *is* an empirical science; he is certainly not saying that proof is unimportant in mathematics. But he is weakening the force of a conventional antithesis.[3]

Mathematical statements, he also argues, are revisable. We have very good reasons for believing that mathematics is substantially correct. There are no alternative hypotheses in view. Nevertheless, he says, one cannot rule out the possibility that some mathematical statements are false. Fresh discoveries may lead us to reject, even, fundamental logical principles, commonly regarded as the extreme instance of the unrevisable. So, according to Putnam, the formalism of quantum mechanics may force us to abandon a two-valued logic. Philosophers, he complains, have still not understood the implications of the overthrow of Euclidean geometry – 'the most important event in the history of science for epistemologists' – just because they are unwilling to admit that it involved the rejection of what had been received as a 'necessary truth', namely, that physical space is Euclidean space, not simply the discovery that one could set up alternative geometries by starting from different axioms. 'The received account', he says, 'is a scandal'.

So much for revisability. What of *realism* in mathematics? Putnam warmly defends realism against nominalism, conventionalism, intuitionism. Neither physics nor logic, Putnam argues, can get along without sets. Nevertheless, he is not entirely happy with the 'Platonic' approach. It might be possible, he suggests, to give an alternative account of the mathematical facts in modal terms – no solace to the nominalist – by regarding a set as a 'permanent possibility of selection'. 'There exists a set of integers satisfying a mathematical condition' is not, he says, significantly different from 'it is *possible* to select integers so as to satisfy this condition'. While he does not want to set up a new, modal, philosophy of mathematics he sees in such alternative renderings a way of stilling our qualms about asserting the reality of sets.

In his philosophy of science, Putnam is just as insistent both on realism and on revisability. On revisability, however, he makes an important proviso: we must not, he argues in 'Philosophy of Physics' (1965), assimilate such statements as 'space has three dimensions' to ordinary empirical generalisations. Kant was right in thinking that they belong to a very special category, even if he was wrong in supposing that they were unrevisable. 'One might indeed say', Putnam sums up, 'if it were not for the appearance of straining after smartness, that there *are* necessary truths in physics, but they can be revised if necessary!' There are, that is, 'framework principles' which *can* be revised but the revision of which 'is quite a different matter from the revision of an ordinary empirical generalisation'. (Quine, of course, took a similar view.)

One of Putnam's defences of realism depends on this distinction. The existence of material objects cannot properly be described, he says, as a 'theory', if by this is meant that some scientist thought it up as a hypothesis, which was then subjected to rigorous criticism and finally accepted as the 'well-confirmed Material Object Theory'. On the contrary, it is taken for granted in science, as was the three-dimensionality of space. It is, then, a 'necessary truth', in the only sense in which there are necessary truths.

In more detail, he wants to argue that not only are electrons real but that the same is true of physical fields and physical magnitudes. This leads him to criticise both Hans Reichenbach and Adolf Grünbaum. These philosophers of science were none the less very important to him. As we earlier remarked, Reichenbach and Grünbaum were in their time exceptional in plunging into the classical problems about space and time and causality as they arise within relativity and quantum mechanics.[4] A considerable part of Putnam's work in the philosophy of science is of this same general character; we have already quoted his remark in 'Philosophy of Physics' that 'the philosophy of physics is continuous with physics itself' as distinct from being a meta-theory about how physicists proceed. Such essays as 'A Philosopher Looks at Quantum Mechanics' (1965) clearly illustrate what he means. Mathematics, science and philosophy all, on his view, interpenetrate one another. (In the heyday of ordinary language philosophy 'that's an empirical question' was used as a discussion-stopper. Not now.)

We shall not, however, follow Putnam into his interpretation of quantum mechanics but shall look rather at what he has to say about the general theory of inquiry. Here again we find him – in such essays as 'What theories are not' (1962) – breaking down distinctions and in that process 'dissolving' familiar philosophical problems. So he rejects the contrast, essential to Carnap, between 'theoretical' terms and 'observation' terms and with it the problem how the one is related to the other. Or at least he rejects it unless by a 'theoretical term' is simply meant a term 'which comes from a scientific theory'. And such terms, he says, may refer to something observable – as 'satellite' does, for example. Theoretical terms, so Putnam tells us, are learnt in the same sort of way as other terms; there is nothing peculiar about them, nothing which ought to make us uneasy until we have somehow reduced them to 'observables'. Simply as they stand, they are perfectly intelligible, in no way eliminable, and refer to entities the existence of which, in general, is quite well established. Indeed, there is no way of sharply distinguishing statements about observables from theoretical statements.[5]

Another notable feature of Putnam's philosophy of science is that he ties science to practice, in what has been the characteristically American fashion. 'The primary importance of ideas', he writes, 'is that they guide practice, that they structure whole forms of life'. True ideas are 'the ones that succeed'. Both Popper and confirmation theorists, on Putnam's view, have placed too much emphasis on the predictive power of hypotheses as distinct from their explanatory power or the ways in which they can be applied. They think of a hypothesis, in consequence, as something which is up for confirmation or falsification rather than as something to be used. And to use a hypothesis the scientist, or the technologist, wants it to be reliable – allowing for an occasional anomaly, which he is prepared to recognise as such.

Putnam acknowledges the influence, at this point, of Thomas Kuhn's *The Structure of Scientific Revolutions* (1962) from which the concept of a 'paradigm', once almost confined to grammarians, has spread like a plague across the intellectual landscape.[6] Kuhn maintains, as against Popper, that 'normal scientists' do not spend their time testing hypotheses as severely as they can but rather in trying to solve 'puzzles'. They do this with the aid of model solutions which they learn to treat as such during the course of their scientific training – along with the information they then acquire and the values they assimilate. This procedure is disrupted by scientific revolutions, not only by those spectacular revolutions, like Einstein's theory of relativity, on which Popper lays such stress, but by relatively minor revolutions, affecting, sometimes, only a quite small scientific community. Between revolutions the paradigms go unquestioned. Collingwood had argued that this was true of metaphysical presuppositions; Kuhn is pointing to scientific presuppositions of a more detailed kind, which may be practices rather than theories.

As a realist, Putnam could not go all the way with Kuhn. Kuhn, indeed, has been taken up by many contemporary anti-realisms in a manner often linked, over the head of Quine's objections, with Quine's 'ontological relativity' or his principle of the 'indeterminacy of translation'. Putnam condemns Kuhn for holding 'views on meaning and truth which are relativistic and, in my view, incorrect'; Quine has spoken of Kuhn's tendency – along with such philosophers of science as Russell Hanson and Michael Polanyi – 'to belittle the role of evidence and to accentuate cultural relativism'.[7]

In his 1969 postscript to *Scientific Revolutions* and the preface to *The Essential Tension* (1977), Kuhn distances himself from some of his admirers and replies to the charge of relativism which Putnam and Quine brought against him. He emphasises the *differentness* of science. Although he is sympathetic to sociological studies of scientific institutions, he criticises those sociologists of knowledge who 'drawing on my work and sometimes informally describing themselves as "Kuhnians" ', reject, sometimes 'stridently', his doctrine that scientists share a unique community of values. And he expresses some dismay at attempts to generalise his ideas by applying them to forms of cultural activity where there is nothing corresponding to the intensive scientific education which serves to 'normalise' scientists.

Nevertheless, he still maintains – and this is where Putnam disagrees – that a change in paradigm brings with it a change in the meaning of such scientific terms as are retained under the new regime. The upholders of the new and the old paradigm are, he says, seeing the world differently, even when they are still using the same words. Hence 'they must be using words differently', speaking from 'incommensurable viewpoints'. Once they recognise the fact that they are members of different language communities, they can try to translate from the old to the new language. But it is unlikely that they will ever succeed in doing this except by 'going native', experiencing a conversion. That is difficult for the older scientists and explains why they are seldom entirely at home with the new language even when they can translate from it; they still speak it 'like a foreigner'.

Kuhn denies the accusation that, on his view, scientists change their paradigms in a quite arbitrary fashion, even although, he admits, the change is not determined in a wholly rational manner. Their conversion can be preceded, he says, by a recognition that the familiar ways of solving puzzles are not working very well, that the 'new men' are solving what were intractable puzzles, puzzles which can be couched in a common language. The new approach sounds less strange as the new language gradually spreads, the new arguments gradually come to seem persuasive. (The analogies with other forms of conversion will be obvious; grounds are necessary, although not sufficient.)

Again, Kuhn is far from denying that science makes progress. He is not asserting, in the manner of a relativist, that one view is as good as another. For him, however, progress consists in an enlarged capacity for solving problems, not, as is commonly supposed, in 'arriving at a better representation of what nature is really like'. Here the antirealism is unmistakable.

Putnam challenges Kuhn by arguing that he fails to distinguish disagreement about the facts from disagreement about the meaning of words. New scientific theories present us with new facts about the world – that, let us say, species evolve – not a new language, or new meanings for old words, in the absolute sense that Kuhn has in mind. If we cannot make this distinction between different kinds of disagreement we should, Putnam argues, abandon the concept of meaning altogether. (Dummett, as we saw, makes a similar point.) The realist, Putnam tells us, has no problems here. No matter how our theory of electrical charge may alter, Putnam contends, the *reference* does not change. We are still talking, in our new theory, about the same physical magnitude and we can still identify it – singling it out, for example, as 'the magnitude which is causally responsible for certain effects' – in a manner that is independent of 'all but the most violent theory change'. He adopts Paul Ziff's motto: 'differences of meaning are not to be postulated without necessity'. A change in belief, on his view, is not such a necessity.

In discussing this issue, Putnam develops – in his 'The Analytic and the Synthetic' (1962) – the first of his theories of 'natural kinds'. (Putnam's Russellian capacity for changing his mind makes him very useful for our purposes. He is the history of recent philosophy in outline). The terms in a developed science, he there argues, are 'natural kinds', in the sense of being 'law-cluster concepts'. 'Energy', for example, appears in a great many different laws in different roles; these various laws and inference roles, not its role in some single law, determine its meaning. The effect is, he concludes, that any one law can be abandoned without affecting 'the identity of the cluster concept involved'. (The influence of Wittgenstein is strong at this point.) The extension of the term remains the same: 'The forms of energy and their behaviour are what they always were and are what physicists talked about before Einstein', even though the law 'e = $\frac{1}{2}mv^2$' has been replaced by a more complicated law. So it would be rash to say that any law about energy is analytic. Sentences about bachelors are in a quite different position. There are no exceptionless laws of the form 'All bachelors are ...' except 'All bachelors are unmarried'. So it cannot hurt – it will not involve deciding in advance not to accept new discoveries – to decide *always* to accept this as a law. And it is helpful for a language to contain a certain number of single-criterion words as an aid to communication. So Putnam weakens the importance of, without quite abandoning, the analytic-synthetic distinction.

Putnam's theory of 'natural kinds' is further developed in 'Is semantics possible?' (1970). On the traditional view, he says, to be a lemon is to possess certain defining characteristics, together making up the 'intension' of 'lemon' – such characteristics as being yellow, having a tart taste – which determine what is to count as a lemon, to constitute its 'extension'. But the trouble is that not all lemons have these characteristics; there are abnormal lemons. (Ryle was fond of the phrase 'with certain boring exceptions'; the exceptions are now being treated as vital.) The most one can say is that there is a 'lemon-stereotype', a 'paradigm' lemon, which has the characteristics mentioned above and to which all lemons are loosely related. But how then rule out plastic lemons, which are certainly like lemons in many of these respects? It takes scientific investigation, Putnam replies, as distinct from 'meaning analysis', to do this. In the case of the plastic lemon this will be, to be sure, a very simple investigation.

In 'Explanation and Reference' (1973), Putnam criticises his earlier paper, while still standing by much of his argument, as not only 'very poorly organised' – a criticism others have directed against many of his articles – but as failing clearly to explain 'the conditions under which a speaker who uses a word (say "aluminium" or "elm tree") is referring to one set of things rather than another' even when the speaker could not himself distinguish aluminium from molybdenum, an elm from a beech, or a lemon from a lime.

He tells at this point a science fiction story. Suppose there is a planet called 'Twin Earth', like our earth – 'Earth One' – in almost all respects, the inhabitants even talking English. But there is this difference – on Earth Two water is not H_2O but has a quite different chemical composition XYZ. This is so even although it tastes, looks and functions just like our water. Then if a chemically-informed visitor from Twin Earth visited Earth One he would at first, no doubt, suppose that 'water' had the same meaning on both planets. But he would eventually decide that he was wrong: 'On Earth One', he would finally report, 'water means H_2O not XYZ'. Now suppose that the date of this visit had been in 1750, before the relevant chemical compositions were known. He could not then have distinguished the two waters. Would he have been mistaken, under these circumstances, to report that water meant the same on the two earths? As a realist, Putnam says 'Yes'.

The anti-realist would maintain, rather, that the visitor was 'fully warranted' in reporting as he did and that 'truth' amounts to nothing more than 'warranted assertibility' – or some comparable concept. It was, on his view, *once* true that water had the same meaning on the two earths; it is no longer true. Or to put the same point differently, the reference of 'water' – what 'water' is 'true of' – once included all those liquids which had a certain taste, use etc. but now includes only such liquids as contain certain molecules. But this response, Putnam argues, is quite inconsistent both with our everyday practice and the practice of scientists, depending as both do on the concept of the growth of knowledge. We should normally say that scientists know more about gold than Archimedes did and would be prepared to accept the consequence, if it follows, that Archimedes mistakenly took some things to be gold which are now known not to be gold. Whether something is of the same natural kind as something else may take a good deal of science to determine and 'future investigation might reverse even the most "certain" example'.

As Putnam's semantic thinking develops, his 'realism' gradually assumes a more Kripkean form. He takes over a variety of the 'causal theory'; he even begins to use such notions as 'necessity' more freely. Rather than pursuing these complications, we shall turn to another main area in his *Collected Papers* – the philosophy of mind. Putnam criticises many of what have been the leading contenders in the field of philosophy of mind. Sometimes, the criticism is along what are now familiar lines, as when, in 'Brains as Behaviour' (1963), he

argues against the 'logical behaviorist' view that 'pain' is to be
identified with some constellation of behaviour. A person, he says,
might be in pain without exhibiting any form of such behaviour. And
there is no 'change of meaning' involved in taking that view. Putnam
is, he insists, talking about the very same pain the logical behaviorist
was analysing.

His criticism of the 'identity' theory – central-state materialism –
leads Putnam, however, into a new approach to the philosophy of
mind, a variety of what has come to be called 'functionalism'. In his
earlier essays on this theme, such as 'Mind and Machines' (1960),
he invokes the notion of a 'Turing machine'. Very roughly indeed,
we can think of a Turing machine as a set of instructions to perform a
set of simple operations on strings of symbols, which constitute the
'input' of the machine. These instructions are gathered into
'machine states', each of them a finite set of instructions, governed
by a master instruction which can switch states, laying down what
sets of instructions are to be followed, stage by stage, in relation to a
particular input. Thus described, to speak of a Turing 'machine' is to
say nothing about of what materials the machine is to be
constructed. The engineer later takes over, with such considerations
before his mind as cost, compactness, speed, reliability; the final
machine one engineer constructs may be very different in its choice
of materials, in the character of its switches, in the details of its
wiring, from the machine another engineer constructs. Two
chess-playing machines, let us say, can be built of very different
metals, can use valves or transistors or silicon chips, yet they can
both be the same Turing machine.

In the identity theory as Putnam states it in order to condemn it,
each type of mental state is identified with a particular type of
physical state, so that, for example, if Jules and Jim both believe that
Jean loves John their brains must be in precisely the same state.
Given what we know about the variety of ways in which the same
Turing machine can be 'realised' in a physical structure, this,
Putnam argues, is quite implausible. There is no reason why an
Extra-Terrestrial or a robot should not share this belief, even if it
wholly lacks brains.

In 'Philosophy and Mental Life' (1973) Putnam sums up his own
earlier view – he had in fact presented it more cautiously – as follows:
he had said '(1) that a whole human being is a Turing machine and

(2) that psychological states of a human being are Turing machine states or disjunctions of Turing machine states'. On that view, Jules, Jim, the Extra-Terrestrial, the robot, in believing that Jean loves John, would all be in the same 'logical' state although they are not in the same physical, or 'structural', state, i.e. we could give the same description of them in terms of the machine's formal design, as distinct from its physical embodiment.

In taking this view, Putnam came to think, he was 'essentially wrong'. For the 'logical' states of a Turing machine can be independently identified. Although a machine may be in a particular state – performing, say, a particular calculation – as a result of what it has in its memory and what it has learnt, we do not have to know this in order to identify the state it is in. In contrast, Putnam argues, identifying a state I am in as 'being jealous of X's regard for Y' will involve 'specifying that X and Y are persons and a good deal about social relations among persons'. So, he concludes, 'jealousy can neither be a machine state or a disjunction of machine states'.

For a fuller development of functionalism, partly inspired by Putnam's work but, as in Davidson's case, owing a good deal to English philosophical psychologists – especially Gilbert Ryle – we shall have to look to Daniel Dennett. In Dennett's work, first presented in *Content and Consciousness* (1969) and developed in the essays published as *Brainstorms* (1978), five lines of investigation meet: artificial intelligence, linguistics, cognitive psychology, evolutionary biology, philosophy of mind – this last conceived of as that segment of the philosophy of science which concerns itself with 'the conceptual foundations and problems of the sciences of the mind'.[8] Two things follow. First, one cannot adequately formulate Dennett's views without moving into these other fields; secondly, he takes up in turn many individual concepts – awareness, thought, pain, consciousness, for example, – in a way that does not permit a description of his work which is at once adequate and brief. We shall have to content ourselves with sketching Dennett's style of approach.

Dennett begins his *Content and Consciousness* by contending that we are not to think of words like 'belief', 'thought', 'intention', even 'pain', referentially. He compares – in Quine's manner – the use of such words to the use of 'sake' in 'for his sake' or, more controversially, to 'voice' in 'she has lost her voice'. There is no entity 'sake', no entity 'voice'. (Losing one's voice is not like losing one's keys.) Similarly, there is no such entity as a 'thought', a 'belief', even though one can quite intelligibly say 'I had a new thought last night.' So to ask whether a thought or a belief or a pain can or cannot be identified with a brainstate or with the state of a Turing machine is to ask a foolish question. The real issue is how 'the mode of discourse in which we speak of persons' – persons, as contrasted with minds are true entities – is related to 'the mode of discourse in which we speak of bodies and other physical objects'. Dennett is not rejecting physicalism, not reverting to dualism, he is simply denying that one ought to be able to find 'referents for the terms of the mental vocabulary' among 'the *things* of science' – unless there turn out to be some mental terms which 'resist all attempts to treat them as non-referential'. The mode of discourse in which we speak of persons is, he agrees with Brentano, 'intentional'. We talk, in our psychological descriptions, of people's desires, beliefs, hopes, intentions, all of which have a content. (There is always *something* that persons desire, believe, intend etc.)

This fact is often used as a refutation of physicalism. Physical states, so it is then said, are purely extensional; they are not directed toward a content. So minds cannot be physical states. Dennett rejects this argument.

Suppose, he says, we wish to predict the actions of a chess-playing machine. Then although the machine is a physical object, and we could in principle predict from a study of its immensely complicated molecular arrangement how it will respond if, for example, its opponent uses a particular opening, to do so would be a Herculean task. We could also, in principle, predict its reaction from a knowledge of its design – assuming that no element in the design malfunctions. (As knowing the design of a television set, I can predict, with this proviso, that if I switch it on and then move a particular control, the sound will come forth with a particular volume.) But the design of chess-machines is now so complex that even their designers cannot always predict how the machine will react to a particular move.

The best hope of prediction, in fact, lies in considering the machine from a 'stance' which is neither the physical stance nor the design stance but the intentional stance. One thinks of the machine as having certain information at its disposal, possessing certain goals and then working out what it is best for it to do. It is then, according to Dennett, 'a small step to calling the information possessed by the computers *beliefs*, its goals and subgoals its *desires*'. A general conclusion follows: 'a physical system can be so complex, and yet so organised that we find it convenient, explanatory, pragmatically necessary for prediction, to treat it as if it had beliefs and desires and is rational'. The reply that the machine does not 'really have' beliefs and desires is misplaced, unless we assume, as Dennett does not, that 'belief' and 'desire' are the names of peculiar entities rather than ingredients in the description of how a system operates.[9] (A very similar story can be told about animal organisms, except that 'the design stance' is then a matter of considering how the animal had to be in order to survive.)

Dennett's *Brainstorms* is rich in diagrams, 'flow-charts', to illustrate the way in which a person thinks. Somewhat in the manner of Plato's *Republic* – he himself makes the comparison – he thinks of a person as a miniature society. Like Ryle, he argues against 'ghost in the machine' theories, criticising Fodor's notion of a 'language of thought' on the ground that it assumes that there is someone to use and read the 'internal' language and just in virtue of this fact can throw no light, short of falling into a vicious regress, on the question what is involved in using a language intelligently.[10] But he does not object to our thinking pictorially of a person, or any system, as being made up of subpersons – homunculi – busily carrying information and the like, provided only that at a further level of analysis we can get rid of them.

It is easy to anticipate the objections which Dennett has had to meet, the objections, for example, that he has left out the immediacy of self-consciousness or the directness of our apprehension of pain, which could have no analogue in any artificial intelligence. His replies are manifold and ingenious. I shall comment on only one feature of them. He is not committed to saying, as I remarked, that every expression we normally use in our psychological descriptions has a reference. Some such expressions, he argues, have no part to play in any theoretical psychology. 'There is a sense', he writes, 'in which I am saying there is no such thing as a thought' – or a pain. The sense in question is that nothing conjoins the characteristics which pains and thoughts are supposed to have; they are not, then, well-formed theoretical concepts. He is not denying, in the case of thoughts, that 'there are episodes whose content we are incorrigible about'. Nor is he denying that there are 'events that control our behaviour and can often be ascribed content'. But nothing, he says, has both these characteristics. 'So much the worse for the ontological status of such things'.

To revert now to Putnam. We have described him so far as the very model of a modern realist, in James's terminology a 'tough-minded' philosopher. But we also remarked that Putnam shared Russell's capacity for changing his mind as a result of learning from his contemporaries. Antirealism is now in the air, a certain sort of 'tendermindedness' flourishes. Science and science-style philosophising, if still predominant, once again have their critics, even in the Anglo-American world; 'coherence', rather than 'correspondence with reality', is again the watchword, as it was for the British Idealists, 'holism' rather than 'logical atomism'. The entire analytic movement, it is even suggested, was just a temporary set-back to the intellectual conquest of the world by Kant and Hegel, whereas the analytic philosophers had supposed that British Idealism was a temporary aberration in the empirical tradition. In his 'Realism and Reason' (1976), writing under the influence of Dummett and Goodman, Putnam announced his partial conversion to these new trends.[11]

True enough, he still stands by what he calls 'internal realism'. That he now takes to be an empirical theory, serving to explain why earlier theories are so often limiting cases of later theories – as well as explaining such 'more mundane' facts as that by using our language we can often achieve goals, get satisfaction. Speakers, he still grants, can 'mirror the world' in the sense that they can construct a symbolic representation of their environment, even if the 'mirroring' is not to be judged, cannot be judged, by comparing its reflections with what it reflects. He now wholly rejects, however, what he calls 'metaphysical realism', defined as providing a 'model' for the relation of '*any* correct theory to all or part of THE WORLD', namely that each term in the theory has a particular relation to a piece, or kind of piece, of THE WORLD. 'Metaphysical realism' differs from 'internal realism' in two ways: first, it purports to be about all theories at once, whereas internal realism is always about a particular theory, and secondly 'THE WORLD is supposed to be independent of any particular representation of it'. It is *there*, a thing in itself, waiting for someone to represent it correctly, whereas for the internal realist there is no getting beyond *some theory or other*. For this reason, metaphysical realism has to leave open the possibility that we are 'totally unable to represent THE WORLD correctly at all'.

More generally, it has the consequence that a theory could be, by all the standards we normally apply, perfect and yet not be true. We might have verified it up to the ideal limit – Peirce's concept of an ideal limit has come to assume great importance in contemporary philosophy – and yet it might be false. That this cannot be so, Putnam tries to show by an argument derived from set theory, which purports to demonstrate that a theory cannot be 'ideal' and yet not satisfy truth requirements.

A later work *Reason, Truth and History* (1981) more clearly brings out the fact that Putnam is not simply criticising a particular epistemology but attempting to construct a total philosophy which would bear as much on ethics and aesthetics as on epistemology and metaphysics. In his characteristic manner, and so far like Derrida, he sets out to destroy dichotomies. The first to go is the absolute dichotomy between objectivity and subjectivity. Because they accept this dichotomy, he says, philosophers are led to believe that there is no third choice between being realists, then accepting some sort of 'copy' or 'correspondence' theory of reality, or collapsing into the 'cultural relativism' of a Feyerabend – who in much recent discussion is an animated *reductio ad absurdum* – or, in certain of his moods, a Kuhn. Metaphysical realism and cultural relativism are the Scylla and the Charybdis between which Putnam hopes to steer his craft, in search of a theory which, in what he takes to be the Kantian manner, 'unites objective and subjective components'.

The second antithesis which has to be 'overcome' is the fact-value dichotomy. Putnam closely connects fact with rationality. 'Crudely', he says, 'the only criterion for a fact is what it is rational to accept'. Using this criterion, he says, we shall regard as facts what philosophers – and not only philosophers – normally distinguish from facts as 'values'. For it can be quite *rational* to accept particular moral and aesthetic judgments. So there are 'value facts' just as there are subjective objective truths.

Rational acceptability, one must add, is not, for Putnam, an absolute notion. 'Our methodological principles', he writes, 'are connected with our view of the world, including our view of ourselves as part of that world, and change with time'. Does not this bring him dangerously close to what he himself calls 'some fancy mixture of cultural relativism and "structuralism", like the French philosophers' – particularly Foucault? A third dichotomy, he replies, has to go; we are not forced to choose between the concept of unchanging canons of rationality and cultural relativism. If canons change, it is for good reason. Here as elsewhere he thinks in terms of a feedback; what we discover can force us to change our canons, our change of canons can affect what we discover, just as our discoveries can change our theories but what we discover can depend on our theories. (Compare the 'hermeneutic circle'.)

Two more false antitheses have still to bite the dust. First, rationality within science is not of a superior or inferior sort to rationality outside science. The canons of rationality apply generally. Secondly, while one must not say that the mind simply *copies* a world which admits of description by One True Theory, a view Putnam ascribes to Physicalism, we must not say, either, that 'the mind *makes up* the world'. If we need a metaphor, he says, it should rather be this: 'the mind and the world jointly make up the mind and the world'. At this point, he bows in the direction of Hegel, who would certainly have complained, however, that he is still far too Kantian.

We cannot follow Putnam through his somewhat tortuous discussion – often making use of arguments he had used previously in a somewhat different intellectual context – although his complex theory of 'reference' would repay attention. Let us consider just one point: his attempt to relate scientific rationality to human flourishing. If we look, he says, at the theories which 'scientists and other people consider it rational to accept', we find that they are 'representations of the world' which have certain virtues: they are 'instrumentally efficacious, coherent, comprehensive and functionally simple'. Why do we regard these as virtues? The 'metaphysical realist' would argue that we hope by this means to arrive at a theory which 'matches' the world. Putnam replies, in a Kantian fashion, that this is nonsense if we are thinking in terms of a match with some independent, noumenal, world. The only 'fit' can be with our empirical world. (His theory of reference makes this same point.) But we accept a particular world as being the empirical world, he continues, only because it is rationally acceptable – even if our ideas of rational acceptability can in turn be modified by our acceptance of that world. Our notion of what counts as 'an optimal speculative intelligence' – an evaluative concept – thus makes possible our concept, even, of our empirical world.

'Optimal' does not here mean something like 'cleverest'. At the crown of Putnam's new position lies the view that our concept of rationality is 'at bottom, just one part of our concept of human flourishing, our idea of the good'. (One is reminded of William James.) Doesn't this mean that there is at least one thing we know once and for all, namely in what human flourishing consists, even if our judgments of what it is rational to believe will change from time to time as the conditions under which human beings flourish change? Not at all: there is no 'ahistorical set of moral principles which determine once and for all what human flourishing consists in'.

We are not to conclude, however, that 'it's all merely cultural and relative'. Again and again, we find him maintaining that 'cultural relativism' is self-defeating. He derives from Wittgenstein an argument which he formulates thus: 'The relativist cannot, in the end, make any sense of the distinction between *being right* and *thinking he is right*; and that means that there is, in the end, no difference between *asserting* or *thinking*, on the one hand, and *making noises* (or *producing mental images*) on the other'. The consequence then follows, he says, that 'I am not a *thinker* at all but a *mere* animal'. And this conclusion he characterises as 'mental suicide'.

This exceptionally emphatic passage leaves us with no doubt that Putnam does not wish to be characterised as a relativist. We find ourselves driven in that direction, he argues, only if we interpret physics in too realistic a fashion, as the One True Theory, or, at least, as the only near approximation to it. Then we are forced to conclude that such concepts as 'human flourishing' or, what is related to this, the properties – such properties as coherence and simplicity – by which we characterise theories, as distinct from the assertions which form part of the theory, must be purely objective. So although metaphysical realism at first sight appears to be a defence against relativism, it ends up, he concludes, by encouraging it, in relation to everything except physics.

Tightrope-treading is very common among philosophers who hope to avoid total relativism while at the same time rejecting 'metaphysical realism'. Putnam said of cultural relativism that it is in fact a form of scientism – taking anthropology rather than physics as its model. But it is often linked, rather, with that historical approach to the philosophy of science which has rebelled against the attempt to describe science as a model of pure rationality, a rationality which works in isolation from political and social pressures, proceeding from one triumph to another by employing a universally applicable scientific method.

When, in 1968, P.H. Nidditch prepared his anthology *The Philosophy of Science*, he commented in his preface on two characteristics of the essays he had selected: the first, that they paid very little attention to actual scientific practice, the second that they analysed science as if it were static, offering no account of scientific progress. There is still a great deal of philosophy of science to which these comments would apply. Nidditch, its authors would say, disregarded Reichenbach's distinction between the context of discovery and the context of justification. If one wants to know how discoveries are made, what scientists actually do when they regard themselves as making progress, we should look, so they tell us, not to philosophy but to psychology or to sociology (the favourite philosophical dustbins). Philosophy of science is only interested in such logical questions as how a theory can be rationally supported by evidence.

In pursuit of an answer to this particular question, philosophers have turned in a variety of directions, in a manner too complex, too technical and too subtly diversified to permit of any but the most summary description. More often than not, they make use of probability theory, refining upon one or the other of the theories described in *A Hundred Years* or drawing upon such subsequent developments as Popper's Peirce-like propensity theory or elaborated forms of Ramsey's subjectivist analysis. These stand poles apart. Popper, as we saw, is bitterly opposed to any form of subjectivism. On his propensity view, the probabilities attaching to the fall of dice are as much objective properties of the dice as are their fields of force. For the subjectivist, in contrast, to say that the dice's falling as double sixes has a certain probability is to say something about our willingness to bet that they will do so. And subjectivists are prepared to take a similar view about the relation between evidence and hypothesis – that the probability of an hypothesis on certain evidence is identical with our willingness to bet upon it, given that evidence, just as, given certain evidence, we might be prepared to bet that a particular horse will win a particular race. Leonard Savage and Bruno de Finetti refined that thesis by developing methods of making our choices more coherent – so that we shall not, for example, make bets of such a character that whatever happens the bookmaker is sure to win – and by calling upon the resources of Bayesian probability theory to take account of prior probabilities. Subjectivist theories have been developed, indeed, to a high degree of mathematical sophistication, even if at the cost, some think, of departing ever further from our intuitive probability judgments and identifying science with a 'closed' rather than an 'open' game. (There are just so many horses in a race, the number of possible hypotheses is not similarly limited.) Other theorists have drawn upon the theory of games or decision theory or consensus theory to justify the acceptance of one particular hypothesis, the rejection of another.[12]

Having noted this considerable literature, however, we shall concentrate on a group of writers who reject all of it, as attempting the impossible. By doing so, they have strengthened the movement towards some form of relativism, whether deliberately or not. Some of them were at one time associates of Karl Popper. An important turning point is the volume of essays edited by Imre Lakatos and Alan Musgrave as *Criticism and the Growth of Knowledge* (1970), designed as a confrontation between Kuhn and Popper. Popper's position is exceptional. He rejected induction, he denied that there was any way in which the probability calculus could be applied to the justification of hypotheses – as opposed to the neo-Bayesian view that while there was no such thing as induction one could correct one's hypotheses by appealing to relative probabilities – he denied, even, that there was any such thing as 'justification' in the full-blooded sense of that word. And yet at the same time he refused to base his philosophy of science on actual scientific practice, to accept any form of that consensus theory according to which (when what is in question is the acceptability of scientific hypotheses) the judgment of scientists is the final court of appeal.

He took, furthermore, a distinctly jaundiced view of both history and sociology – he tended to run the two together – as forms of inquiry. 'The idea of turning for enlightenment concerning the aims of science and its possible progress to sociology or psychology or the history of science', he writes in his reply to Kuhn, is 'surprising and disappointing'. These forms of inquiry, he tells us, are 'riddled with fashions and with uncontrolled dogma'. One would first have to be able to distinguish science from pseudo-science, therefore, in order to know what to count as science in these fields. Without falling into a vicious infinite regress, one cannot use them to distinguish science from pseudo-science – for Popper the question of questions. There is, he believes, a logic of inquiry, even though it is not inductive logic. And logic cannot be overthrown by history.

Many of his students and colleagues were unconvinced by this reply, even when they wanted to dispute Kuhn's more particular views about normal science and scientific revolutions. Popper had said that conjectures and refutations were the path to progress in science. If it could be shown that proceeding thus would have held up the advance of science, at least on some important occasions, then this, they thought, would show that Popper was in error or at the very least – remembering his claim to be putting forward a normative rather than a descriptive theory – that he was giving bad advice to scientists.

Let us look more closely at two of those who took that view, Imre Lakatos and Paul Feyerabend.[13] As we have already briefly seen, Lakatos first came to notice with a philosophy of mathematics, in a series of articles with the Popper-echoing title 'Proofs and Refutations' (*BJPS*, 1963-4, posthumously published in 1976 as a book). In general terms, this applied to mathematics a sophisticated version of Popper's falsificationism. One has to emphasise 'sophisticated'. Lakatos spent a great deal of time distinguishing this from 'naive' falsificationism, the doctrine commonly ascribed to Popper by friend and foe alike. He recognised that Popper, in his more careful moods, is not saying that a theory ought to be dropped as soon as some observation is made which seems to be incompatible with it. But Lakatos gradually, under the influence of historical studies, came to the conclusion that even sophisticated falsificationism would not do. 'In science, we do not learn simply from conjectures and refutations' – so he summed up his conclusion in 'Anomalies versus "crucial experiments"' (1975?). From Popper's long-unpublished *Postscript* he picked up the idea of a 'research programme' and made that central to his thinking. It is not, he says, just a matter of history that scientists often ignore anomalies, objections, apparent refutations, not just a result of their being psychologically weak or under sociological pressure. It is *necessary* for them to do so. If we were to argue that their acting thus is irrational, we should have to conclude that science itself is irrational.

The 'great achievements' of science, its great 'theories' are not, for Lakatos, to be thought of as isolated hypotheses but rather as fruitful research programmes. And once such a 'theory' is lit upon, it is quite irrational, he argues, to abandon a programme which is generating 'dramatic, unexpected, stunning' predictions merely because there are 'known facts' which seem to be incompatible with the principles on which the programme rests, its core doctrines. Contrariwise, the 'central core' of the programme has to be zealously protected against falsifications – so long as it continues to be fruitful. The scientist has a 'negative heuristic', to protect that core by auxiliary hypotheses, as well as a 'positive heuristic', to construct models which serve to modify, in an ever more fruitful way, those protective hypotheses. Its success in doing so will be measured by its ability to protect the core while using the hypotheses to make novel predictions. So far, as he freely admits in his 'Methodology of Scientific Research Programmes' – first published in *Criticism and the Growth of Knowledge* – he is prepared to accept Poincaré's conventionalism. Yet not wholly. For he grants that 'the hard core can crumble'. But that will not be in the face of observations. Perhaps because he began from mathematics and, like so many philosophers of science, constantly has mathematical physics before his mind as the typical science, Lakatos places very little stress on observation. 'If a scientist (or a mathematician) has a positive heuristic', he is prepared to write, 'he refuses to be drawn into observation'. Faced with a problem, he will 'lie down on his couch, shut his eyes and forget about the data'. What destroys his programme is not an anomalous observation but the emergence of a better, more fruitful, programme. His programme, too, may stagnate, degenerate. That will come out in its failure any longer to make novel predictions, to develop auxiliary hypotheses, to turn anomalies into corroborations, thus protecting its central core. Its 'positive heuristic', that is, has weakened and with it its justification as a research programme. But, Lakatos adds, we cannot be quite sure that this 'degeneration' might not turn out to be only a passing phase – as it was, to take an un-Lakatosian example, in the case of the Darwinian theory of natural selection.

Lakatos read Popper in a prison-camp and the (Marxist) scales fell from his eyes. The relation between Feyerabend and Popper is much less straightforward. In his later writings Feyerabend makes it plain that he much dislikes being described as a former (or neo-) Popperian. Yet in his 'How to be a good Empiricist' (1963), he had not hesitated to say that his 'general outlook' derived from Popper and the philosopher-physicist David Bohm.[14] His earlier work – much of it now available, along with more recent work, in his *Philosophical Papers* (1981) – won for Feyerabend a considerable reputation as a philosopher of science who was prepared to think historically and to immerse himself in scientific detail. He defended two principles – realism as against positivism or instrumentalism, proliferation as against the Kuhnian view that science progresses by committing itself to a single paradigm. Realism he links with testability; for the realist it is always possible to envisage the possibility that our observations are erroneous, as is not the case if our starting point is taken to be a sense-datum or some combination of sense-data. And our theories, too, can be erroneous, as on the instrumentalist view they cannot be. Proliferation is a concept he takes over, as he always insists, from J.S. Mill's *On Liberty*. Science flourishes, he argues, when there is a variety of hypotheses in the field; its tendency to harden into dogma, to treat as 'abnormal' alternative views to those which are commonly accepted, is in opposition to the conditions of scientific progress. The history of science, he says, soon reveals how often the scorned view turns out to be the one that is finally fruitful.

It is scarcely surprising that this earlier Feyerabend was read as a dissident Popperian or, at the very least, as a respectable philosopher of science with somewhat unorthodox views. The later Feyerabend, in contrast, is widely regarded as disreputable, a judgment that has to some degree reflected back on his earlier writings. The break began with *Against Method* (1975), originally designed as an open letter to his 'friend, and fellow-anarchist' Lakatos. In his later *Science in a Free Society* (1978), he develops his views further, in large part by way of a series of unprecedently lengthy and vitriolic replies to reviewers. In an essay he prepared for the second volume of his *Philosophical Papers*, under the heading 'Historical background: Some observations on the decline of the Philosophy of Science', he brought together his newer views as a defence of 'democratic relativism'.

One can roughly sum up his extremely elusive argument – he was trained as an actor and likes to assume a mask, if only in the interests of a continuing drama – in two theses. The first is that whenever one tries to set down any procedure whatsoever as a method which has to be adopted if science is to progress – even the 'anything goes' procedure particularly associated with his name – it is possible to point to circumstances under which this is not the best method to adopt. 'There is not a single rule, however plausible, and however firmly grounded in epistemology', he tells us in *Against Method*, 'that is not violated at some time or other' and this not out of ignorance or carelessness but because such violations are '*absolutely necessary* for the growth of knowledge'. So there are times 'when it is advisable to introduce, elaborate, and defend *ad hoc* hypotheses, or hypotheses which contradict well-established and generally accepted experimental results' and so on – with a special eye on Popperian theses. Lakatos, he thought, had really reached the same conclusion even if he was not quite ready to admit it. For Lakatos gave no good formal reason for transferring from one research programme to another. He admits that what appears to be the degenerating programme can in fact turn out to be the progressive programme. To be sure, since Lakatos suggests that grant-awarding bodies, editors and the like are entitled to ignore degenerating programmes, a scientist may have good *prudential* grounds for switching his allegiance. That will not, for Feyerabend, count as rationality.

Feyerabend has a still deeper reason for disagreeing with Lakatos and it is at this point that Feyerabend most sharply separates himself from philosopher-of-science respectability. Lakatos simply presumes, · he says, that science is the best way of coming to understand and control the world. Feyerabend sees science as having become an 'Establishment'. No 'democratic relativist' can accept the view that a particular tradition, whether the scientific or any other tradition, has the kind and degree of authority which science tries to arrogate to itself. His central aim, he tells us, is to remove those obstacles which intellectuals and scientists 'create for traditions different from their own' as, to cite his favourite example, 'scientific medicine' puts obstacles in the way of 'alternative medicine'. Popper, he grants, had also said that there was no such thing as scientific method. But what was at best a set of hints, things sometimes worth taking into account, had hardened at his hands and those of his followers into a set of necessary conditions for 'being rational'. In Feyerabend, the Wittgensteinian 'language game' comes to be thought of as more generally illuminating than the doctrine of conjectures and refutations, applicable as the former is to a wide range of traditions, each with its own method of coping with problems. As for philosophy of science in general, 'almost every journal in the philosophy of science deals with problems that are of no interest to anyone except a small gang of autistic individuals'. Feyerabend is sometimes dismissed as a mountebank. When, however, he puts on the comic mask that is in the interest of exposing what he regards as a tragedy.

Yet another historically minded philosopher of science is Mary Hesse, often cited by sociologists of science. In *The Structure of Scientific Inference* (1974) she had contributed to the debate about the relation between observation statements and the credibility of hypotheses, suggesting means by which a set of individually unreliable observation statements can together lend credibility. But her historical work emphasises the importance in the development of science of analogy, metaphor, imagination – none of them reducible to a method. In the essays collected as *Revolutions and Reconstructions in the Philosophy of Science* (1980) she relates herself to the 'historically orientated' work of Kuhn, Feyerabend and Toulmin, if also to Quine's epistemology and further back to Duhem, who has emerged as a central figure in contemporary philosophy of science.[15] She also has a good deal to say about Habermas and about Gadamer's hermeneutics, just as Putnam refers, not always impolitely, to Foucault, to Apel and to Althusser. That is not surprising; the critique of scientism has long been a Continental specialty.

The degree of parallelism between Putnam and Hesse is striking – is the Spirit of the Age there visible? – given that Putnam does not mention Hesse and that Hesse's references to Putnam are to his earlier realism. They both attack naive realism, the concept of a universal scientific language – physicalism in particular – and the correspondence theory of truth. Hesse places special stress on the Duhem-Quine concept of 'the underdetermination of theory by empirical data', the fact that there are always 'an indefinite number of theories that fit the observed facts more than adequately'. Indeed, Quine, that staunch defender of science, now serves as an armoury for those who wish either to attack science outright or, at the very least, to curb its wings, somewhat as in the sixteenth and seventeenth centuries the arguments of sincere defenders of Christianity were sometimes enthusiastically adopted by its critics, when the defence took the form of arguing that Christianity rests on faith rather than rational demonstration. Popper's attack on induction, Quine's doctrine of indeterminacy, have both been seized upon as demonstrating that scientific theories are in no stronger position, from the standpoint of rationality or truth, than any other imaginative creation. Their protests to the contrary have been set aside as nothing more than a new form of fideism, if with science rather than God as its object.

The defenders of science would commonly reply that scientific theories have peculiar advantages over their rivals. Hesse ascribes to them 'the principle of convergence', the principle that 'accumulating data plus coherence conditions ultimately converge to true theory'. For two reasons this, she says, will not work. The first reason – much emphasised by contemporary sociologists of knowledge – is that data, 'observable statements', have to make use of classificatory descriptive predicates. And the 'natural kinds' referred to in such descriptions are in no sense 'given'; scientists classify in accordance with what they regard as a correct theory. As Putnam also argues in his antirealist papers, things do not *announce* themselves as being of a certain sort. (This Duhemian view that all observations are 'theory laden' is central to contemporary relativisms, moderate or extreme, although it was neither designed for that purpose nor invoked for that reason by Popper or Quine or Hanson.)[16]

So much for 'accumulated data'. The second problem relates to 'coherence conditions' – simplicity, consistency and the like. Where do they come from? Why should we accept them as virtues? They have often been described as 'logically necessary'. In fact, so Hesse replies, any such condition has either already been violated by good science in the past or may well be violated in the future.

Surely, we naturally object, science does in fact converge. To a striking extent, natural scientists come to agree, as philosophers and social scientists do not. This, according to Hesse, is an *instrumental* convergence; science offers us greater control, by the method of theory-construction. The convergence, she adds, 'at best entails increasing approximation of low-level laws and predictions to the subsequently tested data' and is even then limited to what is only a fragment of the universe, spatially and temporally. There is 'no convergence to an ideal conceptual language'. Indeed, 'no empirical theory at any given stage of development can be said to be empirically true in a strictly propositional sense'. When philosophers turn to science for broad theories of the world, for cosmologies, they are turning to it precisely at the point, then, where its claims are weakest, where scientists are most likely to be in error. Engineers, in contrast, turn to science at the point where it is strongest.

Hesse does not see herself as a sceptic, and certainly not as an Idealist. In her 'Reasons and Evaluation in the History of Science' (1973) she attacks those among her fellow-historians who argue that there is no sharp distinction between the 'new science' of the seventeenth century and the magical hermeticism which is contemporary with it. Science *is*, in her view, different; in the seventeenth century 'a new form of rationality can be seen to be distinguishing itself from traditional modes of thought'. A complete relativism, she adds, would make history itself impossible, in so far as 'it has to rely on an accepted form of scientific practice'. She begins to wonder, in 'Truth and the Growth of Scientific Knowledge' (1976), whether her long advocacy of a close relation between history and philosophy of science has not had 'unfortunate consequences'. The historian quite properly asks why, given the indeterminacy of theories by facts, scientists prefer one theory to another. Recognising that there is no purely formal answer to that question, the historian, Hesse thinks, can offer answers in social and political terms. But the purely philosophical task of 'analysing the nature and limitations of our conceptions of truth and rationality' still remains.

One other question worries Hesse. It is characteristic of attempts, from Duhem on, to deprecate reliance on science in its more theoretical cosmological reaches as the sole correct picture of the world, that they hope by this means to 'leave room' for something else – whether religion, or art, or metaphysics, or a sociology whose claims to be a science have been so often disputed. One can plainly see this both in Duhem and Putnam; Hesse is certainly no exception. Yet this leaves her with a problem. The abandonment of naive realism about cosmological theories, means, she says, that 'there can no longer be any straightforward conflict between accounts of the external world given in science and theology'. Since theology is a different theory, its 'facts' will naturally be different. But what is now the status of those doctrines of creation and providence that are so central to the Christianity to which she is committed? In terms of her general view, they must be ideological in the same sense in which, so she argued in 'Truth and Value in the Social Sciences' (1978), 'comprehensive theories in the human sciences' are ideological – they incorporate evaluations, which can be constrained by facts but are not determined by them.

Indeed, in the manner of Emile Durkheim – who, along with Marx and Max Weber, is now a major point of contact between philosophy and sociology – one can think of both religious and scientific cosmologies as belonging, she suggests, to the category of 'collective representations'. They are symbolic systems 'situating human societies in the natural world'. At this point, she concedes, 'the threat of relativism becomes very pressing'. For 'neither scientific realists nor moral absolutists nor religious believers' are prepared to admit that their theories are simply the products of social necessities.

In the case of science, Hesse has suggested, the relativity of its conceptual frameworks does not seriously matter; the assumption that there is some kind of non-relative truth is 'idle' in respect to science's successes – 'the real attainment of *approximate* truth in pragmatic contexts'. In ideological contexts, however, it is far from idle. Our practical decision-making 'depends on commitment to the content of actual conceptual frameworks, historically relative though these may appear to be'. She leaves unsolved this problem of 'how to validate ideology'; she claims, only, that she has shown that the possibility of doing so 'can no longer', if she is right, 'be prejudged by any monopolistic cognitive claims for scientific cosmology'. The fact, that is, that ideologies cannot be 'validated' by some sort of 'scientific method' does nothing to show that they cannot be validated at all; she looks hopefully in the direction of hermeneutics, if it is scarcely made plain exactly how she expects salvation to come from that quarter.

Richard Rorty looks in the same direction but with a somewhat different final intent and as one who once worked within the heartland of professional Anglo-American philosophy. His anthology *The Linguistic Turn* (1967) reveals his mastery of the linguistic philosophising then current, in all its forms. Yet his lengthy introduction already announces the critical themes which were to be more fully developed in his 1972-80 essays, finally collected as *Consequences of Pragmatism* (1982), and in his major work *Philosophy and the Mirror of Nature* (1980).

He there discusses almost every philosopher we have considered in this epilogue – with Popper and David Lewis as notable omissions – never with total acceptance but rarely with quite unmitigated hostility. The exceptions, in this latter respect, are Kripke and Dummett – Kripke as a realist, Dummett because he looks forward to a philosophy which will share the characteristics of a Kuhnian 'normal science'. Such reactionaries apart, Rorty sees philosophy as moving in quite the opposite direction, away from realism and away from the conception of philosophy as being, ideally at least, scientific in character.[17] This applies as much, he thinks, to Quine, Sellars, Davidson as it does to the later Wittgenstein, Heidegger and Gadamer, for all that the American philosophers do not see what they are doing in quite this light.

Sellars, Rorty tells us, destroyed the 'myth of the given' even if he still, mistakenly, clung to analytical propositions; Quine destroyed the analytic, and with it the distinction between the factual and the conceptual, even if he still, mistakenly, stood by the given; Davidson, under Quine's influence, freed us from the idea that there are 'conceptual frameworks' as distinct from empirical theories. In so doing, these philosophers also ruled out the possibility of constructing a scientific philosophy, whether by attempting to build up the world from 'given' foundations, or by taking as a point of departure indubitable analytic truths, or by seeking to determine what our 'conceptual framework' must be, or by 'analysing concepts'.

Looking back at the story I have told, one might well conclude that philosophy has now returned to where it was at the turn of the century, battling between realism and idealism. Rorty disagrees. The new antirealism, he argues, is very different from the old idealism; that idealism competed with realism in giving the One True Picture of the world. The new antirealism, in contrast, sets any such project aside as impossible in principle. What Rorty takes over from such idealists as Hegel, as from Heidegger, is not a philosophical system but the idea of what he calls 'the temporalisation of reality', with its concomitant doctrine that to try to look at the world *sub specie aeternitatis* is to pursue a hopeless task. Indeed, if 'realism' means no more than that most of what we believe is true – as opposed to the idealist doctrine that it is 'only an appearance' of absolute truth – Rorty is willing to call himself a realist. For Quine and Davidson have shown, he believes, that if this were not so we could never learn, or translate, a language.

One might more generally conclude from our story that philosophy still fails to make progress, in the sense in which science progresses. If we mean by 'progress' getting nearer to solving what, from the seventeenth century onwards, have been thought of as the 'great problems', Rorty would agree. (The phrase 'from the seventeenth century onwards' is Rorty's; one might well object that some, at least, of these 'great problems' already raise their head in Plato's *Theaetetus, Parmenides* and *Sophist*. That would not be irrelevant to Rorty's historically-based argument.) But progress *has* occurred, Rorty would continue, in so far as we now see that we can rid ourselves of these 'great problems', not by 'solving' them but by casting them aside as pseudo-problems, generated by our starting from a particular picture of knowledge. If we begin by supposing that there is an entity called 'the mind' and another entity called the 'world', which the mind 'has knowledge of' by way of its privileged access to a set of representations which mirror that world then we are at once faced, automatically, with those problems which make up what Rorty – to mark its official status – capitalises as 'Philosophy'.

We are readily led, too, into the doctrine, for which Rorty holds Kant and the neo-Kantians responsible, that there is a subject called 'epistemology' in which 'Philosophers' are peculiarly expert. It tells us what 'knowledge' is. And this gives 'Philosophy', it is then supposed, a certain supremacy in the realm of culture, since every other kind of inquiry has to look to philosophy before it can be quite sure that it has attained 'real knowledge'. 'Scientific philosophy' is, then, epistemology, sometimes identified with philosophy of science. The situation is not substantially improved, Rorty argues, if linguistic representations (words or sentences) replace mental representations (ideas); the old problems, for the most part, still persist.[18]

What is needed, rather, is a clean sweep, in Wittgenstein's manner. The later Wittgenstein Rorty interprets as a satirist, undermining 'Philosophy' – including his own *Tractatus* – and thereby helping philosophers to shake themselves free from the pictures which have held them in thrall. In the process they will see that the ideal of a scientific philosophy is absurd. Wittgenstein belongs with Nietzsche or Heidegger, as purging 'Philosophical' pretensions, not with Kant or Russell. He does not offer a solution to the 'great problems' – at least in his better moods. Rather, he persuades us to drop them, just as in the seventeenth century so many thinkers dropped theology, as distinct from trying to offer new solutions to familiar theological problems or scrutinising theological arguments point by point.

Then what is left for philosophy to do, now that it sees how to liberate itself from 'Philosophy'? Rorty looks back with evident nostalgia to the days when Dewey and Santayana – the first especially – occupied the centre of American culture. The professionalisation of philosophy, based on the false idea that it should imitate science, has had the effect, he says, that the leading cultural figures are now the literary critics, about whose intellectual proclivities – their name-dropping, their elusive references, their imprecision, their contorted vocabulary – he speaks with a degree of favour many will find surprising. Dewey, in Rorty's eyes, made one bad mistake; he wrote *Experience and Nature*, in which he promulgated a new metaphysics. He was not quite ready, as Rorty is, to abandon the old Platonic distinction between the poet – the sage – and the philosopher. But in writing about art, science, morality, culture, politics, society, education, he saw what philosophy should be like.

One thing 'Philosophers' pride themselves on, and do not find in many of the writers Rorty praises, is close reasoning. They have come to suppose that adversarial argument, of a quasi-legal sort, stands to philosophy as experiment does to science; they have sought out pupils who are gifted in this respect and tried to develop these capacities in them. The real task of philosophy is, according to Rorty, very different – to keep in motion a conversation. (Feminist critics of philosophy, as exemplified in the philosophers brought together by Merrill Hintikka and Sandra Harding in *Discovering Reality*, 1983, have attacked the adversarial method in similar terms, adding that it is a peculiarly masculine device.) The adversarial conception of philosophy, so Rorty goes on to suggest, rests on the notion that 'Philosophy' can by argument establish epistemological foundations, criteria, rules, which are externally valid. But in fact the most an epistemological philosopher can do is to explore the rules, criteria, which a particular form of activity makes use of, and the paradigms on which it relies when it is in a Kuhnian-normal phase.

That is far from being the main task of philosophy. Its more important concern is with 'edifying' rather than analysing, with the abnormal rather than the normal, with trying out new ways of looking at things. 'Edifying' here has some such sense as 'contributing to one's education', to one's *Bildung*. That is the point at which Rorty invokes hermeneutics.[19] It is not to be thought of as a new epistemology, relating in Dilthey's manner to the social as distinct from the physical sciences. Rather, it is an attempt, in Gadamer's manner, to fill the gap in human culture resulting from the demise of epistemology, by creating a theory of understanding, of the ways in which our capacity to understand is tradition-impregnated. This is somewhat as science filled the gap created by the death of theology.

Where does truth come into the picture? In *Consequences of Pragmatism* and especially in the preface to that collection, one sees more plainly to what a degree Rorty is setting out to reinstate pragmatism. (It is an extraordinarily widespread phenomenon, this tendency of American philosophers to turn pragmatist as they grow older.) The pragmatism to which he subscribes, furthermore, is not Peircean pragmatism, relatively rigid and terminating in the concept of an ideal truth, but the much more 'edifying' pragmatism of James and Dewey. Hegel's admonition: 'Philosophy must beware of the wish to be edifying' is nowadays getting less and less of a hearing. Truth, Rorty says, is like goodness, not the sort of thing one can expect to have an interesting general theory about. There are many different morally praiseworthy actions. But their diversity is such as to make it very unlikely that they have any characteristics in common. There are propositions, similarly, which it is morally praiseworthy to assert. But it is equally unlikely, so Rorty tells us, that they have some property – 'truth' – in common.

He is prepared, then, to accept William James's definition of truth: 'The name for whatever proves itself to be good in the way of belief, and good, too for definite assignable reasons.' The natural question whether this itself is true is not, he says, a question about what the word 'true' means, 'nor about the requirements of an adequate philosophy of language, nor about whether "the intuitions of our culture" are captured in the pragmatists' slogans'. It is a question, rather, about whether 'a post-Philosophical culture is a good thing to try for'. Rorty, it would seem, has some vestigial qualms on this point – not surprisingly, perhaps, when one compares the socio-political record of those who have extolled and those who have condemned, whether as poets or philosophers, the ideal of a 'scientific philosophy.'

Notes

AJP	*Australasian Journal of Philosophy*
APQ	*American Philosophical Quarterly*
BJPS	*British Journal for the Philosophy of Science*
HY	*A Hundred Years of Philosophy, 2nd ed., 1966*
JP	*Journal of Philosophy*
JSL	*Journal of Symbolic Logic*
PAS	*Proceedings of the Aristotelian Society*
PASS	*Proceedings of the Aristotelian Society, Supplementary Volume*
PBA	*Proceedings of the British Academy*
PQ	*Philosophical Quarterly*
PR	*Philosophical Review*
RIP	*Revue Internationale de Philosophie*
RM	*Review of Metaphysics*
TLS	*Times Literary Supplement*

N.B. Given contemporary publishing habits, there are often delays between the official and the actual publishing date or between the date of English and American editions, let alone between the date at which a paper was delivered, or circulated, and its publication date. In general, I have tried to give the printed date of the first published edition but I may well be sometimes wrong by a year, or even more. If someone is described as replying to a book or paper not published until after the reply, this is not necessarily an error.

1. Introduction: Change and Continuity

1. A useful point of entry to contemporary philosophy as a whole is T. Honderich and M. Burnyeat (eds), *Philosophy as It Is* (1979), a selection of essays and book extracts, with introductions and prefatory notes. A.J. Ayer's *Philosophy in the Twentieth Century* (1982) is polemical history, Ayer disputing with predecessors and contemporaries. There is a fuller account of some of the philosophers I shall be discussing in W. Stegmüller, *Hauptströmungen der Gegenwarts-Philosophie*, vol.2 (1975). It is particularly strong on logic and semantics but also includes a lengthy study of contemporary developments in science. P. Ricoeur, *Main Trends in Philosophy* is a Unesco Publication, in essence by many hands, first published separately in 1979 but terminating about 1970. The volumes

entitled *Contemporary Philosophy: A New Survey* (1981-) published under
the auspices of the International Institute of Philosophy, contain, like
their predecessors *Philosophy in Mid-Century* (1958) and *Contemporary
Philosophy* (1968), critical surveys of new philosophy in a wide variety of
fields. A.R. Lacey, *Modern Philosophy* (1982) is a systematic introduction
to the central problems of contemporary British philosophy. See also
E.D. Klemke (ed.), *Contemporary Analytic and Linguistic Philosophies* (1983).
J.R. Burr, *Handbook of World Philosophy Since 1945* (1980) is accurately
self-described. It is a useful introduction to Oriental and African
philosophy.

2. One of the many marginal areas I have left unexplored is the philosophy
   of religion. See S. Cahn and D. Shatz (eds), *Contemporary Philosophy of
   Religion* (1982) with bibliography (1965-80) and, subsequently, J.L.
   Mackie, *The Miracle of Theism* (1982). On ethics generally see W.D.
   Hudson, *A Century of Moral Philosophy* (1980). In his *Moral Thinking*
   (1981) R.M. Hare, while still insisting that moral philosophy is
   philosophical logic, gives it content by way of a refined version of
   Utilitarianism (with bibliography). On virtue, see, for example, J.
   Wallace, *Virtues and Vices* (1978); P. Foot, *Virtues and Vices* (1978); A.
   MacIntyre, *After Virtue* (1981) or the more theological P.T. Geach, *The
   Virtues* (1977). As an introduction to a vast field see P. Singer, *Practical
   Ethics* (1979).

3. The general level of Marxist writing in the Anglo-American world, I
   should add, is of a much higher order than it was in the years when it
   was largely devoted to the defence of Soviet ideology. Nevertheless much
   of it is still marked by a refusal to say positively that the founding fathers
   were quite mistaken when they took this or that view, as distinct from
   standing in need of a little reinterpretation. Its atmosphere, that is, is
   distinctly scholastic. The more radical revisionist varieties of Marxism
   have generally been imported from Europe. See especially ch.2, n.5
   below on Althusser. Other common points of reference are Antonio
   Gramsci's *Letters from Prison* (1947, trans.1971) and the Hungarian
   George Lukács, especially his, subsequently disowned, *History and Class
   Consciousness* (1923, trans. 1971). The late translation dates are
   significant, although there were earlier translations of selections from
   Gramsci. The reputation of Lukács has fluctuated, partly as a
   consequence of what was taken to be his readiness to submit to Stalinist
   authority. See, however, A. Heller (ed.), *Lukács Revalued* (1983). For an
   account of the Polish Marxist hybrids see H. Skolimowski, *Polish
   Analytical Philosophy* (1967). For a more orthodox Polish version see A.
   Schaff, *Language and Cognition* (1967). L. Kolakowski, *Main Currents of
   Marxism* (1976-8, 3 vols) tells the story of the fluctuating fortunes of
   Marxism. The series *Issues in Marxist Philosophy*, ed. J. Mepham and
   D-H.Ruben (1979-) attempts to repair the British situation. But they are
   still primarily exegetical. See also G.H. Parkinson (ed.), *Marx and*

Marxisms (1982); T.J. Blakeley et al. (eds), *The Varieties of Contemporary Marxism* (1983). For marxist humanism see E. Fromm (ed.), *Socialist Humanism* (1965). The relation of Marxism to ethics is much disputed. See E. Kamenka, *The Ethical Foundations of Marxism* (1962). Marxists also differ greatly about whether they want to be thought of as philosophers. See A. Callinicos, *Marxism and Philosophy* (1983). The periodical *Radical Philosophy* (1972-) is a good introduction to a wide range of Marx-conscious philosophising. From the immense general literature one can mention S. Avineri, *The Social and Political Thought of Karl Marx* (1968) and J. McMurtry, *The Structure of Marx's World View* (1978). On the ideas that were bandied about during the 1960s see J.A. Passmore, *The Perfectibility of Man* (1970).

4. In *Knowledge and Human Interests* (1968, trans.1971) Habermas criticises, in a largely historical way, the positivist attempt to make of philosophy of science a generalised epistemology 'purged of all the interesting problems', problems, that is, about the place of science in human society and within the broader framework of human 'cognitive interests'. He develops his social theory – his guiding concern – where the concept of an 'ideal speech community', a society of perfect discussants, is central, in the essays translated as *Communication and the Evolution of Society* (1979), in which he also comes to terms with Austin's speech-acts. His theory of language was attacked by Y. Bar-Hillel in *Synthese* (1973). As often, Habermas replies that he has been misunderstood, which, given his manner of writing, is far from improbable. His view that the criticism of ideology is the central task of philosophy goes back to Max Horkheimer's essay on traditional philosophy and critical theory, first published in 1937, for which see his *Critical Theory* (1968, trans. 1972). For the Frankfurt school generally, see A. Arato and E. Gebhardt (eds), *The Essential Frankfurt School Reader* (1979), along with the historical M. Jay, *The Dialectical Imagination* (1974) and the critical P. Connerton, *The Tragedy of Enlightenment* (1980). On Habermas in particular, see T. McCarthy, *The Critical Theory of Jürgen Habermas* (1978); M. Hesse, *Revolutions and Reconstructions in the Philosophy of Science* (1980); G. Kortian, *Metacritique* (1980); J.B. Thompson and D. Held (eds), *Habermas: Critical Debates* (1982); R. Geuss, *The Idea of a Critical Theory* (1982). Theodor Adorno's *Against Epistemology* (1972, trans.1982) is an attack on the pretensions of Husserl's phenomenology. Herbert Marcuse was for a time the most discussed member of the school, but his Freudian marxism lies outside our sphere. I should emphasise that the Frankfurt school entirely rejects the classical version of the sociology of knowledge, as presented by Karl Mannheim in *Ideology and Utopia* (1929, trans.1936) which makes an exception of physical science. See M. Jay, 'The Frankfurt School's criticism of Karl Mannheim' (*Telos*, 1974).

The enormous range of inquiries which now goes under the name of sociology of knowledge can be gathered from J.E. Curtis and J.W. Petras (eds), *The Sociology of Knowledge* (1970). The special numbers of

Philosophy of the Social Sciences (1981) will make the same point for more recent work, especially in relation to the philosophy of science. Two leading exponents are Barry Barnes and David Bloor. See D. Bloor, *Knowledge and Social Imagery* (1976); B. Barnes, *Interests and the Growth of Knowledge* (1976). See also ch.5,n.15 below.

5. For additional bibliographies see notes to *HY* ch.17 and ch.3 below, along with G.F. Fløistad (ed.), *Contemporary Philosophy*, vol.1, 1981, which is entirely devoted to philosophy of language and philosophical logic. On the mathematical front J.N. Crossley et al., *What is Mathematical Logic?* (1972) is a short introduction, particularly useful for its account of 'Turing machines', understood as giving unambiguous instructions which can be followed without any recourse to imagination. They are often referred to in the course of 'physicalist' analyses of minds and knowledge. At the opposite extreme see J. Barwise (ed.), *Handbook of Mathematical Logic* (1977), a vast compilation.

   On the philosophical front see especially N. Rescher, *Topics in Philosophical Logic* (1968) along with such collections as S. Körner (ed.), *Philosophy of Logic* (1976); G.H. von Wright (ed.), *Logic and Philosophy* (1980); R. Haller and W. Grassl (eds), *Language, Logic and Philosophy* (1980); A.C. Grayling, *Introduction to Philosophical Logic* (1982) which discusses most of the authors we shall be particularly considering; G.H. von Wright, *Philosophical Logic* (1983), which brings together his essays on this topic; D.M. Gabbay and F. Guenther (eds), *Handbook of Philosophical Logic*, 4 vols (1983-4).

   S. Haack, *Philosophy of Logics* (1978) has been subjected to some rather severe criticisms but is unique as an introduction to 'the philosophical problems which logic raises'. Mathematical and philosophical logic – the boundaries are indeterminate – are brought together in J. Hintikka et al. (eds), *Essays on Mathematical and Philosophical Logic* (1978); E. Agazzi (ed.), *Modern Logic: a Survey* (1980). See also the periodical *Journal of Philosophical Logic* (1972-). Philosophical logic flows into philosophy of language and linguistics. See such collections as D. Hockney et al. (eds), *Contemporary Research in Philosophical Logic and Linguistic Semantics* (1975); P. French et al. (eds), *Contemporary Perspectives in the Philosophy of Language* (1978); U. Mönnich (ed.), *Aspects of Philosophical Logic* (1981) and chapters 3, 4 below.

6. On these logical innovations see *HY*, ch.17, nn.8-11; on Lewis see ch.12, n.20. See also various references below. On non-classical logics see, although it is incomplete, S. Haack, *Deviant Logic* (1974). It is very difficult to classify them. They are variously combined and their advocates are often most insistent that they do not belong in that category where they are commonly put. They include 'free' logics, which were originally linked with Strawson's doctrine of pre-suppositions, for which see *HY*, ch.18, n.43, and for an extended account of later developments D. Wilson, *Presuppositions and Non-Truth-Conditional*

Semantics (1975). The literature is scattered; it can be approached through K. Lambert (ed.), *The Logical Way of Doing Things* (1969). Logic, so it is argued, has to be capable of dealing with statements which contain references to imaginary, fictional, nonsensical or even inconsistent states of affairs; it cannot adequately do this within the framework of classical logic. See also L. Goddard and R. Routley, *The Logic of Significance and Context* (1973). One interesting side effect has been the rehabilitation of Meinong, for so long regarded as the supreme example of a philosophical *reductio ad absurdum*. See ch.8, n.8 in *HY*, especially R. Routley, *Exploring Meinong's Jungle* (1980) and T. Parsons, *Nonexistent Objects* (1980).

7. On 'relevance' see W.Ackermann, 'Strong Implication' (*JSL*, 1956); A.R. Anderson and N.D. Belnap, *Entailment* (1975); M.R. Diaz, *Topics in the Logic of Relevance* (1981). On the special question of the disjunctive see N.D. Belnap and J.M. Dunn, 'Entailment and the Disjunctive Syllogism' in G. Fløistad (ed.), *Contemporary Philosophy*, vol.1 and the reply by R.K. Meyer, *Why I am not a Relevantist* (1978). The Australian 'relevant' logicians maintain that relevance, although in a weak form a minimal condition for entailment, is something of a 1960s red herring; the crucial thing is to develop a logic which squares with our ordinary logical intuitions. See, as well as Meyer, R. Routley et al., *Relevant Logic and its Rivals* (1982).

The rejection of Lewis's principle that p and not-p together imply any proposition whatsoever has led to the development of 'paraconsistent' logics. See N. Rescher and R. Brandon, *The Logic of Inconsistency* (1979); G. Priest and R. Routley (eds), *On Paraconsistency* (1985); special number of *Studia Logica* (1979). Another supposedly indefensible position has thereby won defenders. See R. Routley and R.K. Meyer, 'Dialectical Logic, Classical Logic and the Consistency of the World' (*Studies in Soviet Thought*, 1976).

There are now many attempts, too, to formalise the indeterminancy relations of quantum mechanics. Hans Reichenbach had suggested in *Philosophical Foundations of Quantum Mechanics* (1944) that this could be done with the aid of a three-valued logic, in which 'indeterminate' is added to 'true' and 'false' as a possible truth-value. For later attempts, often critical of Reichenbach, see B.C. van Fraassen in R.S. Cohen and M.W. Wartofsky (eds), *Logical and Epistemological Studies in Contemporary Physics* (1974); C.A. Hooker (ed.), *The Logico-algebraic Approach to Quantum Mechanics* (2 vols., 1975); H. Putnam, *Philosophical Papers*, vol 1 (1975); P. Mittelstaedt, *Quantum Logic* (1978). It is scarcely surprising if, in the face of such diversities, some logicians have sought to rehabilitate traditional logic. See F. Sommers, *The Logic of Natural Language* (1982). Geach responded strongly in his *TLS* review. But he has a defender in G. Englebretsen, *Three Logicians* (1981).

8. For a critical history of recent German philosophy see R. Bubner, *Modern*

German Philosophy (1981) which closely relates it to contemporary Anglo-American philosophy. The impact of Karl Popper, so long delayed, has been particularly striking. Outside the World Conference of Philosophy in Düsseldorf (1978), German students demonstrated, in the name of the German tradition, against 'Popperian imperialism'. It is significant that his first major defender, Hans Albert, was by training an economist, not a philosopher. See his *Traktat über kritische Vernunft* (1968) and *Plädoyer für kritischen Rationalismus* (1971). A stir was created by the confrontation between Popperians and the Frankfurt school in T. Adorno et al. (eds), *The Positivist Dispute in German Sociology* (1969, trans. 1976). D. Frisby's introduction to that book is a broad survey. See also G. Radnitzky in *Contemporary Schools of Metascience* (1968) and such articles – he is very prolific – as 'From Justifying a Theory to Comparing Theories and Selecting Questions' (*RIP*, 1980). Stegmüller's essays are now translated as *Collected Papers* (1977). See also Hans Lenk, *Metalogik und Sprachanalyse* (1973). Austria, of course, has a long tradition of analytic philosophy. *Erkenntnis* has a special number (1983) on Stegmüller.

In France, there is a growing interest in Wittgenstein, quite a little in Chomsky and in the Austinians, and some in logic. Nevertheless although Vincent Descombes is personally acquainted with the Anglo-American world, his *Modern French Philosophy* (1979, trans. 1980), rich in references to German philosophy, does not find it necessary to mention a single Anglo-American thinker. The contrast with Bubner's otherwise comparable book on modern German philosophy is very striking. See also A. Montefiori (ed.), *Philosophy in France Today* (1983), which includes the essay by Jacques Bouveresse, 'Why I am so very unFrench'.

Italian philosophy is for the most part attached to Franco-German sources and has particularly attempted to come to terms with Marxism. Nevertheless Anglo-American philosophy of science is in some measure cultivated. See, for example, the journal *Epistemologia* (1978-); E. Agazzi (ed.), *Studi sul problema del significato* (1979); M. Dalla Chiara, *Italian Studies in the Philosophy of Science* (1980); M. Pera, *Apologia del Metodo* (1982). For Scandinavian philosophy see R.E. Olsen and A.M. Paul (eds), *Scandinavian Philosophy Today* (1972).

In Spain, in Greece, in South America, there are active groups of analytic philosophers, as still in Poland. See also *The Monist* (1982) on 'Contemporary Continental Analytic Philosophy'. The situation in India is complicated by the existence of strong indigenous philosophical traditions. See, for example, M. Chatterjee (ed.), *Contemporary Indian Philosophy* Series 2 (1974) and the *Indian Journal of Philosophy* (1959-).

9. Ernst Tugendhat has 'placed' himself in R. Bubner et al. (eds), *Hermeneutik und Dialektik* (1970), a Festschrift for the influential 'hermeneutic' philosopher H.G. Gadamer, where he correctly observes that in Germany 'speech-analysis' was for long identified with logical

positivism. He develops his view in *Traditional and Analytical Philosophy* (trans. 1982).

At the hands of the theologian Friedrich Schleiermacher in the first decades of the nineteenth century hermeneutics was a method of Biblical interpretation designed to lessen the risk of misinterpreting the text. See his essays and aphorisms in *Hermeneutik* (1959, ed. H. Kimmerle). For Wilhelm Dilthey it relates to the kind of interpretation possible, he thinks, in the human and not the natural sciences, based on an inner understanding of what fellow human beings have created. See H.P. Rickmann (ed.), *Dilthey: Selected Writings* (1976) and *Wilhelm Dilthey* (1979); R. Makkreel, *Dilthey* (1975); M. Ermath, *Wilhelm Dilthey* (1978); T. Plantinga, *Historical Understanding in the Thought of Dilthey* (1980). Gadamer, basing himself on Heidegger, extended hermeneutics to apply to all our interpretations of experience, always, he argues, a product of our position in a tradition of interpretation. In the ideal case, our 'horizon of meaning' fuses with the 'horizon of meaning' of the text, a fusion in which distinction is still preserved as 'a tension between the text and the present'. See *Truth and Method* (1960; trans. 1965). The Frankfurt School criticised Gadamer as being too subservient to tradition but nevertheless absorbed certain of his ideas into their analysis of ideology. See K.O. Apel et al., *Hermeneutik und Ideologiekritik* (1971).

As the authority of science has come under question in the Anglo-American world, there has been greater sympathy for hermeneutics. But this has attached rather to hermeneutics as text-interpretation or to Dilthey than to Gadamer's attempt to make a total philosophy out of it, by way of the doctrine that all experience is a 'reading'. On its history see R.E. Palmer, *Hermeneutics* (1969). See also D.E. Linge (ed.), *Philosophical Hermeneutics* (1976); J. Bleicher, *Contemporary Hermeneutics* (1980); J.B. Thompson, *Critical Hermeneutics* (1981); C. Taylor, 'Interpretation and the Sciences of Man' (*RM*, 1971). In France, P. Ricoeur has taken up hermeneutic themes. See his *Interpretation Theory* (1976), *The Conflict of Interpretations* (1969, trans.1974) and *Hermeneutics and the Human Sciences* (1981) with bibliography. On Ricoeur himself see D. Ihde, *Hermeneutic Philosophy* (1971); the anthology edited by C.E. Reagan and D. Stewart, *The Philosophy of Paul Ricoeur* (1978); C.E. Reagan (ed.), *Studies in the Philosophy of Paul Ricoeur* (1979) with bibliography of Ricoeur and his critics. For a theological application linking Heidegger, Bultmann, Gadamer and Wittgenstein, see A.C. Thiselton, *The Two Horizons* (1980). Interpretation is discussed with some reference to hermeneutics but from a more Anglo-American point of view in H. von Wright, *Explanation and Understanding* (1971). See also the mixed collection of essays in J. Manninen and R. Tuomela (eds), *Essays on Explanation and Understanding* (1976). P. Connerton (ed.), *Critical Sociology* (1976) includes extracts from both the hermeneutic philosophers and the Frankfurt School. See also R.J. Howard, *Three Faces of Hermeneutics* (1983). The article on Hermeneutics by R.E.

Palmer in G. Fløistad, *Contemporary Philosophy*, vol. 2 contains an exceptionally wide-ranging bibliography. See also G. Shapiro and A. Sica (eds), *Hermeneutics, Questions and Prospects* (1984).

10. Apel and Habermas stand close together. Apel wrote a book on Peirce (1975, trans. 1981) and calls his position *transzendentalpragmatismus*, which brings out its oddity. In his *Transformation der Philosophie* (1973) – a set of essays partially translated under the more modest title *Towards a Transformation of Philosophy* (1976) – he suggests, as against Marx, that philosophy can be so transformed as to be a ground for change and yet retain its transcendental character, not letting the social sciences take over. In his *Analytical Philosophy of Language and the Geisteswissenschaften* (1965, trans.1967) he looks at Wittgenstein and Winch from this point of view. All three are attacked, from a Popperian point of view, in H. Albert, *Transzendentale Traümereien* (1975). For the most part, Anglo-American philosophy has oriented itself in relation to the physical rather than the social sciences, with the notable exception of the Chicago pragmatists and to a lesser degree the Popperians. But the situation is changing, and not only as a result of the resurgence of Marxism. To *HY*, ch.20, n.36 add M. Brodbeck (ed.), *Readings in the Philosophy of the Social Sciences* (1968); C. Borger and F. Cioffi (eds), *Explanation in the Behavioural Sciences* (1970); A. Ryan, *The Philosophy of the Social Sciences* (1970); A. MacIntyre, *Against the Self-Images of the Age* (1971) and *After Virtue* (1981); the essays in *The Proper Study* (Royal Institute of Philosophy Lectures, 4, 1971); P. Winch, *Ethics and Society* (1972); E. Gellner, *Cause and Meaning in the Social Sciences* (1973); A. Ryan (ed.), *The Philosophy of Social Explanation* (1973); R. Keat and J. Urry, *Social Theory as Science* (1975); R. Harrison (ed.), *Rational Action* (1979); S.I. Benn and G.W. Mortimore (eds), *Rationality and the Social Sciences* (1976); J. Elster, *Ulysses and the Sirens* (1979). R. Beehler and A.R. Drengson (eds), *The Philosophy of Society* (1978) illustrates the difficulty in drawing margins between the philosophy of the social sciences and theoretical sociology as also does E. Ullman-Margalit, *The Emergence of Norms* (1977). See also C. Hookway and P. Pettit (eds), *Action and Interpretation* (1978); D. Thomas, *Naturalism and Social Science* (1979), together with much of the literature referred to in the preceding note and in n.3 above.

11. Not so very long ago, the mere suggestion that courses should be given on Hegel could, in British universities, arouse strong opposition. There were always, of course, those who did not acquiesce in this negative judgment, philosophers such as G.R. Mure at Oxford and J.N. Findlay in London, later to migrate to Boston. Findlay's case is particularly interesting. He began as a close student of Meinong, attended classes by Wittgenstein and wrote about them when that was far from being a fashionable thing to do, and finally emerged as a metaphysician in the Hegelian mode. Few philosophers have so consistently moved against

the stream. See his *Hegel* (1958) and his Gifford lectures, *The Discipline of the Cave* (1966) and *The Transcendence of the Cave* (1967). New editions and translations of Hegel appeared in the 1970s and a large-scale critical study by Charles Taylor (1975). See also A. MacIntyre (ed.), *Hegel* (1972). Taylor's 'Theories of Meaning' (*PBA*, 1980) attacks contemporary Anglo-American truth-conditional semantics by appealing to the German Romantic tradition from Herder to Heidegger.

12. Note the range of Armstrong or Rorty below. Anthony Quinton's *The Nature of Things* (1973) is an example of broad metaphysical thinking within an analytic framework. Robert Nozick, after first making his name as a political philosopher in *Anarchy, State and Utopia* (1974) was ready to tackle the entire range of philosophical topics in his *Philosophical Explanations* (1981). On a much larger scale Mario Bunge's *Treatise on Basic Philosophy* (1974-) is announced as extending to seven volumes. In the fashion characteristic of our times it begins from a semantics. The range of contemporary Anglo-American metaphysical interests is illustrated in *Midwest Studies in Philosophy*, vol.4 (1979). K. Campbell, *Metaphysics* (1976) is a useful introduction to that same scene.

13. Gettier's essay can be read in A.P. Griffiths (ed.), *Knowledge and Belief* (1967), which sets it in the context of earlier work from Cook Wilson on. The resulting hue and cry can be approached through G.S. Pappas and M. Swain (eds), *Essays on Knowledge and Justification* (1978). This includes a lengthy bibliography which, even so, is highly selective. The more wide-ranging recent books on traditional epistemological problems, not mentioned previously, would include R. Chisholm, *Theory of Knowledge* (1966) and *The Foundations of Knowing* (1982); B. Aune, *Knowledge, Mind and Nature* (1967); A. Danto, *Analytical Philosophy of Knowledge* (1968); M. Roth and L. Galis (eds), *Knowing* (1970); G.H. von Wright (ed.), *Problems in the Theory of Knowledge* (1972); G. Harman, *Thought* (1973); R. Chisholm and R. Swartz (eds), *Empirical Knowledge* (1973); K. Lehrer, *Knowledge* (1974). P.A. French et al., *Studies in Epistemology, Midwest Studies*, V (1980). Philosophers are still busy defending or responding to scepticism. See, more particularly, P. Unger, *Ignorance* (1975); M. Williams, *Groundless Belief* (1977); N. Rescher, *Scepticism* (1980); J.W. Cornman, *Scepticism, Justification and Explanation* (1980). Somewhat more surprisingly, the representative theory of perception has been re-appraised. See J.L. Mackie, *Problems from Locke* (1976); F. Jackson, *Perception* (1977). The concept of 'information flow' has been prominent in recent epistemology and 'cognitive psychology'. See, for example, F.I. Dretske, *Knowledge and the Flow of Information* (1981). For a general introduction to epistemological controversies see the wide-ranging discussion in G. Macdonald (ed.), *Perception and Identity* (1979) which takes Ayer as its point of departure; J.L. Evans, *Knowledge and Infallibility* (1978); D.J. O'Connor and B. Carr, *Introduction to the Theory of Knowledge* (1982).

For a general introduction which relates epistemological to metaphysical issues see G.N. Schlesinger, *Metaphysics* (1982). R.K. Shope, *The Analysis of Knowing: a Decade of Research* (1983) can serve as a substitute for my omissions. For the 'naturalisation' of epistemology see W.V. Quine, *The Roots of Reference* (1974).

14. Armstrong's views are briefly summed up in his 'The Causal Theory of Mind', most readily accessible in *The Nature of Mind* (1980). Similar views had been presented in D.K. Lewis, 'An Argument for the Identity Theory' (*JP*, 1966). See also B. Medlin, 'Ryle and the Mechanical Hypothesis' in C.F. Presley (ed.), *The Identity Theory of Mind* (1967) and M.C. Bradley, 'Sensations, Brain-Processes and Colours' (*AJP*, 1963), along with his critical notice of Smart's *Philosophy and Scientific Realism* (*AJP*, 1964); K. Campbell, *Body and Mind* (1970); R. Rorty, 'Mind-Body Identity, Privacy and Categories' and his later discussion of the 'the Antipodeans' in *Philosophy and the Mirror of Nature* (1980), as well as Kripke and Davidson, below.
    Armstrong had been encouraged by Donald Davidson's 'Actions, Reasons and Causes' (*JP*, 1963) reprinted in *Essays on Actions and Events* (1980), which also includes a criticism of Armstrong on 'trying', to which Armstrong replies in *The Nature of Mind*. Also relevant is H.P. Grice, 'The Causal Theory of Perception' (*PASS*, 1961) and G. Pitcher, *A Theory of Perception* (1971). See also S. Davis (ed.) *Causal Theories of Mind* (1983). Armstrong's views have been extensively criticised. See for example T. Nagel's review of *A Materialist Theory of Mind* (*PR*, 1970). A.J. Ayer in *Philosophy in the Twentieth Century* concentrates on his account of secondary qualities. See also the more recent literature on materialism in *HT*, ch.20, notes 40-2 and on epistemology (note 13 above). On his theory of universals see also the discussion with Quine and Michael Devitt in *Pacific Philosophical Quarterly* (1981) and L. Goldstein, 'Scientific Scotism' (*AJP*, 1983), which relates Armstrong to Wilfrid Sellars, with an extensive bibliography of Sellars on universals. Armstrong has developed his theory of scientific laws in *What is a Law of Nature?* (1983). For a general account, with bibliography, of work on mind and body – much of it described below – see Armstrong's 'Recent Work on the Relation of Mind and Brain' in *Contemporary Philosophy*, vol.4. For earlier work on universals see M. Loux (ed.), *Universals and Particulars* (1970) and 'Recent Work on Ontology' (*APQ*, 1972).

15. For Ramsey see the new edition of his *The Foundations of Mathematics* (1931), with additional material, published as *Foundations* (1978) and D.H. Mellor (ed.), *Prospects for Pragmatism* (1980). Mellor's own work has been a good deal influenced by Ramsey. See his *The Matter of Chance* (1971). On the concept of 'maps' see R. Downes and D. Stea, *Maps in Minds* (1977). In 'Cognition and Representation' (*AJP*, 1980) J. Heil relates Armstrong's view to Wittgenstein's 'picture' theory. See also *HT*, ch.15 and Stalnaker (below).

16. A later version of his *Identity and Spatio-temporal Continuity* (1967). See also the essays in M.K. Munitz (ed.), *Identity and Individuation* (1971); J. Perry (ed.), *Personal Identity* (1975) and, especially, A. Rorty (ed.), *The Identities of Persons* (1976), with an extensive bibliography. Bernard Williams, *Problems of the Self* (1973) collects essays by one of the cleverest but least prolific of contemporary British philosophers. See also Derek Parfit, *Reasons and Persons* (1984). Other contributions include T. Penelhum, *Survival and Disembodied Existence* (1970); J.L. Mackie, *Problems from Locke* (1976); R.M. Chisholm, *Person and Object* (1976); B.R. Brody, *Identity and Essence* (1980); E. Hirsch, *The Concept of Identity* (1982); the debate between S. Shoemaker and R. Swinburne, *Personal Identity* (1984).

    In Thomas Nagel's *Mortal Questions* (1979), questions about personal identity run through a book which clearly illustrates the ways in which barriers have broken down in contemporary philosophy.

17. As exponents of relative identity see P.T. Geach, *Reference and Generality* (1962) and *Logic Matters* (1972), together with his contribution to M.K. Munitz (ed.), *Logic and Ontology* (1973); N. Griffin, *Relative Identity* (1977); N. Griffin and R. Routley, 'Towards a Logic of Relative Identity' (*Logique et Analyse*, 1979); H. Noonan, *Objects and Identity* (1980). Wiggins's textual notes should be consulted, as well as the final bibliography. It should be observed that this apparently technical issue can have theological implications, if the question is whether the three persons of the Trinity can be one without having all their properties in common. Dummett criticises Geach and develops a position rather like Wiggins's in his *Frege* (1973).

18. Wiggins here draws upon Hilary Putnam's theory of natural kinds, as developed in his 'Is Semantics Possible?' (1970), reprinted in H. Putnam, *Mind, Language and Reality* (1975). See also Kripke and Putnam below. Wiggins, characteristically, traces a Putnam-like view back to Aristotle and Leibniz, finding it adumbrated, indeed, even in the Pre-Socratics.

19. See, for example, J.M. Shorter, 'Personal Identity, Personal Relationships, and Criteria' (*PAS*, 1970). It is a general tendency of our time, however, to swing between the view, developed by such sociobiologists as E.O. Wilson in his *Sociobiology* (1975) and a good deal more tentatively in *On Human Nature* (1978), that to understand society we have to turn to biological laws and the quite opposite view, under the influence of the sociology of knowledge, that what we call 'nature' has to be understood as a social phenomenon.

20. 'Empiricism' is by no means a sharply defined concept; although Quine once attacked 'two dogmas of empiricism' he has himself been attacked as an empiricist. H. Morick has brought together an astonishing range

of philosophers in his *Challenges to Empiricism* (1972), ranging from Carnap, Quine and Popper through Feyerabend to Chomsky. The Kantian revival is so widespread as scarcely to lend itself to illustration. But see, for example, W. Sellars, *Science and Metaphysics* (1968). It should be added, however, that there is much sympathetic re-reading of Locke, in particular, as by Wiggins and Mackie, and that scholarship on Hume has reached a highly developed point.

21. The quotation is from M. Platts, *Ways of Meaning* (1979). It can be matched elsewhere, as in R. Scruton's dismissal of Oxford linguistic philosophy in his *From Descartes to Wittgenstein* (1982).

22. For the theory of speech acts see *HY*, ch.18, n.35. Criticism of Searle can scarcely be separated from criticism of Austin. But see Searle's 'Austin on Locutionary and Illocutionary Acts' (*PR*, 1968), along with J.J. Katz, 'Literal Meaning and Logical Theory' (*JP*, 1981). Many of the major articles are in J. Rosenberg and C. Travis (eds), *Readings in the Philosophy of Language* (1971). Searle's theory of mind has been published as *Intentionality* (1983). See R.M. Kempson, *Semantic Theory* (1977) both for linguistic applications of speech acts and the conflict between such analyses and contemporary truth-conditional semantics, of the type later to prevail at Oxford. See also J. Sadock, *Toward a Linguistic Theory of Speech Acts* (1974); K. Bach and R.M. Hamish, *Communication and Speech Acts* (1980). Searle particularly criticises J.R. Ross, 'On Declarative Sentences' in R.A. Jacobs and P.S. Rosenbaum (eds), *Readings in Transformational Grammar* (1970). Searle's troubles with metaphor are by no means peculiar to him. See, for example, A. Ortony (ed.), *Metaphor and Thought* (1979); M. Johnson (ed.), *Philosophical Perspectives on Metaphor* (1981).

For the new wave of transcendental arguments see P. Bieri et al. (eds), *Transcendental Arguments and Science* (1979). There is an extensive bibliography in the article in that volume by Jonathan Bennett.

23. Paul Grice, for many years an Oxford tutor before he moved to the United States, exerted his influence through his Oxford seminars, widely attended by sabbatical visitors, as much as through his articles. 'Utterer's Meaning', first published in *Foundations of Language* (1968), is a highly schematic summary of his 1967 William James lectures at Harvard. See also his reply to critics in 'Utterer's Meaning and Intentions' (*PR*, 1969). Along with critical articles by P.F. Strawson, his former pupil, and J.R. Searle on his earlier 'Meaning' (*PR*, 1957), it is reprinted in J.R. Searle (ed.), *The Philosophy of Language* (1971). See also P. Ziff, 'On H.P. Grice's Theory of Meaning' (*Analysis*, 1967); A. Mackay, 'Professor Grice's Theory of Meaning' (*Mind*, 1974); T.E. Patton and D.W. Stampe, 'The Rudiments of Meaning: on Ziff on Grice' (*Foundations of Language*, 1969); N.L. Wilson, 'Grice on Meaning' (*Noûs*, 1970); S.R. Schiffer, *Meaning* (1972); D.M. Armstrong, 'Meaning

and Communication' (*PR*, 1971); P.F. Strawson, *Logico-Linguistic Papers* (1971); M. Black, 'Meaning and Intention' in *Caveats and Critiques* (1975); J. Bennett, *Linguistic Behaviour* (1976). Grice's 'Meaning' and Ziff's criticism, along with other criticisms *en passant*, can be read in D. Steinberg and L. Jakobovits (eds), *Semantics* (1971). B. Loar, *Mind and Meaning* (1981) defends a neo-Gricean theory of meaning.

24. One of Grice's William James lectures, published in P. Cole and J.L. Morgan, (eds), *Syntax and Semantics*, vol. 3 *Speech Acts* (1975), where it is discussed, and formalised, by a group of philosophers and linguists, and in D. Davidson and G. Harman, *The Logic of Grammar* (1975). The basic idea was first presented in P. Grice, 'The Causal Theory of Perception' (*PASS*, 1961), examined in M. de B. Platts, *Ways of Meaning* (1979). For a formalised theory of 'conversational postulates' see D. Gordon and G. Lakoff, 'Conversational Postulates' in *Papers from the Seventh Regional Meeting of the Chicago Linguistic Society* (1971), criticised as 'too strong' by J.R. Searle in *Expression and Meaning* (1979).

2. Structure and Syntax

1. There is some controversy about the degree to which this version reflects Saussure's intentions. (A new translation with annotations by R. Harris appeared in 1983.) See R. Godel, *Les Sources manuscrites du Cours du linguistique générale* (1957). For Saussure see J. Culler, *Saussure* (1976) or, for a short account, John Lyons in D. Robey (ed.), *Structuralism* (1973). F. Jameson in *The Prison-House of Language* (1972) condemns the criticisms of Saussure by Ogden and Richards in their *The Meaning of Meaning* (1923) as an example of 'the vice of Anglo-American empiricism' which lies in its 'preference for segments and isolated objects'. This preference, Jameson darkly and characteristically suggests, is itself 'a means to avoid observation of those larger wholes and totalities which if they had to be seen would force the mind in the long run into uncomfortable social and political conclusions'. On the other side, Saussure's approach is sometimes condemned as totalitarian. Saussure does not refer to C.S. Peirce, on whose theory of signs see *HT*, pp.140-2. He was, however, considerably influenced by the American linguist W.D. Whitney. For an extensive Bibliography see H. Parret, *Language and Discourse* (1971) and on linguistics generally P.H. Salus, *Panini to Postal: a Bibliography in the History of Linguistics* (1971).

2. See Roman Jakobson: *Selected Writings*, 4 vols (1962-). Particularly influential has been his 'Closing Statement: Linguistic and Poetics' included in T.A. Sebeok (ed.), *Style in Language* (1960). Unlike Saussure, he cites Peirce. For the link between Saussurean linguistics and Russian formalism see F. Jameson, *The Prison-House of Language* (1972). Of the other linguists in the same general school the Danish L. Hjelmslev in his

Prolegomena to a Theory of Language (1943; revised English ed. 1961) has been particularly influential. The important Prague school of linguists with N.S. Troubetskoy as a leading representative can be read in J. Vachek (ed.), *A Prague School Reader in Linguistics* (1964). See also his *The Linguistic School of Prague* (1966). 'Structuralism' as a movement is sometimes dated back to a set of theses presented at a linguistic conference at Prague in 1929. See E. Benveniste, ' "Structure" en linguistique' in R. Bastide (ed.), *Sens et Usages du terme 'structure' dans les sciences humaines et sociales* (1962). Benveniste's *Problems in General Linguistics* (1966, trans. 1971) has exerted a considerable influence, especially through its emphasis on 'discourse' as distinct both from individual sentences or simple narratives. See the bibliography in J. Ehrmann, *Structuralism* (1970). Some notion of the range of contemporary linguistics can be gathered from J. Lyons (ed.), *New Horizons in Linguistics* (1970) with an extensive bibliography. The periodical *Linguistics and Philosophy* (1979-) covers a lot of ground. See also H. Parret, *Language and Discourse* (1971). T.K. Seung, *Structuralism and Hermeneutics* (1982) is a philosophical criticism which places structuralism in a broader context of interpretation-theory.

3. See J. Piaget, the genetic psychologist, in *Structuralism* (1971). For 'genetic structuralism' in general see M. de Gandillac, L. Goldmann and J. Piaget, *Entretiens sur les notions de genèse et de structure* (1965). Piaget looks for 'structuralism' in a wide range of mathematicians, linguists, psychologists, sociologists and scientists, attacking Lévi-Strauss, Foucault, Althusser for trying to make of structuralism the *sole* method. In D. Robey (ed.), *Structuralism: an Introduction* (1973) – a set of essays by English writers – it is more narrowly defined as the attempt to analyse human culture as a set of signs. (The article in that volume by J. Mepham illustrates the way 'structuralism' has been taken up by some younger English philosophers with a Marxist bent.) P. Pettit, one of the few 'Anglo-American' philosophers to take structuralism seriously, in his *The Concept of Structuralism* (1975) objects to counting Althusser, Foucault, Lacan as 'structuralists' on the ground that nothing in their subject-matter corresponds to a sentence. J. Parain-Vial in her highly critical *Analyses structurales et idéologies structuralistes* (1969) includes Lacan, Althusser and Foucault among the 'structural ideologists'. The various collections of readings, most of them with excellent bibliographies, differ notably in whom they include or exclude. J. Ehrmann (ed.), *Structuralism* (1970) contains an essay by the influential French linguist A. Martinet – reprinted from the special *RIP* number *La Notion de structure* (1965) – and one on Merleau-Ponty, of whom it has been said 'had he lived longer he would have been the philosopher of structuralism', but otherwise restricts itself to Lévi-Strauss and Lacan. T. Hawkes (ed.), *Structuralism and Semiotics* (1977), with an excellent analytical bibliography, is mainly interested in language and literary criticism. R. and F. de George, *The Structuralists* (1972) come closer to

my text with essays by Marx, Freud, Jakobson, Barthes, Lévi-Strauss, Althusser and Foucault. R. Macksey and F. Donato (eds), *The Language of Criticism and the Sciences of Man* (1970) reports an international symposium with essays by leading structuralists. See also the critical essays contained in J. Sturrock (ed.), *Structuralism and Since* (1979) on Lévi-Strauss, Barthes, Foucault, Lacan and Derrida. The Tel Quel volume *Théorie d'ensemble* (1968) contains a series of essays by leading structuralists, including, as well as the writers already mentioned, J. Kristeva and P. Sollers. 'Tel Quel' is the name assumed by a Parisian publishing house, once devoted to the publications of the more radical structuralists. For French periodical debates on structuralism, see the bibliography in M. Poster, *Existential Marxism* (1975, p.306). From Germany, J.M. Broekman, *Structuralism* (1971, trans. 1974) is relatively detailed, in a brief monograph, on Moscow and Prague. F. Wahl in O. Ducrot et al., *Qu'est-ce que le structuralisme?* (1968) defends the view that what is essential to structuralism is the primacy of the sign. The 'semiology' which de Saussure only sketched has come to be more influential than his theory of language as such. See the lengthy series of works published under the editorship of T. Sebeok as *Approaches to Semiotics* (1969-). For a neo-Marxist analysis see R. Coward and J. Ellis, *Language and Materialism* (1977). See also F. Kurzweil, *The Age of Structuralism* (1980), which moves from Lévi-Strauss to Foucault; P. Kemp, 'Le structuralisme français' in G. Fløistad (ed.), *Contemporary Philosophy*, vol.2 (1982) and the extensive multi-disciplinary bibliography *French Structuralism* compiled by J.M. Miller (1981).

4. Foucault's theory of history is somewhat differently, and even more obscurely, developed in his *The Archaeology of Knowledge* (1968, trans. 1972). More widely read have been his studies of madness (1961), hospitals (1963), prisons (1975) and sexuality (1976-). See the special number of *Magazine littéraire* (1975), as well as the general works mentioned above. Derrida studied under Foucault. His critique of Foucault's interpretation of Descartes' 'Cogito' – 'Cogito and the History of Madness' in *Writing and Difference* (1967, trans. 1978) – points to the kind of weakness in interpretation to which Foucault's historical and scholarly critics have also drawn attention. (But note Foucault's vigorous reply in the second edition of his *Histoire de la Folie*, 1972.) See, for example, G. Huppert, 'Divinatio et Eruditio: Thoughts on Foucault' (*History and Theory*, 1974). Yet some historians still find him 'perceptive' and 'suggestive'; he has the artist's gift for making the familiar look strange. Inevitably, Foucault has been severely criticised by French existentialists and phenomenologists. These traditions were carried on in France by such philosophers as M. Dufrenne, P. Ricoeur and E. Levinas. See especially P. Ricoeur, *The Conflict of Interpretations* (1969; trans. 1974). For Sartre's reply to structuralism, see 'Anthropologie' in *Situations*, vol. 9 (1972); for French Marxist criticisms L. Sebag, *Marxisme et structuralisme* (1964); H. Lefebvre, *Au-delà du structuralisme*

(1970). Foucault's theory of history, as that of the structuralists generally, has been influenced by Gaston Bachelard's *La Philosophie du non* (1940) in which he argues that a change in scientific theory will often involve an apparent negation of what preceded it by the introduction of a new structure. See the Bachelard number of *RIP* (1963) and D. Lecourt, *Pour une critique de l'epistemologie: Bachelard, Canguilhem, Foucault* (1972), trans. as *Marxism and Epistemology* (1975); M. Vadée, *Gaston Bachelard* (1975); G. Canguilhem, *Études d'Histoire et de Philosophie des Sciences* (1968). See the illuminating interviews, M. Foucault, *Power/Knowledge*, ed. C. Gordon (1980) for Foucault's later emphasis on power. For a general study see A. Sheridan, *Michel Foucault* (1980). The twist and turns in Foucault's thinking are brought out in H. Dreyfus and P. Rabinow, *Michel Foucault: Beyond Structuralism and Hermeneutics* (1982). In his *Michel Foucault and the Subversion of Intellect* (1983), K. Racevskis considers Foucault as a critic of Western intellectual traditions. M. Clark has prepared an annotated bibliography (1982).

5. Althusser was for a time very widely read by philosophically-minded Marxists. For an extremely vigorous attack see the monograph on Althusser included in E.P. Thompson, *The Poverty of Theory and Other Essays* (1978) and Derek Sayer, 'Science as Critique: Marx vs. Althusser' in J. Mepham and D. Rubin (eds), *Issues in Marxist Philosophy* (1979). For Althusser's complicated relationship to French communism see J. Rancière, *La Leçon d'Althusser* (1974) – Rancière had been a disciple of Althusser – and J.M. Vincent (ed.), *Contre Althusser* (1974), as well as the invaluable Poster, with his running bibliographies. Althusser's rejection of the Hegelian Marx is carried to its extreme point in his *Lenin and Philosophy* (1968, trans. 1971). For a comparison of Lévi-Straus and Althusser see M. Glucksmann, *Structuralist Analysis in Contemporary Social Thought* (1974). See also A. Callinicos, *Althusser's Marxism* (1976). Althusser's criticisms of socialist humanism are brought together in his *For Marx* (1965, trans. 1969). For bibliography see *Essays in Self Criticism*, an English translation (1976) of a set of essays (1973-4). The periodical literature is of enormous proportions. See, for example, M. Poster, 'Althusser on History without Man' (*Political Theory*, 1974), with bibliography. Like Foucault, Althusser was considerably influenced by Bachelard. For a broader study see M. Kelly, *Modern French Marxism* (1982). It makes an interesting contrast with P. Piccone, *Italian Marxism* (1983). On Althusser see also S.B. Smith, *Reading Althusser* (1984).

6. Lacan's influence was for a time largely exerted through his seminars, in course of translation into English (1978-), beginning with *The Four Fundamental Concepts of Psycho-analysis*. Barthes, Foucault, Derrida, Althusser all attended these seminars. See especially Althusser's account of Lacan in *Lenin as a Philosopher*. His 'linguistic' interpretation

of Freud first took shape in the 'Discours de Rome', delivered in 1953: 'The function and field of the word and of language in Psycho-analysis.' It was reprinted in *Écrits* (1966) and has been translated by A. Wilden as *The Language of the Self* (1968), where it is accompanied by sixty-four pages of notes and a hundred-and-fifty page essay on Lacan. Even so the Anglo-American philosopher is scarcely likely to complain that he is being over-illuminated. Lacan's seminar on 'The insistence of the letter in the unconscious', specifically designed for philosophers, is translated in J. Ehrmann (ed.), *Structuralism*, with an introductory essay by J. Miel, and a lengthy bibliography. Lacan's career in the psycho-analytic movement has been a turbulent one. For a relatively sympathetic account see S. Turkle, *Psychoanalytic Politics* (1979); for a distinctly hostile account, F. George's oddly-titled *L'effet 'yau de poêle* (1978). See also C. Clément et al., *Jacques Lacan* (1974); A. Sheridan's translated selection from *Écrits* (1977); R. Coward and J. Ellis, *Language and Materialism* (1977); M. Stanton, *Outside the Dream* (1983). In S. Felman, *Le Scandale du corps parlant* (1980) Austin and Lacan are compared. For a not-unrelated French hermeneutic study see P. Ricoeur, *Freud and Philosophy* (1970). For a broader range of philosophical commentary on Freud see R. Wollheim (ed.), *Freud* (1974); R. Wollheim and J. Hopkins (eds), *Philosophical Essays on Freud* (1982).

7. Lévi-Strauss won a wide audience with his *Tristes Tropiques* (1955, complete trans. 1974), personal reflections on his travel and work as anthropologist. See especially §39: 'A little glass of rum.' *The Savage Mind* (1962, trans. 1966) struck a fashionable note with its elevation of the 'savage' and depreciation of the Western mind. His fullest theoretical statement is in *Structural Anthropology* (1958, trans. 1963). *The Elementary Structures of Kinship* (1949, trans. 1969) puts his method into practice as do the series of works on mythology beginning with *The Raw and the Cooked* (1964, trans. 1969). For a brief statement of his method see 'The Structural Study of Myth', *Journal of American Folklore* (1955), reprinted in R. and F. de George, *The Structuralists*. G. Charbonnier, *Conversations with Claude Lévi-Strauss* (1961, trans. 1969) conveys his general attitude over a wide range of topics. For an introductory essay see E. Leach, *Claude Lévi-Strauss* (1970). O. Paz, *Claude Lévi-Strauss*, (1967, trans. 1970) contains reflections on Lévi-Strauss by a Mexican critic. See also E. Leach, *Culture and Communication* (1976). E.N. and T. Hayes, *Claude Lévi-Strauss: the Anthropologist as Hero* (1970) contains a series of essays on Lévi-Strauss, with some book-extracts and an extensive bibliography of his writings up to 1968. For an account of his reception in England see N. Dyson-Hudson in R. Macksey and E. Donato, *The Language of Criticism and the Sciences of Man* (1970). Lévi-Strauss's analysis of myths is criticised by P. Pettit in *Structuralism* as 'hardly more than a licence for the free exercise of the imagination in establishing associations'. See also N. Chomsky, *Language and Mind* (2nd ed., 1972). For Derrida's criticisms see especially *Of Grammatology* (1967,

trans. 1974). There is a lengthy bibliography in J. Ehrmann, *Structuralism* (1970).

8. No less consequential, however, is the fact that the French Communist Party, to which the structuralists were to some degree committed, remained faithful to Leninist-Stalinism, turning its back on 'Socialist humanism'. In the 1970s things began to change. In his *Le Système des objets* (1968) J. Baudrillard offered a Marxist-structuralist analysis of consumer goods as essentially signs of prestige. In *The Mirror of Production* (1973, trans. 1975) he rejects Freud, Marx and structuralism alike, partly in reaction to the events of May 1968. He condemns structuralism on the sufficiently obvious ground that it has nothing to say about the referential character of language, about language as a form of communication, and both Marx and Freud as the final expression of bourgeois society. The 'new philosophers' in France reacted against Marx on a variety of grounds; they became the latest media-discovery in the mid-1970s. See, for example, B-H. Lévy, *Barbarism with a Human Face* (1977, trans. 1979) and A. Glucksmann, *The Master Thinkers* (1977, trans. 1980). What is really astonishing is how long it took for French intellectuals to divorce themselves from the Soviet Union, as if they were prepared to believe nobody but a novelist – Solzhenitsyn – about life in that country.

9. Derrida has exerted a considerable influence on literary critics. See, for example, the Derrida number of *The Oxford Literary Review* (1978) or H. Bloom et al., *Deconstruction and Criticism* (1979). For a more general discussion of his ideas see F. Jameson, *The Prison-House of Language* (1972); the very Derridean introduction by G. Spivak to the English translation of *Of Grammatology*; R. Rorty, 'Philosophy as a Kind of Writing' (*New Literary History*, 1978) and the short account by J. Culler in J. Sturrock (ed.), *Structuralism and Since* (1979). W.W. Fuchs, *Phenomenology and the Metaphysics of Presence* (1976) discusses the background against which Derrida is writing. For French reactions, see L. Finas et al., *Écarts* (1973). In *Annexe III* to that volume it is suggested that Derrida is more highly regarded outside France than within it, where he is read mainly by students at the new Universities, by psycho-analysts and by writers. For a comparison between Derrida and Wittgenstein see N. Garver's introduction to the English translation of *The Voice and the Phenomenon* and M. Grene, *Philosophy In and Out of Europe* (1976). For an American Derridean study see R. Rorty, *Philosophy and the Mirror of Nature* (1979). Unlike the structuralists, Derrida rarely grants interviews. But see his *Positions* (1972, trans. 1981), which contains his comments on marxism and psycho-analysis. C. Norris, *Deconstruction: Theory and Practice* (1982) relates Derrida to contemporary literary criticism. There is an extensive bibliography in the periodical *Research in Phenomenology* (1978) and a useful selection in Norris. Derrida has been severely criticised by Marxists as the death-agony of liberal humanism.

But in his *Marxism and Deconstruction* (1982), M. Ryan suggests that Marxism can at once use Derrida's methods in its critique of capitalism and fruitfully turn it against its own dogmatism.

10. Derrida began as a translator and commentator (1962) on Husserl's *The Origin of Geometry*; his detailed commentary on Husserl's theory of signs in *Speech and Phenomena* (1967, trans. 1973) continues to be of central significance in his thinking. It was Rousseau's turn in *Of Grammatology* (1967, trans. 1976). These – especially the first two – were still relatively conventional commentaries. But in *Glas* (1974) in which Hegel is juxtaposed with the French writer, Jean Genet, Derrida proceeds in a manner which even his warmest admirers have regarded with dismay, in which argument is displaced by free associations and bad puns. (We are reminded of Bradley's remark that no one ever set out to break logic without in the end logic breaking him.)

11. The publishing history is rather complicated. Derrida read his paper 'Signature, Event, Context' to the Congrès international des Sociétés de philosophie de langue française in 1971. It was reprinted in *Marges de la Philosophie* (1972) and translated in the Johns Hopkins periodical *Glyph I* (1977), where it was replied to by J.R. Searle. Derrida's very lengthy reply is published in *Glyph II* as 'Limited Inc., a b c'. It can be read in *Margins of Philosophy* (trans. 1983). The battle between Searle and the Derrideans did not end with this article. See his review of Culler (27 Oct. 1983) and reply to Mackey's counterblast (2 Feb. 1984) in *The New York Review*.

12. A useful approach to Chomsky's work is J.P. Allen and P. van Buren (eds), *Chomsky: Selected Readings* (1971). For his philosophical views see especially his *Language and Mind* (enlarged edition 1972) and *Reflections on Language* (1976). See also J. Lyons, *Chomsky* (1970); G. Harman (ed.), *On Noam Chomsky* (1974); J. Leiber, *Noam Chomsky* (1975); G. Sampson, *The Form of Language* (1975); F. D'Agostino, *Chomsky's System of Ideas* (1984); Chomsky's introduction to *The Logical Structure of Linguistic Theory* – written in 1955, first published in 1975 – contains an account of his intellectual development. He is exceptionally articulate; the interviews in B. Magee, *Men of Ideas* (1978) and H. Parret, *Discussing Language* (1974) are illuminating. For Chomsky's relationship to Carnapian and to 'ordinary language' philosophy of language see J.J. Katz, *The Philosophy of Language* (1966) and *The Underlying Reality of Language and its Philosophical Import* (1971). (The English edition, 1972, bears the title *Linguistic Philosophy*.) In *Philosophy and Psycho-Linguistics* (1973) E.L. Erde sets out to show that Wittgenstein and Chomsky are complementary. See also the essays in S. Hook (ed.), *Language and Philosophy* (1969). W. Stegmüller, *Hauptströmungen der Gegenwarts-philosophie* (1975), has an extensive bibliography, especially on the now considerable German work on Chomsky. See also M. Gerhardt

(ed.), *Linguistik und Sprachphilosophie* (1974). For Chomsky in the context of French structuralism see J. Parain-Vial, *Analyses structurales et idéologies structuralistes* (1969) and the debate between Chomsky and Foucault in F. Elder (ed.), *Reflexive Water* (1974). Useful introductions to Chomsky-style transformational grammar include E. Bach, *Syntactic Theory* (1974) and J.T. Grinder and S.H. Elgin, *Guide to Transformational Grammar* (1973). See also the collection J.A. Fodor and J.J. Katz (eds), *The Structure of Language* (1964); R. Jacobs and P.S. Rosenbaum (eds), *Readings in Transformational Grammar* (1970). The theory as a whole is detailed in J. Katz and P. Postal, *An Integrated Theory of Linguistic Descriptions* (1964). For linguistic critics, C.F. Hockett, *The State of the Art* (1968); the wide range of criticisms in H. Parret (ed.), *Discussing Language*; P. Matthews, *Generative Grammar and Linguistic Competence* (1979). A more 'literary' criticism, from a neo-Wittgensteinian point of view, is Ian Robinson's *The New Grammarian's Funeral* (1975). See also F. Householder (ed.), *Syntactic Theory* (1972) and N. Smith and D. Wilson, *Modern Linguistics: the Results of Chomsky's Revolution* (1979). P. Jacobsen and G. Pullum (eds), *The Nature of Syntactic Representation* (1982) indicates the ways in which later linguists have at once departed and parted from Chomsky. For a criticism from the speech act point of view see the essay by John Searle in G. Harman (ed.), *On Noam Chomsky* (1974). For a detailed account of the changes which have occurred in Chomsky's linguistic theory and the reactions of his associates and his critics see F.J. Newmeyer, *Linguistic Theory in America* (1980). See also the questions asked in D.T. Langendoen and P.M. Postal, *The Vastness of Natural Languages* (1984).

13. See N. Chomsky, *Problems of Knowledge and Freedom* (1972) and *For Reasons of State* (1973), which takes as its epigraph a long quotation from Bakunin. His wide-ranging shorter pieces are most easily read in C. Otero (ed.), *Radical Priorities* (1981). For a discussion of the interrelation between Chomsky's political views and his linguistic theories see G. Sampson, *Liberty and Language* (1979). The Polish Marxist philosopher, Adam Schaff, is distinctly more sympathetic to Chomsky than he is to Althusser. See his *Structuralism and Marxism* (1978).

14. No less important is the influence of that remarkable late-eighteenth-century thinker Wilhelm von Humboldt. For a general introduction to his thought see M. Cowan (ed.), *Humanist without Portfolio* (1963) or the introduction to J.W. Burrow's translation (1969) of *The Limits of State Action*, written in 1791 although not fully published until 1852. For Humboldt's theory of language in particular see E. Cassirer, *The Philosophy of Symbolic Forms* (vol.1, 1923, trans. 1953). Also influential was that maverick among American linguists Edward Sapir. See his *Language* (1921) and D.G. Mandelbaum (ed.), *Selected Essays by E. Sapir* (1949). There is a good brief account in Grinder and Elgin's *Guide to Tranformational Grammar* of what Chomsky owed to Harris. See

also Z. Harris, *Papers on Syntax* (ed. H. Hiż,1981). For Harris's later views see his 'A Theory of Language' (*APQ*, 1976). Paul Ziff applies Harris philosophically in his *Semantic Analysis* (1960). Chomsky's theories were developed at a time when simple computer-style theories of language were all the rage and are sometimes confused with them. But he was quite dissatisfied with the 'finite state' grammars which developed out of Claude Shannon's work on information theory. See, for example, C.F. Hockett, *A Manual of Phonology* (1955), reviewed by Chomsky in the *International Journal of American Linguistics* (1957). Such theories describe a speaker as proceeding in the manner of an automaton from an initial state through a choice of words, the choice at any point being limited by the preceding word. The 'grammar' of a language represents the restriction on such operations. Having chosen 'the' we cannot make 'a' our second word; having chosen 'boy' to follow 'the' we cannot choose 'go' as our third word and so on. Chomsky's objection is that we often cannot make our choice without referring back beyond the preceding word to earlier words. So in 'The man who told us is not coming', the choice of 'is' depends on 'man' not on 'us'. In Hockett's version, finite state grammars are linked with 'probabilistic' theories of language use. See also P. Suppes, 'Probabilistic Grammars for Natural Languages' (*Synthese*, 1970). On the broader contributions of this far-ranging thinker see R.J. Bogdan (ed.), *Patrick Suppes* (1979). For 'communication theory' in general use C. Cherry, *On Human Communication* (1966).

15. On the relationship between logical form and deep structure see the essays by G. Harman, J.J. Katz and W.V. Quine in D. Davidson and G. Harman (eds), *The Semantics of Natural Language* (1972). See also the comments by G. Lakoff in H. Parret (ed.), *Discussing Language*. For Chomsky's later views see also 'Deep Structure, Surface Structure and Interpretation' (1970) reprinted in his *Studies on Semantics in Generative Grammar* (1972). J.J. Katz defends semantic representation against traditional logical form in *The Monist* (1977). Chomsky returns to this theme in *Rules and Representations* (1980). See also *The Monist* (1973) on 'Philosophical Analysis and Deep Structure'.

16. This essay can be read in J.A. Fodor and J.J. Katz (eds), *The Structure of Language* (1964). See also 'Some Empirical Assumptions in Modern Philosophy of Language' in S. Morgenbesser, P. Suppes, M. White (eds), *Philosophy, Science and Method* (1969) which directs its fire more widely, against Quine and Wittgenstein as well as Skinner.

17. These distinctions – 'ungrammatical' and 'unacceptable', 'competence' and 'performance' – have been widely criticised, as have been Chomsky's evaluative procedures. Sometimes they are rejected as confining linguistic theory far too narrowly, so as to exclude, let us say, C.F. Hockett's analysis of 'Freudian slips'. (See his *The View from*

Language, 1977.) Chomsky's 'performance', G. Lakoff has written, is a 'waste-basket for all the phenomena that cannot be accommodated by whatever theory he happens to be maintaining at a given time'. Chomsky's own view is that he has no objection to attempts to work out a theory of 'performance' but that it is logically posterior to a theory of 'competence' and cannot expect to be either as general or as intellectually satisfying as that theory. His ambition, one might say, is to be the Galileo of linguistics; a falling feather is a 'performance'; we shall never discover the laws of fall by describing its movements. A broader question is whether Chomsky's linguistics does in fact constitute a well-formed theory or whether it resembles, rather, the 'occult qualities' of pre-Galilean physics or at best a 'neo-taxonomy' disguised as a theory. But it is, of course, by no means clear what constitutes a well-formed theory, or how theories are to be evaluated. See D. Cohen (ed.), *Explaining Linguistic Phenomena* (1974); D. Cohen and J. Wirth (eds), *Testing Linguistic Hypotheses* (1975). The most systematic account of Chomsky's methodology is the introductory section to *Aspects of the Theory of Syntax* (1965). See also essays 4,5, in H. Putnam, *Philosophical Papers*, vol.2 (1975).

18. Naturally enough, Chomsky's revival of innateness – philosophical theories die only to be reincarnated, after a decent interval – has not gone unchallenged. See the debate with N. Goodman and H. Putnam in *Synthese* (1967) reprinted in R.S. Cohen and W.M. Wartofsky (eds), *Boston Studies in the Philosophy of Science*, vol. 3 (1967) and Chomsky's further reply, first published in S. Hook (ed.), *Language and Philosophy* (1969), where other critics have their say, and reprinted in *Language and Mind*. See also R. Edgley, 'Innate Ideas' in G. Vesey (ed.), *Knowledge and Necessity* (1970); D. Cooper, *Philosophy and the Nature of Language* (1973) and *Knowledge of Language* (1975); S.P. Stich (ed.), *Innate Ideas* (1975); N. Chomsky, *Rules and Representations* (1980); M. Halle et al. (eds), *Linguistic Theory and Psychological Reality* (1980).

Chomsky refers to the psychologist K.S. Lashley in support. R. Gregory, *Eye and Brain* (1966) is a later contribution to cognitive psychology; Gregory has acknowledged Chomsky's influence. Chomsky has also inspired much work in psycho-linguistics. See, for example, J. Fodor, T. Bever and M. Garrett, *The Psychology of Language* (1974) or B. Derwing, *Transformational Grammar as a Theory of Language Acquisition* (1973). J.A. Fodor, *The Language of Thought* (1975) illustrates the interplay between psychology and Chomsky-style linguistics. Among the psychologist-critics of Chomsky one of the most notable is Piaget. See M. Piatelli-Palmarini, *Théories de Langage* (1979), a debate between Piaget and Chomsky, (trans. as *Language and Learning*, 1980). For alternative views of language-acquisition see P. Fletcher and M. Garman (eds), *Language Acquisition* (1979); K. Wexler and P.W. Culicover, *Formal Principles of Language Acquisition* (1980); E. Wanner and L.R. Gleitman (eds), *Language Acquisition* (1983).

19. On universal grammar see, as an introduction, E. Bach, *Syntactic Theory* and E. Bach and R. Harms (eds), *Universals in Linguistic Theory* (1968).

3. From Syntax to Semantics

1. A much disputed question. Most of the leading post-Chomskyan linguistic theorists – with R.T. Lakoff, J.D. McCawley, P.M. Postal, C.J. Fillmore as leading figures – bring syntax and semantics into closer relationship with one another. For an introduction to their work and some of Chomsky's criticisms see the essays included in D.D. Steinberg and L.A. Jakobovits (eds), *Semantics* (1971). See also E.L. Keenan (ed.), *Formal Semantics of Natural Language* (1975); P. Seuren (ed.), *Semantic Syntax* (1974). Chomsky argues that many of the points at issue are merely terminological. See his *Reflections on Language*. His opponents reply that Chomsky both wants to say this *and* that they are mistaken. For a comparison between Chomsky and Harris and the confusions created by their different concepts of 'transformation' see R.C. Dougherty, 'Harris and Chomsky at the Syntax-Semantics Boundary' in D. Hockney, W. Harper and B. Freed (eds), *Contemporary Research in Philosophical Logic and Linguistic Semantics* (1975).

2. J.D. Fodor, *Semantics* (1977) relates generative grammars to their rivals; J.J. Katz in *Semantic Theory* (1972) links them to philosophical logic and in *Propositional Structure and Illocutionary Force* (1977) to Austin. For a general survey – not always to be trusted at the more philosophical level – see J. Lyons, *Semantics* (2 vols, 1977). R.M. Kempson, *Semantics* (1977), with excellent bibliographies, is more argumentative. See also J.M.E. Moravcsik, *Understanding Language* (1975). In his *Componential Analysis of Meaning* (1975) C.A. Nida looks at translation. See also F. Guenthner and M. Guenthner-Reutter (eds), *Meaning and Translation* (1978). The Katz-Fodor approach is criticised by Y. Bar-Hillel in *Aspects of Language* (1970). See also R. Baüerle et al., *Semantics from Different Points of View* (1979). S. Peters and E. Saarinen (eds), *Processes, Beliefs and Questions* (1981) indicates just how broadly semantics is now conceived. See also H. Parret and J. Bouveresse (eds), *Meaning and Understanding* (1981). The overlap with, and difference from, traditional logical concerns comes out in such books as S. Cushing, *Quantifier Meanings* (1982). See also *The Monist* (1977); S. Kanger and S. Öhman (eds), *Philosophy and Grammar* (1980). From the appearance of J.J. Katz and P. Postal, *An Integrated Theory of Linguistic Descriptions* (1964), the classical attempt to work out Chomsky's suggestion that semantic interpretation should be related to deep structures, a battle raged about whether this could be done, described in detail in F.J. Newmeyer, *Linguistic Theory in America* (1980). Two collections which relate semantics on the one side to logic and on the other to epistemology are R. Stern and A. Orenstein (eds), *Development in Semantics* (1981) and H.

Leblanc et al., *Essays in Epistemology and Semantics* (1981). For a large-scale discussion of the central issues in the following pages, see G.P. Baker and P.M. Hacker, *Language, Sense and Nonsense* (1984).

3. For Katz's reply see 'Logic and Language' in K. Gunderson (ed.), *Language, Mind and Knowledge* (1975). See also G. Harman, 'Meaning and Semantics' in M. Munitz and P. Unger (eds), *Semantics and Philosophy* (1974). In his later work Katz rejects a mentalistic in favour of a 'Platonist' approach. See his *Language and Other Abstract Objects* (1981). In his 'Literal Meaning and Logical Theory' (*JP*, 1981) he criticises not only Searle and Grice but Davidson and Dummett (below). On Fodor see also ch.5, n.10.

4. See *HY*, ch.17, n.20. Hilary Putnam, in the same spirit, has accused not only Carnap but Katz of dressing up traditional mistakes in modern garb. See his 'Is Semantics Possible?', first published in H.E. Kiefer and M.K. Munitz (eds), *Languages, Belief and Metaphysics* (1970). In a later essay on 'The Meaning of "Meaning" ' in K. Gunderson (ed.), *Language, Mind and Knowledge* (1975) he is much more sympathetically inclined towards, at least, the 'markers-distinguishers' analysis, for all that Katz later abandoned it. (Both these essays are in H. Putnam, *Philosophical Papers*, 1975.) The most systematic attempt to work out an 'ordinary language' approach to grammatical analysis is B. Rundle, *Grammar in Philosophy* (1979). Note Peter Geach's adverse review in *Times Literary Supplement*, March 7, 1980. In his *An Introduction to the Philosophy of Language* (1979), Bernard Harrison defends a late-Wittgensteinian analysis of language, after critically surveying a wide range of contemporary alternatives. For the view that the post-Fregeans misunderstand Frege, whose work is quite at odds with theirs, see G. Baker and P. Hacker, *Frege* (1980). See also J. Hintikka, 'Semantics: a Revolt against Frege' in G. Fløistad (ed.), *Contemporary Philosophy* (1981).

5. His more philosophical essays were collected by R.H. Thomason as *Formal Philosophy* (1974), with a very useful introduction and a bibliography. B. Partee relates Montague to Chomsky in a number of articles, most fully in 'Montague Grammar and Transformational Grammar', *Linguistic Inquiry* (1975). See also the essays she brought together as *Montague Grammar* (1976) and particularly the introductory exposition in C.L. Hamblin, 'Questions in Montague English'. Montague is discussed in K.J. Hintikka (ed.), *Approaches to Natural Language* (1973) and J.M.E. Moravcsik, *Understanding Language* (1975). See also the account of Montague in W. Stegmüller, *Hauptströmungen der Gegenwarts-philosophie* (1975 ed., vol.2) and, for an adverse judgment, R.M. Martin: 'Why I am not a Montague Grammarian' in *Pragmatics, Truth and Language* (1979). See also J. Hintikka, 'On the Proper Treatment of Quantifiers in Montague Semantics' in S. Stenlund (ed.), *Logical Theory and Semantic Analysis* (1974). For a more detailed work

.constructed in Montague's spirit see M.J. Cresswell, *Logics and Languages* (1973). See also S. Davis and M. Mithun (eds), *Linguistics, Philosophy and Montague Grammar* (1979); G. Link, *Montague-Grammatik* (1979).

The essays included in E.L. Keenan (ed.), *Formal Semantics of Natural Language* (1975) range broadly over the field, but include critiques of Montague's approach. See also S. Kanger and S. Öhman (eds), *Philosophy and Grammar* (1980); F. Guenthner and S.J. Schmidt (eds), *Formal Semantics and Pragmatics for Natural Languages* (1979) and M. Przelecki: 'A Model-Theoretic Approach to the Problem of Interpretation of Empirical Languages' in M. Przelecki and R. Wojcicki (eds), *Twenty Five Years of Logical Methodology in Poland* (1977). For a textbook style introduction see D. Dowty et al., *Introduction to Montague Semantics* (1981). Dowty's *A Guide to Montague's PTQ* (1978) reads Montague as he wanted to be read – 213 pages on a 24-page article. Even then, few will complain that Dowty is unnecessarily verbose. See also N. Cocchiarella, 'Richard Montague' in G. Fløistad (ed.), *Contemporary Philosophy* (1981). For an example of the way in which linguists bring together Chomsky and Montague see R. Cooper, *Quantification and Syntactic Theory* (1983). Montague's work is now widely discussed in Belgium and the Netherlands, as well as in West Germany. As is frequently the case in the more technical branches of philosophy, much of the discussion finds its way into circulated papers rather than into books or articles. For an alternative, purely intentional, approach see G. Bealer, *Quality and Concept* (1982).

6. Alonzo Church's article first appeared in *Proceedings of the American Academy of Arts and Sciences* (1951). It is reprinted in J.A. Fodor and J.J. Katz, *The Structure of Language* (1964). See also Church's review of Carnap's *Introduction to Semantics* (*PR*, 1943). Church's brief articles and reviews have exerted an influence on contemporary philosophy which could scarcely be guessed from their number and length. His logic is most fully formulated in *An Introduction to Mathematical Logic* (1956). In his 'Truth and Meaning', *Synthese* (1967), Donald Davidson had suggested that formal semantics might be extended to natural languages as did Terence Parsons in his unpublished but widely circulated *A Semantics for English* (1968). For an attempt to develop a logic of such 'fuzzy concepts' as 'tall' see G. Lakoff, 'Hedges' in D. Hockney et al. (eds.), *Contemporary Research in Philosophical Logic and Linguistic Semantics* (1975) together with the comments of B.C. Van Fraassen. Van Fraassen's *Formal Semantics and Logic* (1971) is a rigorous introduction to the field. See also the work of L. Zadeh, especially his contribution to W. Leinfellner et al. (eds), *Language and Ontology* (1982). This is partly a criticism of Montague. It includes a bibliography of Zadeh's work. For a more general treatment of metaphor, vagueness etc., see I. Scheffler, *Beyond the Letter* (1979) and ch.1, n.22 above. For a set of West German essays on this theme see T.T. Ballmer and M. Pinkal (eds), *Approaching*

Vagueness (1983). See also H.J. Skala et al. (eds), *Aspects of Vagueness* (1984).

7. See notes 9 and 10 to *HY* ch.17. On tense logic, the work of A.N. Prior was particularly important. See his *Time and Modality* (1957) and the sets of papers collected after his premature death as *Past, Present and Future* (1967); *Papers on Time and Tense* (1968); *Objects of Thought* (1971). *Doctrine of Propositions and Terms* (1976); *Papers in Logic and Ethics* (1976); *Worlds, Times and Selves* (1977). For a general account of Prior's work see the obituary notice by A. Kenny (*Proceedings of the British Academy*, 1970). More generally see N. Rescher and A. Urquart, *Temporal Logic* (1971). There is some dispute about the relationship between tense logics and the use of tenses in natural languages. See especially D.M. Gabbay, *Investigations in Modal and Tense Logics* (1976), critically reviewed by J.W. Gerson (*International Studies in Philosophy*, 1978). D. Dowty, *Word Meaning and Montague Grammar* (1979) compares Montague and Chomsky-style grammars on tenses and verbs generally. In *Word and Object* (1960) Quine defends his characteristic view that by the use of such descriptions as 'John at time *t*', the argumentative force of temporal distinctions can be incorporated within classical logic. Prior, always influenced by the Polish logicians, wants to extend the classical apparatus. Questions have also been raised about adverbial expressions, as by R. Clark in 'Concerning the Logic of Predicate Modifiers' (*Noûs*, 1970) and T. Parsons, 'Some Problems concerning the Logic of Grammatical Modifiers' (*Synthese*, 1970), reprinted in D. Davidson and G. Harman (eds), *Semantics of Natural Language* (1972) and most fully, within the context of Church-style set theory, in M.K. Rennie, *Some Uses of Type Theory in the Analysis of Language* (1974).

8. Quine's objections can be read in, for example, 'Three Grades of Modal Involvement' (1953) reprinted in *The Ways of Paradox* (1966). There is a good selection from the vast resulting literature in Leonard Linsky's collection *Reference and Modality* (1971) with an extensive bibliography, equally select. Of the articles in Linsky, D. Kaplan, 'Quantifying In' has been particularly discussed. It first appeared in D. Davidson and J. Hintikka (eds), *Words and Objections* (1969). The basic texts are in F. Zabeeh et al., *Readings in Semantics* (1974). Another useful collection is D. Davidson and G. Harman (eds), *The Logic of Grammar* (1975). See also the particularly lucid account of contemporary disputes about modal logic by R. Barcan Marcus in G. Fløistad, *Contemporary Philosophy*, vol.1.

9. Saul Kripke became something of a legend in the 1970s. See the *New York Times* (August 14, 1977). At the age of 18 he published his first article on 'A Completeness Theorem of Modal Logic' in *JSL* (1959). His articles on modal logic are extremely succinct and widely scattered; his semantical analyses were published in the *Zeitschrift für mathematische Logik* (1963), *Acta Philosophica Fennica* (1963) and J. Addison, L. Henkin

and A. Tarski (eds), *The Theory of Models* (1965). The second of these articles is reprinted in Linsky. For a discussion of the degree to which 'possible-world' semantics is indeed Leibnizian see B. Mates, 'Leibniz on Possible Worlds' in B. van Rootselaar and J.F. Staal (eds), *Logic, Methodology and Philosophy of Science* III (1968). Carnap had already invoked the concept of possible worlds in his *Meaning and Necessity* (1947), influenced by Wittgenstein's *Tractatus* references to 'possible states of affairs', as, earlier still, had C.I. Lewis. Kripke's semantics had been substantially anticipated in S. Kanger, *Provability in Logic* (1957). But it was Kripke's version which caught the eye. (Kanger had published in Stockholm.) For modal logic generally see *HT*, ch.17, n.9. Among those who defended modal logic against Quine one of the most forceful was Ruth Barcan (Marcus). The major contributions to this controversy are printed in Linsky and in F. Zabeeh et al., *Readings in Semantics*, section 7 (1974). See also D. Scott, 'Advice on Modal Logic' in K. Lambert (ed.), *Philosophical Problems in Logic* (1970); E.J. Lemmon and D. Scott, *Introduction to Modal Logic* (1977); M.J. Loux (ed.), *The Possible and the Actual* (1979); Scott's approach is developed in J. Stoy, *Denotational Semantics* (1977). See also S. Haack, *Philosophy of Logics* (1978).

10. Ajdukiewicz's essay was first published (in German) in *Studia Philosophica 1* (1935), trans. in S. McCall (ed.), *Polish Logic* (1967). See also Y. Bar-Hillel, *Language and Information* (1964); J. Pelč (ed.), *Semiotics in Poland* (trans. 1978); A. Church, 'A Formulation of the Simple Theory of Types' (*JSL*, 1940) and *The Calculi of Lambda-conversion* (1941). On Lésniewski see E.C. Luschei, *The Logical Systems of Lésniewski* (1962). M. Creswell's *Logics and Languages* (1973) should particularly be consulted in this context. See also J. Szrednicki and V. Rickey, *Lesniewski's Systems* (1983).

11. 'Pragmatics' is usually defined much more broadly; the work of Austin and his followers is often included in its ambit. See, for example, J.R. Searle (ed.), *Speech Act Theory and Pragmatics* (1980); S.C. Levinson, *Pragmatics* (1982). For German pragmatics see K.-O. Apel (ed.), *Sprachpragmatik und Philosophie* (1976) and ch.1, n.10. For Polish pragmatics see K. Ajdukiewicz, *Pragmatic Logic* (1965, trans. 1974). The suggestion that pragmatics should concentrate on indexical expressions Montague derived from Y. Bar-Hillel, 'Indexical Expressions' (*Mind*, 1954), reprinted in Y. Bar-Hillel, *Aspects of Language* (1970). See also Y. Bar-Hillel (ed.), *Pragmatics of Natural Languages* (1971); R.C. Stalnaker, 'Pragmatics' in D. Davidson and G. Harman, *Semantics of Natural Language* (1972); the sections on 'Pragmatics' in A. Kasher (ed.), *Language in Focus* (1976) and E.L. Keenan (ed.), *Formal Semantics of Natural Language* (1975); R.M. Martin, *Pragmatics, Truth and Language* (1979). For an account of the interrelation between syntax, semantics and pragmatics within the general field of linguistics see J. Pelč, 'The Place of the Philosophy of Language' in G. Fløistad (ed.), *Contemporary*

Philosophy (1981). See also *The Journal of Pragmatics* (1977-) and W. Sellars, *Pure Pragmatics and Possible Worlds* ed. J. Sicha (1980) – although these are earlier essays than the publication date suggests.

12. Lewis's general semantics is reprinted in D. Davidson and G. Harman (eds), *Semantics of Natural Language* (1972). For his 'Languages, Language and Grammar' see G. Harman (ed.), *On Noam Chomsky* (1974). Lewis's use of game-theory, it should be observed, is very different from Hintikka's game-theoretical semantics. Hintikka's starting-point is a competitive game: 'an attempted verification of a given sentence *S* resisted by an actively malicious opponent which can be identified with nature.' For game-theoretical semantics see J. Hintikka, *Logic, Language Games, and Information* (1973); E. Saarinen (ed.), *Game-Theoretical Semantics* (1979); F. Guenthner and S.J. Schmidt (eds), *Formal Semantics and Pragmatics for Natural Languages* (1979). Hintikka relates his semantics to a modified version of Wittgenstein's 'language games'. There is still another application of game theory in the 'dialogical logic' of P. and K. Lorenzen (*Dialogische Logik*, 1978). This takes as its point of departure the logic of argumentation, as illustrated in a philosophical dialogue. For Hintikka's work in general see E. Saarinen et al., *Essays in Honour of J. Hintikka* (1979). Lewis acknowledges his indebtedness to E. Stenius, 'Mood and Language Game' (*Synthese*, 1967) for his theory of truthfulness conventions. Lewis's articles are collected as *Philosophical Papers* (1983). As an example of the use that is made of his theory of convention see *New Literary History* (1981 and 1983) with contributions by Putnam and Goodman. His theory of communication is criticised in A.J. Jones, *Communication and Meaning* (1983).

13. Goodman is a staunch nominalist, for whom nothing exists except individuals. He joined with Quine in writing his 'Steps towards a Constructive Nominalism' (*JSL*, 1947). But whereas Quine moved away from nominalism as a result of his doctrine of 'ontological commitment', Goodman has remained faithful. See the third edition of *The Structure of Appearance* (1977), with an introduction by G. Hellman, and *Problems and Projects* (1972).
    For an example of the sort of controversy aroused by Goodman's 'green-grue' example, see the articles in *JP* 1966-1967, including Goodman's comments and D. Davidson, 'Mental Events' (1970), republished in his *Essays on Actions and Events* (1980). It is typical of the historian's difficulties nowadays that some of the *JP* writers, in spite of the relative publication dates, refer to Davidson's argument. On Goodman's nominalism see M. Dummett, *Truth and other Enigmas* (1980), including a 'Critical Notice' from *Mind*, 1955 and articles in *PR* 1956 and 1957. On nominalism generally see *The Monist* (1978). The range of Goodman's interests is illustrated in his *Of Mind and Other Matters* (1984).

14. Like Armstrong, Mackie was a very independent pupil of the Australian

philosopher John Anderson although, unlike Armstrong, he spent most of his life outside Australia, much of it at Oxford. His views about probability are most fully expounded in *Truth, Probability and Paradox* (1973) which is part-dedicated to Anderson. It includes a criticism of possible world theories. In *The Cement of the Universe* (1974) he develops a conditional theory of causality. See also E. Sosa (ed.), *Causation and Conditionals* (1975) along with the highly compressed articles on causality and on hypotheticals in John Anderson, *Studies in Empirical Philosophy* (1962). For Anderson see also *HY* ch.11, n.10. For subsequent causal theories see M. Bunge, 'The Revival of Causality' in G. Fløistad (ed.), *Contemporary Philosophy*, vol.2 (1982), together with the essay in the same volume by I. Niiniluoto on 'Statistical Explanation'. B. Skyrms, *Causal Necessity* (1980) explores similar themes.

15. The controversy can be followed in W.L. Harper et al., *Ifs* (1981). One can also pursue in that volume the closely related issue of conditional probability, to which Lewis has also contributed. See also D. Nute, *Topics in Conditional Logic* (1980); W.L. Harper et al., *Ifs, Conditionals, Belief, Decision, Chance and Time* (1980). Once more, Lewis goes in search of a 'higher synthesis', in this case of a subjective theory of probability and a chance or propensity theory. See also ch.5, n.12 below. One major point at issue is whether it is possible to give a single account of counter-factual and ordinary conditionals, whether in terms of truth conditions or, as Brian Ellis has suggested, of 'acceptability conditions'. See the debate between Ellis, F. Jackson and A. Appiah (*AJP*, 1984).

16. Lewis propounded his counterpart theory in 'Counterpart Theory and Quantified Modal Logic' (*JP*, 1968). It has been much criticised, as in A. Plantinga, *The Nature of Necessity* (1974); K. Fine's critical review (*Mind*, 1975); D. Nute (*Noûs*, 1975); S. Haack (*RM*, 1976); F.M. and J.J. Katz (*PR*, 1977). See also Kripke, below. On the broader theme see also J.L. Pollock, *Subjunctive Reasoning* (1976). For earlier work on counter-factuals see *HY*, ch.18, n.21, along with the introduction by W.C. Salmon to the 1976 edition of H. Reichenbach: *Laws, Modalities and Counterfactuals*, originally published as *Nomological Statements and Admissible Operations* (1954), a pioneer study of counterfactuals. R. Chisholm, 'Identity through Possible Worlds' (*Noûs*, 1967) is an important alternative. See also the textbook of R. Bradley and N. Swartz, *Possible Worlds* (1979). Other problems for possible world semantics relate, as usual, to indexical statements and propositional attitudes. See R. Stalnaker, 'Indexical Belief' in *Synthese* (1981) and J. Bigelow, 'Believing in Semantics' (*Linguistics and Philosophy*, 1978). There are many other varieties of possible world semantics, developed by N. Rescher, M. Cresswell and others. For a starting point see M. Loux (ed.), *The Possible and the Actual* (1979). Possible worlds are also invoked in deontic logics, as one might expect, given the resemblances between deontic and modal logics. See, for example, R. Hilpinen (ed.), *Deontic*

Logic (1970) and *New Studies in Deontic Logic* (1981).

17. Kripke's views have been extensively discussed, if by no means amid unanimous approval. The best entry-point is S.P. Schwartz (ed.), *Naming, Necessity and Natural Kinds* (1977) which includes an earlier essay by Kripke on 'Identity and Necessity' (1971). See also many articles in *Philosophical Studies* and in *JP* from 1973 onwards along with *Midwest Studies in Philosophy* (1976, 1977). A collection by J. Woods and L.W. Sumner (eds), *Necessary Truth* (1969) illustrates the state of the discussion when Kripke intervened. For a full-length study of necessity, with a special concern for theology, see A. Plantinga, *The Nature of Necessity* (1974). For links between essentialism and modal logic see *Noûs* (1967) and the essay on modal logic by R.B. Marcus in G. Fløistad (ed.), *Contemporary Philosophy* (1981). See also the comments on Kripke in D. Wiggins, *Sameness and Substance* (1980). Although R. Sorabji, *Necessity, Cause and Blame* (1980) is basically a commentary on Aristotle it has a good deal to say about Kripke. See also ch.3, n.9 above for Kripke on modal logic. T. Parsons has argued in his 'Essentialism and Quantified Modal Logic' (*PR*, 1969) that such a logic is not necessarily essentialist. See for Kripke's central article, Parsons and other basic papers L. Linsky (ed.), *Reference and Modality* (1971). For alternative approaches see S. Blackburn (ed.), *Meaning, Reference and Necessity* (1975).

18. See S. Kripke, 'Is There a Problem about Substitutional Quantification?' in G. Evans and J. McDowell (eds), *Truth and Meaning* (1976). This is in part a criticism of J. Wallace, 'On the Frame of Reference' in D. Davidson and G. Harman (eds), *The Semantics of Natural Language* (1972). John Wallace is another philosopher whose influence, often exerted through personal discussion, is much wider than his rather scattered publications would suggest.

19. On proper names see also J. Searle, 'Proper Names' (*Mind*, 1958), developed in his *Speech Acts* (1969). He would object to Kripke's account of his views. 'To use a proper name referringly,' he says, 'is to *presuppose* the truth of certain uniquely referring descriptive statements, but it is not ordinarily to *assert* these statements or even to indicate which exactly are presupposed' (my italics). See also three articles by K.S. Donnellan: 'Reference and Definite Descriptions' (*PR*, 1966), 'Proper Names and Identifying Descriptions' (*Synthese*, 1970) and 'Speaking of Nothing' in D. Hockney et al. (eds), *Contemporary Research in Philosophical Logic* (1975), along with Kripke's 'Speaker's Reference and Semantic Reference' (*Midwest Studies*, 1977). Donnellan is a member of that not inconsiderable group of contemporary philosophers – another example is D. Kaplan – whose works, often described as 'unpublished', are much referred to but whom the schematic, as distinct from the encylopedic, historian has to pass by. See also C. Peacocke, 'Proper Names, Reference and Rigid Designation' in S. Blackburn (ed.), *Meaning,*

Reference and Necessity (1975); P. Ziff, 'About Proper Names' (*Mind*, 1977); L. Linsky, *Names and Descriptions* (1977). In his *Frege* (1973), M. Dummett comments at length, and severely, on Kripke's theory of proper names as also in *Truth and Other Enigmas* (1978). Kripke replies in the preface to *Meaning and Necessity*. Many of the issues had been taken up by Paul Ziff in *Semantic Analysis* (1960) and developed in his *Understanding Understanding* (1972). A good idea of the older controversies about proper names can be gathered from the essays on 'names and descriptions' in D. Davidson and G. Harman (eds), *The Logic of Grammar* (1975), with selections from Russell and Quine and later essays by T. Burge (1973) and D. Kaplan (1970) or in the section on 'reference' in D. Steinberg and L. Jakobovits (eds), *Semantics* (1971). Naturally, linguists have also interested themselves in this theme. See, for example, C. Sloat, 'Proper Names in English' (*Language*, 1969) which, like Kripke, assimilates proper and common nouns. See also B. Mates, 'On the Semantics of Proper Names' in W. Abraham (ed.), *Ut Videam* (1975). In Schwartz's anthology see G. Evans, 'The Causal Theory of Names' (*PASS*, 1973). P.T. Geach, 'Names and Identity' in S. Guttenplan, *Mind and Language* (1975) is mainly about Frege but departs from Frege in respect to what counts as a name. For a philosophico-linguistic study see Z. Vendler, *Linguistics in Philosophy* (1967). The 'causal' theory of proper names is sometimes ascribed to Donnellan; it has been developed by M. Devitt. See his *Designation* (1981).

The classical problems about substitution in belief sentences arise in a special form in respect to the substitution of a proper name like 'Tully' for 'Cicero' if names are taken to be rigid designators. On this theme see Kripke's essay, 'A Puzzle about Belief' in A. Margalit (ed.), *Meaning and Use* (1979).

20. On natural kinds, see several of the essays in H. Putnam, *Mind, Language and Reality* (1975), beginning with 'Is Semantics Possible?' (1970) and running on, with special reference to Kripke, in 'The Meaning of "Meaning" ' (1975), together with W.V. Quine, 'Natural Kinds' in the Schwartz anthology, D.H. Mellor, 'Natural Kinds' (*BJPS*, 1977) and David Wiggins, above.

On mass terms see F.J. Pelletier (ed.), *Mass Terms* (1979).

On names and necessity see R.B. de Sousa, 'Kripke on naming and necessity' (*Canadian Jnl of Phil.*, 1973); H.S. Chandler, 'Rigid Designation' (*JP*, 1975) and, especially, N. Salmon, *Reference and Essence* (1982). In his 'Names and Identity' P.T. Geach totally rejects 'the distinction of syntactical category between proper names and common names'. (In S. Guttenplan (ed.), *Mind and Language*, 1974.)

21. For comment see, for example, the articles in *JP*, 1974 and the discussion by Wiggins, Marcus and Hacking in S. Körner (ed.), *Philosophy of Logic* (1976) which concentrates on the broader logical issues. See also T. Nagel, 'What is it like to be a bat?' (*PR*, 1974),

reprinted in *Mortal Questions* (1979) for a defence of Kripke.

4. Davidson and Dummett

1. For a general introduction to the work of this school and to Davidson and Dummett generally, see M. Platts, *Ways of Meaning* (1979); G. Evans and J. McDowell (eds), *Truth and Meaning* (1976); and M. Platts (ed.), *Reference, Truth and Reality* (1980). More specialised studies include C. Peacocke, *Holistic Explanation* (1979); B. Loar, *Mind and Meaning* (1981) – a defence of a neo-Gricean approach to meaning; the posthumously published G. Evans, *The Varieties of Reference* (1982), ed. J. McDowell. See also Quine's review of the Evans and McDowell volume (*JP*, 1977). M. Davies, *Meaning, Quantification, Necessity* (1981), provides a relatively graduated approach. The work of this group, however, is necessarily difficult, in the light of their topics, and also unnecessarily so, as a consequence of the peculiar opacity of their style, as if they were intent on concealing rather than revealing. There is a representative criss-cross of views in *The Monist* (1979) on 'Truth, Meaning and Reference', with contributions by Quine, Evans, Strawson.

2. Davidson is particularly good at referring both to those who have influenced him and those who have taken up his ideas. In the former group fall most of the philosophers mentioned in *HY* ch.20. *Actions and Events* includes several replies to critics – especially, on the question of events, to R.M. Chisholm.

3. The position adopted by Smart and Lewis, Davidson calls 'nomological monism'. For doctrines like his own he refers us to T. Nagel, 'Physicalism' (*PR*, 1965) and P.F. Strawson in D. Pears (ed.), *Freedom and the Will* (1963). Kripke refers to Davidson-Nagel identity theories but does not specifically contest them.

4. For general discussions of Davidson's semantics see, as well as the books mentioned in ch.4, n.1, I. Hacking, *Why does Language Matter to Philosophy?* (1975); R.M. Kempson, *Semantic Theory* (1977); B. Harrison, *An Introduction to the Philosophy of Language* (1979); A.R. Lacey, *Modern Philosophy* (1982); C. Peacocke and J. Hintikka in G. Fløistad (ed.), *Contemporary Philosophy*. Of Davidson's articles 'Truth and Meaning' first appeared in *Synthese* (1967) and is reprinted in J.F. Rosenberg and C. Travis (eds), *Readings in the Philosophy of Language* (1971). 'On Saying That' appeared in D. Davidson and J. Hintikka (eds), *Words and Objections* (1969), with Quine's comments, and is in D. Davidson and G. Harman (eds), *The Logic of Grammar* (1975), along with 'Semantics for Natural Languages' and other relevant essays, especially G. Harman on 'Logical Form'. For 'In Defense of Convention T' see H. Leblanc (ed.), *Truth, Syntax and Modality* (1973); 'Radical Interpretation' is in *Dialectica*

(1973). The reply to Foster is in Evans and McDowell. See also H. Putnam, 'The Meaning of Meaning' (1975), reprinted in his *Philosophical Papers* vol.2 (1975); C.H. Chihara, 'Truth, Meaning and Paradox' (*Noûs*, 1976). But as in Kripke's case discussion of Davidson has been too extensive for enumeration. He replies to Lewis and Quine in *Synthese* (1974).

5. Barry Taylor in the course of developing 'A Truth-theory for Indexical Languages' in M. Platts (ed.), *Reference, Truth and Reality* ascribes to Davidson the view that underlying English 'there exists a formal language ("Base English") in which every surface sentence of English finds at least one paraphrase ("a base paraphrase")' – 'surface sentences' being linked to such paraphrases 'by a series of meaning-preserving Chomskyan transformations'. This is very close, indeed, to Chomsky. One might well hesitate at such an interpretation. See Davidson, 'Semantics for Natural Languages' on Chomsky.

6. First published in *Dialectica* (1977), reprinted in Platts. Compare on 'reference' and 'meaning' J. Hintikka, 'Semantics for Propositional Attitudes' in J.W. Davis et al. (eds), *Philosophical Logic* (1969); S. Leeds, 'Theories of Reference and Truth' (*Erkenntnis*, 1978); E. Saarinen (ed.), *Demonstrative and Indexical Reference* (1981).

7. For Tarski see *HT*, ch.17, n.16. There is a truncated version of 'The Concept of Truth' in Davidson and Harman. Lacey, Platts and Hacking all attempt expositions of Tarski, of varying degrees of complexity. Hartry Field's reformulation of Tarski (*JP*, 1972) and his suggestion that Tarski reduced truth to other semantic notions rather than defining it without the use of semantic notions has been widely discussed. It is reprinted in Platts along with a critique by McDowell. See also the account of Tarski in W.V. Quine, *Philosophy of Logic* (1970).

8. See, as well as 'Radical Interpretation' Davidson's article on 'Thought and Talk' in S. Guttenplan (ed.), *Mind and Language* (1975) along with the critical essay by D. Føllesdal. A Norwegian philosopher, Føllesdal has written extensively on contemporary philosophy of logic and language and has sought to reconcile phenomenology and analytical philosophy. See his 'An Introduction to Phenomenology for Analytic Philosophers' in R.E. Olsen and A.M. Paul (eds), *Contemporary Philosophy in Scandinavia* (1972). Quine's essay in Guttenplan is a good introduction to this theory of language-learning. Davidson thinks that indeterminacy in translation is rather less consequential than Quine supposes.

9. The question of propositional attitudes continues to be widely discussed. For a post-Davidsonian view see H. Burdick, 'A Logical Form for the Propositional Attitudes' with comments by Quine (*Synthese*, 1982).

10. Most of Dummett's essays up to 1976 are included in *Truth and Other Enigmas* (1978). The two essays on the theory of meaning are in S. Guttenplan (ed.), *Mind and Language* (1975), which also includes important essays by Anscombe, Quine, Davidson, Geach and Føllesdal, and in G. Evans and J. McDowell, *Truth and Meaning* (1976). There is some discussion of Dummett in this volume but more in M. Platts (ed.), *Reference, Truth and Reality* (1980). For Dummett's 'Science and Commonsense' see G.F. Macdonald (ed.), *Perception and Identity* (1979) with Ayer's reply.

Among philosophers who stand close to Dummett, although not uncritically so, one should mention Crispin Wright. See his discussion with Roger Scruton on 'Truth Conditions and Criteria' (*PASS*, 1976) and, for criticism, Strawson's remarks as chairman (*PAS*, 1977). Wright's *Wittgenstein on the Foundations of Mathematics* (1980) is also relevant, as is his defence of finitism (*Synthese*, 1982). On use and meaning see A. Margalit (ed.), *Meaning and Use* (1979). Dummett's anti-realism and the link between it and Wittgenstein's 'criteria' are further discussed by John McDowell in his 'Criteria, Defeasibility and Knowledge' (*PBA*, 1982) with some reference both to his own 'Anti-realism and the Epistemology of Understanding' in H. Parret and J. Bouveresse (eds), *Meaning and Understanding* (1981) and Wright's 'Anti-realist Semantics' in G. Vesey (ed.), *Idealism: Past and Present* (1982).

11. For Hintikka's semantics see above ch.3, n.12.

12. A central reference for the discussion not only of Dummett but of the whole realist versus anti-realist controversy is *Synthese* (1982) with three numbers devoted to this theme. For a distinctly hostile critique of Dummett, see M. Devitt, 'Dummett's Anti-realism' (*JP*, 1983). He did not have the opportunity of reading Dummett's 1982 article.

On the issue of bivalence, see also W.V. Quine, 'What Price Bivalence?' in *Theories and Things* (1981).

5. Realism and Relativism

1. For Goodman, see also ch.3, n.13 above. Many of his major themes are more clearly presented in *Problems and Projects* (1972). Ayer criticises Goodman as, more briefly, Dummett in *Philosophy in the Twentieth Century* (1982). *The Structure of Appearance* should be read in the third edition (1977), with an important introduction by G. Hellman. Dummett's discussion is in three essays (originally published in 1955-7) in *Truth and Other Enigmas*. Quine criticises Goodman in *Theories and Things* (1981). Goodman's approach to art is influenced by E.H. Gombrich, whose *Art and Illusion* (1960) did so much to make art theory respectable in the eyes

of philosophers. My own 'Art and Truth' (*Tanner Lectures on Human Values*, 3, 1982) is at some places close to Goodman – if at other places not at all so – although developed independently. See also the discussion by Hempel and Scheffler in *Synthese* (1980) with Goodman's reply. Hempel interestingly relates Goodman to Neurath. See also Hilary Putnam's more favourable comment in *JP* (1979).

2. See also Popper's *Realism and the Aim of Science* (1983). For criticism see P. Feyerabend, 'Popper's *Objective Knowledge*' in *Philosophical Papers*, vol.2 (1981). Naturally his views have been unenthusiastically received by sociologists of knowledge. See D. Bloor, 'Popper's Mystification of Scientific Knowledge' (*Science Studies*, 1974). See also the more recent commentaries in *HY*, ch.17, n.27.

3. This article, like several others in *Collected Papers*, was not previously published; otherwise, I give the date of publication.

   For approaches to mathematics which do not assimilate mathematical reasoning to Euclidean-style proofs see, as well as the discussion of Wittgenstein's philosophy of mathematics in *HY*, G. Pólya, *Mathematics and Plausible Reasoning* (1954); I. Lakatos, *Proofs and Refutations* (1976) and *Mathematics, Science and Epistemology* (1978) – his original publications were in *BJPS* (1963-4); H. Lehman, *Introduction to the Philosophy of Mathematics* (1979); P. Kitcher: *The Nature of Mathematical Knowledge* (1983). Putnam refers to Pólya but not to Lakatos.

   The subtitle of Lakatos' book is 'the logic of mathematical discovery'. When N.R. Hanson wrote his *Patterns of Discovery* (1958), Reichenbach's contrast between 'the context of justification' and 'the context of discovery', with the associated doctrine that only the first of these is of any interest to the philosophy of science, was still widely taken for granted. But now see, for example, H.A. Simon, *Models of Discovery* (1977); T. Nickles (ed.), *Scientific Discovery, Logic and Rationality* and *Scientific Discovery* – both 1980; M.D. Grmek et al. (eds), *On Scientific Discovery* (1981).

4. See also *HY* ch.20, n.29. Later writings in this same area are particularised in the article by R.B. Angel and M.L. Dalla Chiara, with P.A. Metelli, in G. Fløistad, *Contemporary Philosophy*, vol.2 (1982). On space-time see M. Bunge, *Philosophy of Physics* (1973) and his many other writings detailed in J. Agassi and R.S. Cohen (eds), *Scientific Philosophy Today* (1981), with an extensive bibliography of Bunge's work; R. Swinburne, *Space and Time* (1968, rev.1980); J.R. Lucas, *A Treatise on Time and Space* (1973); L. Sklar, *Space, Time and Spacetime* (1974); I. Hinckfuss, *The Existence of Space and Time* (1975); G. Nerlich, *The Shape of Space* (1976); J. Earman et al., *Foundations of Space-Time Theories* (1977); H. Margenau, *Physics and Philosophy* (1978); R. Swinburne (ed.), *Space Time and Causality* (1982); special number of *Synthese* (1982) on 'Philosophical Problems of Modern Physics'; D. Mayr and G. Süssman (eds), *Space, Time and Mechanics* (1982).

Many of these works also include studies of quantum mechanics. But see also ch.1, n.7 above; C.A. Hooker (ed.), *Contemporary Research in the Foundations and Philosophy of Quantum Theory* (1973); M. Jammer, *The Philosophy of Quantum Mechanics* (1974); L.J. Lopes and M. Patey (eds), *Quantum Mechanics* (1977); D. Bohm, *Wholeness and the Implicate Order* (1980); P. Suppes (ed.), *Studies in the Foundations of Quantum Mechanics* (1980); P.K. Feyerabend, *Realism, Rationalism and Scientific Method* (1981); K.R. Popper, *Postscript* (1982), especially *Quantum Theory and the Schism in Physics*.

See also two volumes of translated essays, H. Reichenbach, *Selected Writings, 1909-1953* (1978) and H. Mehlburg, *Time, Causality, and the Quantum Theory* (1980).

Like many philosophers of science, Putnam concentrates most of his attention on that very untypical science, theoretical physics. But biology is beginning to attract more attention. See D.L. Hull's article in Fløistad along with his *Philosophy of Biological Science* (1974); M. Ruse, *Philosophy of Biology* (1973); F.J. Ayala and Th. Dobzhansky (eds), *Studies in the Philosophy of Biology* (1974); U.J. Jensen and R. Harré (eds), *The Philosophy of Evolution* (1981).

For a wider conspectus on the philosophy of science see P. Asquith and H. Kyburg (eds), *Current Research in Philosophy of Science* (1979); J.A. Passmore, 'Why Philosophy of Science?' in R.W. Home (ed.), *Science under Scrutiny* (1983); R. Harré, *An Introduction to the Logic of the Sciences* (2nd.ed.,1983), which includes a discussion of the sociological approach.

5. Compare *HY* ch.17, n.33. There is a general approach to a range of such issues in J.D. Sneed, *The Logical Structure of Mathematical Physics* (1971) as in H.A. Simon, *Models of Discovery* (1977).

6. Kuhn wrote as a physicist turned historian but his influence on the philosophy of science has been extensive. In respect to incommensurability, his theories resemble Feyerabend, but in respect to the desirability of 'normal science' they stand poles apart; Feyerabend favours the maximum proliferation of theories. For a confrontation between the two and more generally between Kuhn and Popperians or ex-Popperians see I. Lakatos and A. Musgrave (eds): *Criticism and the Growth of Knowledge* (1970). In his *Tradition and Innovation* (1978), Kuhn discusses his method and its origins. J.D. Sneed has sought to formalise Kuhn's paradigm changes. See the discussion between Kuhn, Sneed and Stegmüller in R.E. Butts and J. Hintikka (eds), *Historical and Philosophical Dimensions of Logic, Methodology and Philosophy of Science* (1975). See also G. Pearce and P. Maynard (eds), *Conceptual Change* (1973); F. Suppe (ed.), *The Structure of Scientific Theories* (1974); T. Kisiel, 'Paradigms' in Fløistad, *Contemporary Philosophy* vol.2; G. Radnitzky and G. Andersson (eds), *Progress and Rationality in Science* (1978) and (eds), *The Structure and Development of Science* (1979); D. Papineau, *Theory and Meaning* (1980); G. Gutting (ed.), *Paradigms and Revolutions* (1980); I.

Hacking (ed.), *Scientific Revolutions* (1981); C. Dilworth, *Scientific Progress* (1981); G.L. Pandit, *The Structure and Growth of Scientific Knowledge* (1982). For the historical approach see J.A. Passmore, 'History and the Philosophy of Science' in N. Rescher (ed.), *Scientific Explanation and Understanding* (1983). For a wide range of articles on this theme see *Studies in History and Philosophy of Science* (1970-). There is a different approach to these topics in Clark Glymour, *Theory and Evidence* (1980). Making free use of the history of science, he argues against Kuhn and his followers that science adopts a 'bootstrap' strategy, with a constant interplay between theories and observations. See the discussion in *JP*, 1980 and J. Earman (ed.), *Testing Scientific Theories* (1983). For the social sciences, as seen by a sociologist of knowledge, see B. Barnes, *T.S. Kuhn and Social Science* (1982). See also Lakatos and Feyerabend (below).

7. For Michael Polanyi see especially his *Personal Knowledge* (1958). Polanyi particularly emphasised the degree to which scientific 'judgment' rather than formal considerations determine what is to be taken seriously, whether as a theoretically interesting observation, a falsification – as distinct from an unimportant anomaly – or an hypothesis worth pursuing. Lakatos discusses him extensively. For a very favourable account see R. Gelwick, *The Way of Discovery* (1977). For related views see G. Holton, *The Scientific Imagination* (1978). J. Agassi, *Science and Society* (1981) is dedicated to Polanyi and shows his influence.

8. The relationships between cognitive psychology and philosophy can be explored in the two volumes of N. Block (ed.), *Readings in Philosophy of Psychology* (1980); J.M. Nicholas (ed.), *Images, Perception and Knowledge* (1977). Images are having something of a comeback; the dispute about whether we think in images or propositionally is very much alive, and discussed by Dennett. See also S.N. Thomas, *The Formal Mechanics of Mind* (1978) and W.I. Matson, *Sentience* (1976), in which he defends an identity theory against Dennett. For a criticism from the standpoint of the older 'philosophical psychology' see D.W. Hamlyn, *Perception, Learning and the Self* (1983). On functionalism generally see J.A. Fodor, *Psychological Explanation* (1968); C.W. Savage (ed.), *Perception and Cognition* (*Minnesota Studies*, IX, 1978); special number of *Philosophical Topics* (1981) on 'Functionalism and the Philosophy of Mind'. W.G. Lycan, 'Mental States and Putnam's Functionalist Hypothesis' (*AJP*, 1974) has a wider application than its title suggests. S. Shoemaker, 'Functionalism and Qualia' (*Philosophical Studies*, 1975) sets, along with T. Nagel's 'What is it like to be a bat?' (*PR*, 1974, now in *Mortal Questions*, 1979) problems Dennett tries to solve. For the connection between cognitive psychology and epistemology see T. Mischel (ed.), *Cognitive Development and Epistemology* (1971) which includes a criticism of cognitive psychology by Norman Malcolm. In his *Persons and Minds* (1978), J. Margolis defends a version of materialism which has functionalist overtones but emphasises the cultural role of mental

functions. C. McGinn, *The Character of Mind* (1982) is a general introduction to contemporary controversy.

9. For intelligence and machines see *HT* ch.20, n.33 to which can be added A. Sloman, *The Computer Revolution in Philosophy* (1978); M.A. Boden, *Artificial Intelligence and Natural Man* (1978); M.D. Ringle (ed.), *Philosophical Perspectives in Artificial Intelligence* (1978); J. Hungeland (ed.), *Mind Design* (1981).

10. At the same time Dennett is very sympathetic to Fodor's general approach in his *The Language of Thought* (1975), for all that he reviewed it critically. (See *Brainstorms*.) For further discussion of the points at issue see J.A. Fodor, *Representations* (1981). In his *Philosophy and the Mirror of Nature* (1980), Richard Rorty criticises the view that Fodor is involved in a regress. See also Fodor's later *The Modularity of Mind* (1983) which he revealingly sub-titles 'An Essay in Faculty Psychology'.

11. The argument about realism, especially in relation to scientific entities, continues apace. See ch.4, n.12 above; R. Bhaskar, *A Realist Theory of Science* (1978); B.C. van Fraassen, *The Scientific Image* (1980) – an antirealist analysis; P.M. Churchland, *Scientific Realism and the Plasticity of Mind* (1979) – a defence of realism; P. Smith, *Realism and the Progress of Science* (1981); P.K. Feyerabend, *Realism, Rationalism and Scientific Method* (1981); *PQ*, 1982, and *HT*, ch.17, n.33.

   See also the controversy between Putnam, Field and Harman in *JP* (1982) and Churchland's critique of van Fraassen (*Pacific Philosophical Quarterly*, 1982) along with W.P. Alston, 'Yes, Virginia, there is a Real World' (*Proceedings and Addresses of the American Philosophical Association*, 1979). The difficulty in giving a coherent account of quantum mechanics in realist terms disturbs even convinced realists. So in his 'Difficulties for Realism in the Philosophy of Science', J.J.C. Smart suggests that one might have to combine an 'ultimate metaphysical realism' with 'an instrumentalist view of present-day microphysics' (*Logic, Methodology and Philosophy of Science*, VI, 1979). Quantum mechanics continues to be extraordinarily resistant to incorporation in any coherent world-picture. From the work of John Bell, in particular, the most far-reaching cosmological conclusions, of an anti-realist sort, have been drawn. His article on 'The Problem of Hidden Variables in Quantum Mechanics' appeared in *Review of Modern Physics* (1966). For a (relatively) informal exposition see A.D. Mermin, 'Quantum Mysteries for Anyone' (*JP*, 1981). Putnam presents his formal argument against 'metaphysical realism' in 'Models and Reality' (*JSL*, 1980). His anti-realist papers are brought together in *Collected Papers*, vol.3 (1983). For criticism and alternative views, see I. Hacking, *Representing and Intervening* (1983), which is unusual in the stress it puts on experimentation as distinct from theorising, and N. Cartwright, *How the Laws of Physics Lie* (1983) which is realistic about electrons but not laws.

12. Subjectivist theories have won fresh friends because frequency theories, as we saw (*HT* ch.17), met with problems in defining 'in the long run' and did not allow direct assertions about the probability of individual events. The subjective approach was developed by the statistician L.J. Savage in his *The Foundations of Statistics* (1954), discussed by his fellow-statisticians in L.J. Savage et al., *The Foundations of Statistical Inference* (1962). Also important is the work of B. de Finetti, now summed up in his *The Theory of Probability* (1975), but dating back to a 1937 memoir. See also H.E. Kyburg and H.E. Smokler (eds), *Studies in Subjective Probability* (1964); R.D. Rosenkrantz, *Inference, Method and Decision* (1977). Other relevant books would include D.H. Mellor, *The Matter of Chance* (1971); R.C. Jeffrey, *The Logic of Decision* (1965) – and much subsequent work; E.W. Adams, *The Logic of Conditionals* (1975); Brian Ellis, *Rational Belief Systems* (1979); E. Eells, *Rational Decision and Causality* (1982). Among logicians who have helped to formalise conditional probabilities, B. Van Fraassen and R. Thomason are particularly influential.

Subjective theories have been severely criticised, as by G.H. von Wright in E. Nagel et al. (eds), *Logic, Methodology and Philosophy of Science* (1962) and, more generally, by Karl Popper as part of his broader onslaught on subjectivism. His own propensity theory is presented in *BJPS* (1959). A similar view was suggested by C.S. Peirce. See also the extensive bibliographies in the articles by R. Hilpinen and R. Jeffrey in G. Fløistad, *Contemporary Philosophy* (1981); the criticisms of Popper by T. Settle and P. Suppes in P.A. Schilpp (ed.), *The Philosophy of Karl Popper* (1974) along with Popper's reply. See also the lengthier discussions of quantum mechanics in his *Postscript* (1982).

Objective probabilities of a Popperian sort are defended in D.A. Gillies in *An Objective Theory of Probability* (1973) and in J.H. Fetzer, *Scientific Knowledge* (1981). One reason, we said, why frequency theories fell out of favour is that they did not seem to be able to give a satisfactory account of the probability of individual cases; this Fetzer attempts. It is an indication of the complexities of the present scene that Fetzer finds it necessary to distinguish between logical Bayesians, subjective Bayesians, empirical Bayesians, critical Bayesians and quasi-Bayesians, with several distinguished names in each area. The statistical approach is defended by R.N. Giere in *Understanding Scientific Reasoning* (1979). See also W. Harper and C. Hooker (eds), *Foundations of Probability Theory, Statistical Inference and Statistical Theories of Science* (1976); I. Hacking, *The Emergence of Probability* (1975); I. Niiniluoto, 'Statistical Explanation' in G. Fløistad, *Contemporary Philosophy*.

For a formalised consensus theory see K. Lehrer and C. Wagner, *Rational Consensus* (1981). For Lehrer generally, see R.J. Bogdan (ed.), *Keith Lehrer* (1980). See also J.C. Harsanyi, *Papers in Game Theory* (1982). Isaac Levi, in his *Gambling with Truth* (1967) and *The Enterprise of Knowledge* (1980), relates the acceptance of propositions to the taking of gambling risks, the value of modifying one's existing corpus of knowledge being set against the risks in doing so. In the manner typical of the last decades, induction is thought of holistically, as a matter of modifying an existing set of beliefs rather than of accepting an isolated generalisation. See the discussion of Levi in R.S. Cohen (ed.) *Language, Logic and Method* (1982). See also R.J. Bogdan (ed.), *Local Induction* (1976) with a far-reaching bibliography. This includes a summary by Jonathan Cohen of the position he works out more fully in *The Implications of Induction* (1970) and *The Probable and the Provable* (1977). In his case, inductive reasoning is related to legal reasoning, with the same emphasis on an existing corpus. See also *HY* ch.17, n.48 on induction and R.J. Bogdan (ed.), *Henry Kyburg and Isaac Levi* (1982), along with H.E. Kyburg, *Epistemology and Inference* (1983).

13. For a vigorous attack on Popper, Lakatos, Kuhn and Feyerabend as 'four modern irrationalists' see D.C. Stove, *Popper and After* (1982). Not incidentally, he blames the historical approach for what, in his judgment, has gone wrong. For a milder criticism see W.H. Newton, *The Rationality of Science* (1981). A.F. Chalmers, *What is this thing called Science?* (1976) is a more elementary critical survey. For realism see his 2nd ed. (1982). On the general issues see R. Hilpinen (ed.), *Rationality in Science* (1980); D. Shapere, *Reason and the Search for Knowledge* (1983); G. Andersson (ed.), *Rationality in Science and Politics* (1983). For Lakatos see R.S. Cohen et al. (eds), *Essays in Memory of Imre Lakatos* (1976). He is deployed and developed, in conjunction with a defence of realism, by D. Papineau in *Theory and Meaning* (1979). For the earlier Feyerabend see also *HY*, ch.20. There is a broader discussion of his work in H.P. Dürr (ed.), *Versuchungen* (1981). For other post-Popperian writings on scientific progress see L. Laudan, *Progress and its Problems* (1977), on which Feyerabend comments severely, and such essays by G. Radnitzsky as his contribution to G. Radnitzsky and G. Anderson (eds), *Progress and Rationality in Science* (1978). This is more generally relevant, along with *The Structure and Development of Science* (1979) with the same editors. See also *The Monist* (1977) on 'Historicism and Epistemology' and ch.5, n.5 above.

14. See Feyerabend's review of David Bohm's *Causality and Chance in Modern Physics* (1957) in *Philosophical Papers* vol.1. See also D. Bohm, *Wholeness and the Implicate Order* (1980).

15. As in Putnam's case, I have dated such of the articles as were previously published. The volume contains an extensive bibliography of Hesse's work. See especially *Models and Analogies in Science* (1963). Her essay on 'The Strong Thesis of Sociology in Science' will help to place her in her relationships to her sociological admirers. For Toulmin see his *Foresight and Understanding* (1961) and his *Human Understanding* (1972). Toulmin was a good deal influenced by Wittgenstein. See also his *The Return to Cosmology: Postmodern Science and the Theology of Nature* (1982). On some of

the general issues raised in Hesse's work see also M. Hollis and S. Lukes (eds), *Rationality and Relativism* (1982); J.W. Meiland and M. Krausz (eds), *Relativism* (1982). M.J. Mulkay, *Science and the Sociology of Knowledge* (1979) will serve as an example of the use made of Hesse – along with Duhem, Hanson and Kuhn – by the new breed of sociologists of knowledge. See also ch.1, n.4 above.

16. The discussion of this issue in N.R. Hanson, *Patterns of Discovery* (1958) has been particularly influential. Subsequent discussion has been extensive. See I. Scheffler, *Science and Subjectivity* (1967) and E. Nagel, S. Bromberger, A. Grünbaum, *Observation and Theory in Science* (1971). Nagel particularly refers to Hesse. Popper, Feyerabend and Kuhn all stress that observations are theory-laden. See also W.V. Quine, 'Epistemology Naturalised' in *Ontological Relativity* (1969) and W.V. Quine et al., *Experience and Theory* (1970). For criticisms see C.R. Kordig, *The Justification of Scientific Change* (1971). The importance of this controversy in current philosophy of science is brought out in the Critical Introduction by F. Suppe to the symposium-based collection he edited as *The Structure of Scientific Theories* (1974), with important contributions by many of the leading figures at the time when the 'new wave' of philosophers of science was beginning to assume the proportions of a tidal-wave. Together with the Afterword he added to the second edition (1977), Suppe has written a general account of the history of recent philosophy of science. The uncertainties of Putnam and the reservations of Kuhn are interesting features of the volume but they by no means exhaust its value.

17. For examples of what Rorty is reacting against, see the volume entitled *The Owl of Minerva*, eds C.J. Bontempo and S.J. Odell (1975), in which various well-known philosophers present their views about the nature of philosophy. See especially Smart's hopes for a professional philosophy, Popper on the theory of knowledge as 'the very heart of philosophy', Blanshard's remark that 'science is logically dependent on philosophy', Lorenzen's 'constructivism' and contrast Hook on 'Philosophy and Public Policy'. See also J.A. Passmore, 'The Place of Argument in Metaphysics' in W.E. Kennick and M. Lazerowitz (eds), *Metaphysics* (1966), for its distinction between the philosopher and the sage. Rorty is discussed in *JP*, 1980. For a much more fully developed contemporary version of pragmatism see N. Rescher, *Methodological Pragmatism* (1977). In his *Philosophical Relativity* (1983) P. Unger displays scepticism about the traditional doctrine that philosophy presents us with problems to which there must in principle be answers, whatever the difficulties philosophers have encountered in discovering them.

18. For a study of this 'replacement' see I. Hacking, *Why Does Language Matter to Philosophy?* (1975). Hacking, however, does seem to think that it constitutes progress although he warns against the possible emergence

of linguistic phenomenalism, a new version of Berkeley. That warning was fully justified.

19. For hermeneutics see ch.1, n.9. The Davidson article to which Rorty particularly refers is 'On the Very Idea of a Conceptual Scheme' (*Proceedings of the American Philosophical Association*, 1973). But as so often, he also has unpublished material in mind. See also B. Stroud, 'Conventionalism and the Indeterminacy of Translation' in D. Davidson and J. Hintikka (eds), *Words and Objections* (1969).

The general issues we have been considering are further discussed in R.J. Bernstein, *Beyond Objectivism and Relativism* (1983) with special reference to contemporary German thought.

Index

1. Names

N.B. In the case of edited works, only the name of the first editor is cited.

168   *Index*

2. Subjects